The
Launching
Years

The Launching Years

Strategies for Parenting from Senior Year to College Life

**Laura S. Kastner, Ph.D.,
and Jennifer Wyatt, Ph.D.**

THREE RIVERS PRESS
NEW YORK

Published by Clarkson Potter/Publishers, New York, New York.
Member of the Crown Publishing Group, a division of Random House, Inc.

www.randomhouse.com

CLARKSON N. POTTER is a trademark and POTTER and colophon are registered trademarks of Random House, Inc.

Printed in the United States of America

Design by Maggie Hinders

Library of Congress Cataloging-in-Publication Data
Kastner, Laura Scribner.
The launching years : strategies for parenting from senior year to college life /
Laura S. Kastner and Jennifer Wyatt.
Includes index.
1. College student orientation—United States.   2. Education—Parent
participation—United States.   3. College students—United States—Conduct of
life.   4. Parent and teenager—United States.   5. Adolescent psychology.
I. Wyatt, Jennifer Fugett.   II. Title.
LB2343.32.K37   2002
378.1'98—dc21   2002024691

ISBN 0-609-80806-0

10 9 8 7 6 5 4 3 2

First Edition

To our next generation:

Cameron and Lindley

Megan, Molly, Andy, and Jay

Acknowledgments

Encouragement and sound direction came from many individuals, including our agent, Pam Bernstein, and our editors, Margot Schupf and Lance Troxel. Ann Vander Stoep's astute review of our manuscript, an act of true friendship, strengthened our thinking. Thanks are also due to the many friends, relatives, and colleagues who listened attentively and responded generously as we bounced ideas off them. We are grateful to the parents and launching adolescents whose stories are reflected in this book. No acknowledgment would be complete without paying tribute to our parents, our children, our caring husbands, Philip Mease and Scott Wyatt, and to the relationships that will sustain us through our families' launching years.

Contents

Notes from the Authors

This book was created collaboratively by Laura Kastner and Jennifer Wyatt through a process of talking, drafting, exchanging ideas, and redrafting. Laura Kastner is the psychologist whose knowledge, insight, and clinical experiences are represented in the book. Jennifer Wyatt's background in writing, editing, and parenting made her the indispensable expresser and translator of ideas. For clarity's sake, we made the decision to speak to readers in the first person.

Families represented here are mostly fictionalized composites of real families from Laura Kastner's experiences clinically and in launching workshops. Letters, quotations, situations, and dialogues have either been generously provided by parents or re-created in a way that is true to an actual experience.

Introduction: Going on Tilt

During a two-year period beginning with the senior year of high school, most parents find themselves confounded by unanticipated challenges. "Why are my daughter and I fighting like cats and dogs now that she's about to leave?" a mother might ask. "I can't make one request, remark, or recommendation without infuriating my senior. Whether it's college-application issues, homework, or his social life, he expects to be treated as an adult, but is there no parenting role left for me anymore?" another might wonder.

Vastly underrated as a complicated transition for parents and children alike, the launching years rival any two years of parenting for the formidable events they contain, the challenges and questions they raise, and their sheer emotional intensity. With so little emphasis in our culture on so large a phenomenon, families traveling through this passage can be taken by surprise, particularly since parents experience the lurch of life-transition issues at the same time as their child.

A child leaving home is a momentous developmental juncture, now more so than ever because today's parents are more focused on their children and their relationships with them. Pioneer child psychologist Jean Piaget used the term *disequilibrium* to describe the lack of stability individuals experience when moving from one developmental stage to the next. To say that families lose their balance and orientation during this transition is no exaggeration. Making matters worse, some families are now faced with a highly competitive, anxiety-provoking college-admission process, exacerbating the stresses of launching.

The Launching Years guides families through this exciting, inspiring, discomforting, and humbling two-year period filled with sentiments deep and rich. Written for families whose children are considering leaving home for college, it explores and emphasizes the following issues.

Parents who understand the developmental transition of launching and all that it entails will be more effective in parenting. They can maintain greater harmony in their family life and in their relationship with their child, present and future. Just as it's helpful to know how to interpret a two year old's temper tantrum as an assertion of self, it's wise to understand that *launch anxiety* on the part of parents and senior can be behind much of the havoc of senior year. A heightened awareness of the specific hurdles they are facing, along with an appreciation for why everyone is behaving as they are, can help parents navigate this stage more successfully and set themselves up for a mutually satisfying future relationship.

The elongation of adolescence leaves many parents surprised by how much longer they are actively parenting. The question is—What is the nature of parenting as children mature? Now that military service, marriage, or employment are no longer the staples of life after high school, young people ages 18 to 25 within our culture are "emerging adults."[1] During this prolonged period, young people actively explore possibilities in love, work, and worldviews; and this process often involves risky behaviors, which, surprisingly enough, can be even more prevalent than during the teen years. Since the average age at marriage for Americans is 25 for women and 27 for men, parents remain their primary family unit much longer than a generation ago. The reality is that until our emerging adults are securely established, parents need to provide the continuing help young people need to cross the threshold to adult roles.[2] Depriving them of support during this crucial period has been shown to inhibit their ultimate independence.[3]

It takes extraordinary resourcefulness for families to negotiate this new parenting terrain, unmapped by previous generations who engaged in far less parenting after their children turned 18 than we do today. To parent optimally through this period, parents need an ingenious blend of support and challenge.[4] In times of trouble, parents support, guide, and even rescue their emerging adults whenever necessary. Likewise, for their growth and increased competence, we challenge them to be more independent and to learn their way in the world. Vignettes in *The Launching Years* bring this delicate dance to life.

Senior year of high school is inherently tricky to manage. Parenting during this year is orchestrated around preparing children for greater independence and, for many, around leave-taking. Although many students live at home while attending college, higher education has become a rite of passage with the majority of youth participating. Within our culture, heading to college is one of the ways that young people separate from their families.[5]

The college years are not only an academic experience, but also the means whereby young people shed their reliance on parents, becoming less emotionally dependent on their support and authority—rarely a smooth process. With stress in college life at an all-time high, challenges of mental health, ideological dilemmas, substance abuse, and love-life and career decision-making abound. For various reasons, often practical in nature, many young people will drop out of college, and more students than not will take more than four years to complete a Bachelor's degree. *The Launching Years* shows parents ways to be helpful and not harmful.

Knowing the ingredients for a successful launch from home gives parents some guideposts for building their child's competen-

cies during this two-year period. Not all young people are ready for the independence of today's college campuses at age 18. Young people who leave home successfully have accomplished a series of developmental tasks, as described in our book *The Seven-Year Stretch: How Families Work Together to Grow Through Adolescence.* Likewise, *The Launching Years* provides parents with information to determine whether their child is ready to launch and what the best path might be, given today's diverse timetables and paths to autonomy.

The Launching Years is a companion volume to all of the how-to books on college admissions in that it focuses on family relationships during this transition. It explains why young people move through the launching years in different ways and what parents can do to prepare their child not just to be accepted into college but also to be successful and self-reliant in life.

Parenting during this transition involves an inspired mixture of letting go, within a context of staying connected. Even as parents' roles shift and young people become more independent in every way, parents continue to stay connected to their children, providing them with both roots and wings. When we say good-bye at the college gate, we don't simply let go with blind trust. Young people leave home with 18 years of our relating to them within them, as well as all their competence developed over that time. Emerging adults can draw on these internal resources for guidance, feelings of security, and a means of coping with the adversities they'll inevitably face. Still, the degree to which they can draw on their strengths will be mitigated by their temperament and the magnitude of the stresses they incur. Delineating obstacles that some parents and children will confront, *The Launching Years* provides parents with the means to assess whether they should make a leap of faith that their child can handle a challenge or, conversely, move in with direct assistance.

This transition involves a range of thorny issues and dilem-

mas that families may face. The Launching Years *walks parents through many tough, multilevel problems.* Situations covered include these:

- You're beside yourself over the application process but your senior is doing nothing except procrastinate;
- Your senior, whose learning issues suggest a different timetable, looks as if he's trying *not* to graduate;
- You're puzzling over what *launching* means to you personally, since over the last 18 years, three-quarters of your life has revolved around parenthood;
- Your just-graduated daughter, who has always been so perfect, winds up in the emergency room from alcohol poisoning, and it looks as if she's developing an eating disorder;
- Your college freshman calls you in a tizzy, "dumping" all her upset on you, and you're not sure how to calm her down;
- Your feisty daughter has issued an ultimatum about sleeping in your home with her boyfriend;
- You find condoms in your son's pockets, and since he's a single guy, this indicates he's engaging in casual sex;
- Your son's level of alcohol consumption has always worried you, and now he's in deep trouble over a fraternity brawl involving extensive vandalism.

At any stage, parents can feel buffaloed by problems, but the gargantuan issues that may arise during launching can make potty training or a child sleeping through the night feel like small potatoes. As with earlier challenges, though, there are resourceful ways to see them through.

Once our children are more established and independent, they're still ours, but in a more liberated way. The overarching task for families during the launching years is to negotiate the transition to a close adult-adult relationship. Resolving the loss of our old parent-child relationship, we forge a new one, based less on direct control and more on consultation and mutually-agreed-upon ways of staying close. Still, it involves a certain amount of "growing pains" to get there, with the toughest times starting senior year. What an amazing two years these can be, but what a payoff when parents know how to both support their child through inevitable setbacks and challenge them to make the most of their assets. Then, as young people begin to come into their own, parents enjoy the fruit of an easier, more open relationship.

PART I

SENIOR YEAR

The Big
Shake-Up

CHAPTER ONE

The Fall Flurry

How to keep the college-application process and planning for the next year from getting out of hand

*"Little children disturb your sleep . . .
big ones your life."*
—PROVERB

There's an uncanny resemblance between parents-to-be in a childbirthing class and parents at a college-information night, preparing for their high schooler's launch from home. Throughout the challenges of the adolescent years, differences among families are striking—differences in parenting decisions, values, types of children, levels of challenge, life circumstances, and experiences. But like childbirth, the mutual anticipation of change unites parents collectively from various walks of life during launching.

Similar questions weigh on parents' minds: Is my child ready to leave home? If college is the next step, which one? Where will he get in? If not college, what else? Will my child be safe, successful, and happy once he's gone? And more secretly, will I be? What will the quieter house, their perpetually made bed, and the empty place at the dinner table feel like?

Questions proliferate during this unsettling time. Like previous generations, today's parents wonder whether their child can handle the academic demands of college. Can she stay on top of the workload? Does she have enough self-discipline to manage the social whirlwind? Parents acquire a heightened awareness of the thousands of little skills needed for daily living—from remembering to set the alarm in the morning, to meeting crucial deadlines, to making travel arrangements. What will happen once she's on her own?

Control over the purse strings remains a perennial struggle between parents and nearly grown children, and with the cost of education skyrocketing, financial issues feel particularly urgent. Few families are immune from worrying about tuition expenses and whether to saddle their child with debt accrued from college loans. What, parents wonder, should the limits of our monetary support be when our children are not directly under our wing?

Some concerns are specific to our time. Many parents are alarmed by media reports on risks of campus life such as date rape and unprecedented levels of student inebriation. A generation ago, colleges enforced curfews, requiring students to sign in and sign out of dorms, but today's students are virtually free agents. Are the stories we hear about the freedom on today's campus and the lack of adult oversight true? Which young people are potentially binge drinkers or the ones who will eschew relationships for casual sex?

The upsurge in interest in emotional intelligence (strengths related to social and emotional competence) has led parents to wonder whether their soon-exiting children are emotionally mature enough and capable of forming healthy relationships and coping with life's inevitable slings and arrows. Knowing that in one short year they won't be physically present to help their children face difficult problems, parents ask themselves: Does my child have the persistence and initiative to handle responsibilities ahead? What if my son gets depressed after his heart is broken? What if my daughter loses motivation to study when she can't make the grades she got in high school?

The senior year is packed with intense, contradictory emotions and—invariably—increased family friction. With so many launching concerns, parents wonder where to put their energy. Sometimes, we'll feel confident, joyful, and excited in the widening of our children's horizons—and, potentially, ours. Then there are moments when they seem too young to be heading out into this complicated world. What parent doesn't sometimes long to hang on a little tighter, a little longer? The decisions our children are making—their college choices, use of time, evolving values, and relationships—carry significant life consequences, so parents hope to make their influence felt. We have our preconceptions, dreams, and expectations for our children, which rarely match theirs 100 percent, potentially creating more family fray.

Significant parental soul searching takes place senior year. Have I done a good job? What might I have done differently in my child-rearing? How can I continue to have a close relationship with my child after launching? What's next in my life when parenting is no longer my day-to-day job? Despite the reflective mood of senior year—which is natural and necessary because it helps parents prepare for their child's leave-taking—parents still need to remain attentive to their senior's needs in the present. And those needs are often considerable. Right as

COUPLES GIVE BIRTH TO BABIES, AND EVERYONE KNOWS IT'S A BIG DEAL. AND THEN YOUR "BABY" LEAVES HOME. IT'S ALSO A MAJOR DEVELOPMENTAL HURDLE, SO WHY SHOULDN'T A CHILD'S SENIOR YEAR BE THE MOST CHAOTIC YEAR OF YOUR LIFE?

seniors are planning their exits, parents are often surprised by being pulled closely into their seniors' lives, whether it's through their child's unexpected clinginess and dependency or increased risk-taking.

Whether described as "emerging adults" or "late adolescents" (some developmental psychologists lump these years into adolescence itself), 18 year olds in our culture straddle the worlds of childhood and adulthood and are not fully self-sufficient. Most will spend the next several years setting their direction and acquiring the necessary competencies to be on their own. During this stage—and particularly during senior year and the first year post–high school—parents play a crucial role in moving their children toward increased independence. Ideally, this occurs in a context of support and close relationships; research shows that late adolescents who describe their parents as "available" have greater resilience.[1] Even when our children are living elsewhere, we can continue to nurture their development. The fall of senior year, however, many families are focusing on applying to college, trying to decide whether to apply early (a controversial trend), or, in some cases, determining other options.

"JELLING" INTO COLLEGE

My best advice for parents of college-bound seniors is this: Beware of the feeding frenzy around college ratings, and do whatever it takes to keep the college-application process calm and contained so that it doesn't engulf what's likely to be your last year with your child at home. Though they may not show it, most seniors worry about leaving home at least as much as their parents do. Relatives, neighbors, and strangers on airplanes make conversation with high-school seniors by asking them where they're applying to college. In this year of feeling sized-up and judged, seniors need cool-headed, supportive parents, not or

best hand we can le

process is to provide

trolling our own and

That said, where

tion process? One u

their child's school r

been sending about

is she? Where do in

nesses? Your child's

expect. Although

bloomers catch on 1

whether their child takes a lot of prodding to buckle

schoolwork or is the focused, goal-setting type.

College counselors and admissions officers tell families to seek "the best fit." That's terrific advice, since too many families fixate only on "the best school." Parents who set their minds on finding the school that matches their child are savvy consumers of higher education, since the value of an education depends on individual effectiveness rather than intrinsic worth.

Think of the college decision as an identity decision. Throughout adolescence, young people are slowly forming and "jelling," a process shaping who they are, the experiences they pursue, the values they embrace, the aptitudes they build on, and where their passions lie—what they'll stay up after midnight to complete and what leaves them cold. The decision of what to do after high school should be an

> CONSIDER CAREFULLY: DO THE COLLEGES MY CHILD IS CONSIDERING MATCH WHO MY CHILD IS AS A STUDENT OR AM I CREATING UNREALISTIC EXPECTATIONS FOR MY SENIOR?

outgrowth of their solidifying identity. A high-school senior is a sum total of 18 years of development. If there are disap-

...erns, or features that make parents
...cessful launch, anxiety will undoubt-
... college-application time.

...g parents who have been chronically dissat-
...ir child's B's and C's can be distressed over
...e as limited options. When their seniors have less
...ar GPA's, parents can feel like they're on the edge of
...ing board over uncertain waters, but in actuality, there
... great matches in higher education for different student
profiles. With over 3,000 accredited colleges in the United
States, nearly every high-school graduate can be accepted
into a college. Over 1,000 colleges admit students with C
averages, and B students can attend all but the 200 most
selective institutions.[2]

Pressure mounting, parents can get worked up over the
quirkiness of college admission, a particular danger when
parents over-identify with their child. As acceptance becomes
increasingly more competitive, it's every parent's worst night-
mare to think that their deserving child might be rejected
from the school his heart is set on attending. Playing the college financial-aid game creates additional uncertainties. With
students experiencing the pinched acceptance rate of top colleges, parents are having their own parallel version of the desperate feelings seniors often experience during this time.

Parents whose children are driven to excel are often genet-
ically wired for ambition themselves, which can interfere with
the kind of calm, emotional support and reassurance that
help seniors most. When everyone in the family is hardwired
to "go for it," parents may need to put a check on their own
drives so they can stay composed as their senior flips out.

Launching a child to college can feel as if it's one of our
last hands-on parenting acts. The college choice appears to be
our child's link to the future, and, hoping to control as much
as we can, we want it to be the best possible link. Invested in
our child's future, we start to view college choice as the key

to everything we want for our child, when in fact, no set of empirical data has been able to establish that *where* a young person attends college automatically correlates with success. What does correlate with eventual occupational success is the number of years of higher education; it matters that young people finish their degrees, but the specific college has no statistical significance, nor, interestingly enough, do grades in high school or college.[3]

Wise parents adopt a broader framework. Instead of asking, "where will my child go to college?" as the benchmark of success, look to questions that truly are vital to one's future, such as these:

- Is my child building strong interests and pursuing them both inside and outside school?
- Does he seem motivated to do well, wherever he goes?
- Does he know how to take full advantage of whatever resources a college has?
- Is he engaged, aware, resilient, responsible, and committed to living a productive life?
- Is my child developing a life based on worthy values and goals?

Since our parenting goal is the development of a well-adjusted adult, not just college admission, parents may need to monitor their reactions and remind themselves: There are many paths children can take to be happy and successful. Any room full of accomplished adults is likely to contain more people who graduated from mid-ranking colleges than from top-tier schools.

Only too easily does the tail start to wag the dog, and college choice begins to influence what a teen does—all for the sake of the college application. Parents of seniors can direct too much energy away from child-rearing, project into the future, and lose track of all of the developmental tasks of an 18 year old. During this culminating year, there's usually ample room for growth in areas like building character, making ethical decisions, or developing healthy habits.

> **TRY NOT TO FIXATE ON COLLEGE RANKINGS. THINK INSTEAD ABOUT THE FULLER PICTURE OF YOUR CHILD'S DEVELOPMENT AND ALL OF THE QUALITIES OTHER THAN A'S THAT WILL MAKE FOR A FRUITFUL AND PRODUCTIVE LIFE FOR YOUR CHILD.**

To make it a good senior year, keep up your parenting, look beyond college rankings, and find the school that realistically matches the gifts and passions of your child. Then make a leap of faith that where he ends up is probably the best place. A healthy motto for parents is this: *Whatever school rejects my child doesn't deserve him!*

UNHINGED OVER APPLICATIONS FAMILY STORY

Many seniors send their parents into a tailspin by completing college applications at the eleventh hour. Parents' own developmental challenges and worries about launching can exacerbate family friction. How can families best contain the application process?

"I'm really losing it," sighed Mattie, a poised and personable mom, describing to me how stirred up she is over her daughter's college application process. "I *know* I'm supposed to let Lauren be responsible for her applications. I *know* I shouldn't nag her. I *know* in my heart that she will attend college somewhere next fall, but I can't seem to help myself!"

Like Mattie, many parents find themselves nagging, fretting, and engaging in power struggles that are reminiscent of eras of child-rearing they thought they'd outgrown. To say that just about everybody "regresses" sounds clinical and minimizing, but the word is descriptive. Likewise, adolescents express their anxiety about their momentous transition to college in anything but direct ways.

Mattie had attended a college-launching talk I'd given at her daughter's school and as part of the evening had completed a survey on parent and adolescent readiness for launching. By taking the launching survey, parents can get an overview of issues that might be working below the surface to heat things up on the home front. The survey can help parents size up how well they and their seniors, posed on the launch pad, are doing.

> UNWILLING OR PERHAPS UNABLE TO VERBALIZE THEIR MIXED FEELINGS ABOUT LAUNCHING, SENIORS OFTEN WASTE TIME AND FUNCTION BELOW THEIR PAR INSTEAD.

READY FOR THE LAUNCH? AN ADOLESCENT- AND PARENT-READINESS SURVEY

The following quiz is for parents to assess the readiness of their seniors as well as themselves for launching. Please indicate to what degree you agree with these statements. Answer on a scale of 1–5, where 1 = strongly agree; 2 = agree; 3 = uncertain; 4 = disagree; 5 = strongly disagree.

PART I: THE SENIOR

1. I feel confident that my adolescent has the problem-solving abilities to handle most challenges that will come with life after high school.

2. My adolescent has the necessary social skills she/he will need for living in a new social setting and interacting with new people.

3. My adolescent has the intellectual and academic skills she/he needs for the kind of experience she/he will choose after high-school graduation.

4. I do not believe my adolescent needs time off after high school for maturational purposes before taking full advantage of a college experience.

5. My adolescent will be emotionally secure enough to leave home after graduating from high school.

6. My adolescent makes good decisions related to her/his use of money.

7. I believe my adolescent possesses age-level emotional skills for handling romantic involvements.

8. I do not think that my adolescent will have problems with homesickness upon leaving home.

9. My adolescent has the capability to set goals and meet them.

10. For the most part, my adolescent possesses the moral values to guide his actions and understand the consequences of his behavior.

PART II: THE PARENT

11. Despite my major commitment to parenting, I have other parts of my life I look forward to developing after my last child leaves home.

12. My marital status does not concern me at this point in my life.

13. If married, I'm satisfied with the quality of my marital relationship, or if single, I'm satisfied with my current intimate relationship(s).

14. I know there will be plenty of pleasures in my role as a parent after my children leave home.

15. I feel capable of both supporting my adolescent's independence and her/his needs for extra help during setbacks.

16. I have not expected that my adolescent's graduation automatically means stressful changes for me.

17. Facing the challenges of middle age does not overwhelm me.

18. My current employment status is satisfactory to me.

19. I am happy with the friends I have at this point in my life.

20. My emotional and physical health is currently satisfactory.

This survey, representing important areas for families during their child's senior year, can help everyone zero in on tender spots. Reviewing their responses, parents can identify 4's or 5's as a warning flag. The survey is a means for sorting through issues and determining what you need to work on, either personally or with your child, over the next few years—whether it be money management, emotional maturity, or goal-setting. Generally speaking, the better off you are with respect to the areas in this survey, the smoother the transition through the launching years is likely to be.

THE PARENT TRAP: COMPARING KIDS

Responding to the survey, Mattie realized that Lauren's scores surpassed hers and that her own wobbliness was sparking fireworks, hampering her ability to deal optimally with Lauren's postponing. Mattie articulated a range of worries related to work, friendships, and the "big hole" Lauren's departure would leave. Issues like these latch subversively onto the application process and are rarely as highlighted as they should be.

Consider, for example, the following tussle between Mattie and Lauren, which she described to me. From a fly-on-the-wall perspective, it *looked* as if Lauren's procrastination were the problem to be fixed, but notice Mattie's own contribution:

We hit a low point the other night. Lauren was watching TV—a favorite show she watches regularly. It sent me over the edge, even though she's not a big TV-watcher. I kept thinking about the deadline for her college essay next week, her lip service about doing well in English this semester, how she's borderline for getting into the U, and on and on—and I lost it.

I wagged my finger, lecturing Lauren on the insanity of being glued to the TV with so much on her platter. Then I stepped over the line. I thought about her friend Ellie, who is an ultra-performer and Ivy-League bound, and blurted out, "I bet Ellie isn't watching TV right now!"

Lauren sliced through my ire with a cool put-down, replaying the words of the school guidance counselor, "School and college applications are my responsibility. Your job, Mom, is to support me."

Lauren hit a bull's-eye with that retort, and that's the thing. She's pretty squared away, but she drives me crazy with the way she always postpones until the last minute. I like to have all my ducks in a row. We've always differed on this.

Mattie's last remark signaled a deep truth about mother and daughter. Despite her aggravation, Mattie knew Lauren was a last-minute artist. Normally, Mattie tolerated Lauren's style, but interacting with other parents, particularly parents of seniors pursuing elite schools and merit scholarships, had thrown her off balance, as she listened to others describe their own interesting lives, their child's accomplishments and impressive college list, and the massive effort their child was putting into the application process.

PARENTS OFTEN FEEL INTIMIDATED BY THE RADICAL NOSINESS OF THE APPLICATION SEASON. UNDER THE GUISE OF FRIENDLY CHIT-CHAT, OTHERS FEELS ENTITLED TO INQUIRE ABOUT COLLEGE PLANS AND TO SIZE UP A SENIOR ON THAT BASIS.

The college application process activates something primal. We know, of course, that this process doesn't divide seniors into the winners and the losers, but anxiety can skew our thinking. Though it's often covert or unconscious, parents at this juncture are comparing themselves by comparing their children's flight patterns toward various college choices. Seniors do it, too.

At its worst, every senior is reduced to a single dimension: a college applicant. Most adolescents are deft enough with an "I dunno" to fend off the barrage of usually unwelcome questions about their college plans. Parents may need to arm themselves with a couple of short, effective responses to protect themselves from others' invasiveness. Something vague like, "Oh, she's lining up lots of good options," may not deter emboldened inquisitors. A strategic non-sequitur—such as "Oh, she's making plans. What about you? Do you have plans for next year?"—shifts the subject more effectively.

We all know it's inaccurate and unfair and try to resist it, but there is a deceptive rating of an adolescent's life prospects (and by association the parenting they received) by their GPA's, SAT's, and college choices. What a trap it is to believe that an A in school is commensurate with an A in child-rearing, but the whole process can create doubts and subvert our basic trust in our teenager as we obsess on the relatively narrow measure of college admission.

FALL'S MIASMA: WORRIES, WORRIES EVERYWHERE

Mattie's anxiety had caused her to lose her bearings and be overly influenced by external voices and circumstances, instead of being guided by her own internal compass. Though her marriage was solid, her husband, Al, had little patience. When she tried to talk to him about how bad she felt about nagging Lauren, he replied, "Well, just don't nag her."

In a sense, Al was on target, but he wasn't appreciating Mattie's burden. Moms are often in a vulnerable position during application season because they are likely to be the overseer of school-related matters. Many mothers also hold the role of "feeler" around emotional issues related to child-rearing generally. Fathers often compensate for mothers during this phase, since the worrying-badgering role is already taken.

Mattie needed to remind herself of what she already knew about herself and her daughter: "Lauren always waits until the eleventh hour, but she nearly always gets it done. I'm anxious, and I do things ahead of time. That pit in my stomach says more about me than her."

Excessive anxiety narrowed Mattie's wisdom, and she was feeling panicked, emotionally and physically. Mattie's worries were all over the map: What do I do when Lauren won't take the SAT prep review course? Should we have gone on college visits last spring like the other families? Why isn't the school tracking Lauren's applications better? The school says, "It's her responsibility," but she's not doing it! If Lauren's relaxed about it, the school is relaxed, and my husband is relaxed, it's up to me to be the alarm clock, right?

FOR PARENTS, LAUNCHING RELATES TO QUESTIONS LIKE "IS SHE READY?" "WILL SHE BE SAFE AND HAPPY?" "HAVE I DONE A GOOD JOB?" SINCE THESE QUESTIONS ARE ABSTRACT AND HARD TO ANSWER AND COLLEGE ACCEPTANCE IS CONCRETE, WE PUT ALL OUR EGGS IN ONE BASKET AS A MEASUREMENT OF OUR CHILDREN AND OURSELVES.

In counseling Mattie and I pulled together numerous issues that were churning up distress. She was experiencing a convergence of all of her postponed developmental challenges barking at her heels, as shown in her survey, *and* her maternal feelings of loss related to her daughter's launch, *and* her antipathy to the intrusive, competitive college-application environment, *and* her distress over Lauren's procrastination.

Like many parents, Mattie, anticipating Lauren's launch, was undergoing a midlife reckoning. "If three-fifths of everything I do and experience is 'mother,' what happens when that role becomes less everyday?" she wondered. "Who will I be? What will I do with the time I put into parenting?" Mattie had to grapple with life conflicts that had been brewing for some time. How much easier it would be if the family uproar were only about Lauren's dilly-dallying!

LETTING SENIORS BE THEIR OWN ALARM CLOCKS

When students have consistently performed well in school and made their deadlines one way or another, they deserve their parent's trust that they will complete their applications—albeit on their own time clocks and in keeping with their own standards. Most of Lauren's dawdling on applications is the postponing that is her usual habit, heightened by the enormousness of what she faces, but some of her resistance is in opposing her mom.

When parents are overly engaged in a child's college-application process, they are short-circuiting the child's own feelings about her responsibilities and impending deadlines. What takes up most of the senior's attention is resisting the oppressive hounding so they don't have a chance to experience their own drive and motivations.

Mattie and Lauren are stuck in a dance with the steps already established: Mom badgers, and daughter reacts. It's up to the adult to change the pattern with an original and compelling proposal. With deadlines looming, Mattie can introduce a new approach to the problem.

She can go to Lauren for two expressed purposes: a sincere apology and a negotiation. First of all, she can acknowledge her part in the problem by saying calmly, "I'm sorry.

I've been too involved in trying to make sure you meet your deadlines. I know you want to go to college, so it's yours now. It's between you and you, and not you and me."

But Lauren isn't off the hook; next comes the negotiation. In exchange for Mom's great effort to back off, Lauren needs to come forward with her intentions of how she plans to finish applications and promise to follow through. Mattie might say, "We've always been different in how we get things done—you know that. You're not as anxious as I am, but we've got to negotiate. I'll give you a wide berth, but you have to set a deadline for your applications that has a safety net of one week before they're actually due. This is as much for me as it is for you."

I recommended an exchange like this for Mattie and Lauren because their relationship already contained a lot of warmth, humor, and mutual respect. The goal for this family was to return to their usual rapport, which would follow once Mattie calmed herself, put her energy into the concerns she pinpointed in the survey, and realized she had a choice *not* to react to Lauren's foot-dragging.

SPINNING THEIR WHEELS: HOW MUCH PROCRASTINATION OVER APPLICATIONS IS NORMAL?

Typically, high-school seniors deal with their own tidal wave of emotions about leaving home by doing anything other than filling out applications. A lot depends on your child, though; some seniors make quick work of applying to get it over with, and others maintain a secret front, both of which can also be less than ideal.

Superficially, the obvious reason for postponing is the application essay. Consider the build-up when you're faced with writing THE essay of your life. How can it possibly be good enough? Even diligent seniors sometimes falter under the burden of summing themselves up in 250 words.

It's also normal for parents to feel torqued over their child's procrastination because we only see the negative consequences of the behavior, not the undertow of dread, panic, worry, and fear. Time-wasting is a symptom. Even when relationships with parents are open and warm, some seniors clam up as they did during early adolescence, hoping to avoid the whole overwhelming issue of college applications with their parents. The more intense the parents, the more likely children are to stonewall. Many seniors minimize, "Don't sweat it, Mom." And "I've got it under control, Dad." Stirring up more conflict through procrastination may have another function: It serves as confirmation for the senior, ambivalent about leaving home, that parents are hard to live with, so college with all its uncertainties looks very appealing.

Because the whole process is potentially crazy-making, many families accept that along with applications comes an ebb in the parent-child relationship. They simply get through it the best they can, steeling themselves for some frustration, staying cognizant of all the contributing factors, choosing battles carefully, minimizing the number of blow-ups, and trying to stay as calm and upbeat as possible. If you're one of the rare families who find this process smooth as silk, consider yourself blessed.

PARENTS ARE SET UP FOR CONFLAGRATION DURING THIS TIME. FEARS AND DREADS OF LAUNCHING REGRESS FAMILIES INTO POWER STRUGGLES OF YESTERYEAR. THAT FRICTION ALLOWS SENIORS THE GREAT "OUT" OF FOCUSING ON FIGHTING WITH THEIR PARENTS INSTEAD OF DEALING WITH THEIR OWN ACCOUNTABILITY. IT'S VERY HANDY FOR SENIORS.

Having some empathy for your senior helps. Most young

people are at once excited and terrified about leaving home. Do I really want to cut loose from my parents? Where will I go? What's it going to feel like when I say good-bye? Will I make it in college? What if I don't belong or I hate my roommate?

SOME PRACTICAL TACTICS FOR HANDLING HEEL-DRAGGING

Knowing not to hound the competent senior is one thing, but what if you're concerned that your senior is in the danger zone of not completing applications on time? One important gauge is your child's pattern of fulfilling responsibilities. If your child is a postponer, like Lauren of the previous vignette, consider negotiating as Mattie did: Have a tête-à-tête wherein you agree not to talk about applications and deadlines if your senior agrees to turn everything in at least a week before it's due.

Although an arrangement like this provides parents a stopgap, unfortunately not every senior will comply. If your child has always been one to knock on your bedroom door at midnight asking you to proof an essay—and you've consistently relented—you might need to brace yourself for that same pattern or bring in outside help to avoid it.

One option is to ask a friend your child knows and

RIGHT AS YOU'RE TEARING YOUR HAIR OUT OVER YOUR SENIOR'S APPLICATIONS DURING THE HOLIDAY BREAK, SOME EARLY-DECISION APPLICANTS ARE RECEIVING ACCEPTANCE LETTERS. A REVERSE PROCESS HAPPENS IN SPRING: EARLY-DECISION CANDIDATES OFTEN HAVE SECOND THOUGHTS AS THEIR FRIENDS BASK IN MULTIPLE CHOICES.

respects for a big favor you'll return some day. This friend could work with your child, setting up deadlines, proofing the essay, and double-checking applications for completeness, based on the assumption that it's emotionally cleaner for a child to deal with anyone other than one's own parent.

If you have a high-conflict relationship, a child whose history of meeting deadlines is shaky, and you don't have a friend or relative to lean on, see if your school counselor can closely supervise the process, or you may want to hire a private college counselor. Like private tutoring, private college counseling has experienced a huge upswing because it shifts some of the anxiety to an independent third party. Although some feel it's a luxury, families prioritize funds for both tutoring and college counseling when they know from experience that anything less sets the teenager up for failure and the family up for quarrelling.

With any kind of student, be on the lookout for extremes. If a senior misses a less-than-essential deadline, say, signing up for an SAT prep course, it may be that he never really intended to take the course in the first place. On the other hand, if he "forgets" about taking the actual test, there's greater cause for concern. It's classic for even earnest teens to slip up once or twice with something like forgetting one college counselor appointment, skipping the first deadline for handing in an essay, and not sending away for college material in the summer.

However, when a teen persistently misses his deadlines, and it looks as if he's not going to pull through, doubts about launching could accelerate to the level of self-sabotage. Do you have grounds to suspect that he's truly undermining his chances of leaving home by delaying his applications? It is common for students to feel aimless, not quite ready for more school, and muse about taking some time off from school— or something deeper might be at work that could be identified through clinical consultation. Review the larger picture of what's going on in your child's life, whether there is, for example, a pattern of truancy, unrelenting arguing, or withdrawal from the family. When application avoidance is persistent, look into it.

If you determine that your child's last-minute scrambling is normal, consider doing what most parents do: Remind yourself that you won't be able to hover like a helicopter in college, then take a leap of faith and turn the job over to the senior—mostly.

I'm using the qualifier "mostly" deliberately. Some highly directed seniors handle the whole process themselves, but in truth many parents aren't entirely able to wash their hands of the process. After 18 years of service as our children's monitors on many vital tasks, ranging from orthodontist appointments to birthday plans to school functions, how can we expect ourselves to leave something as monumental as college applications solely up to our children—especially if they're dragging their feet?

Badgering, pleading, bribing, and threatening are off-limits, but small acts of behind-the-scenes technical support are legitimate and usually acceptable to seniors, though often tricky to get right. Grounding your senior for two weeks until applications are done will strike most seniors as overbearing, just as rescuing your child by micromanaging the process is a problem. On the other hand, some busy seniors who have trouble prioritizing competing interests will benefit from a parent's gentle nudging and setting up of a quiet space and time—plus great snacks. By all means, make sure your child stays in charge and does the real work

IT MAY BE TOO BLACK OR WHITE FOR PARENTS TO STAY OUT OF THE APPLICATIONS PROCESS ENTIRELY. ASSISTING WITH SOME OF THE "SECRETARIAL" DETAILS GIVES PARENTS A MEANS TO NURTURE THEIR CHILDREN—AND THEMSELVES!

(anything else would be unethical), and if your senior resists your efforts, know to back off. Whatever help you provide should be nurturing, supporting, and in the background, perhaps making a phone call to set up an appointment, or addressing envelopes, or photocopying forms, for example.

A primary benefit of providing some of the legwork for your senior is that it can be tremendously soothing for parents. Being able to do something—anything—concrete often eases the tension and can avert a power struggle. The calmer parents feel, the less likely they'll be to nag, and the more likely seniors will be assume ownership of the process—in their own way.

KEEPING BOUNDARIES

Like marriage, childbirth, and your child's first day of school, launching is a major developmental threshold that throws parents into a whirlwind. If not over applications per se, launch anxiety will rear its head somewhere, and when special circumstances—such as illness, a difficult divorce, or spirited temperament—made growing up difficult, launching can be an even stormier process.

Even amicably divorced parents can experience turmoil during the application process, since it requires coordination, cooperation, and negotiation between parents and child. High-conflict divorced parents run a particular risk for creating havoc. I've heard numerous single parents complain of an uninvolved ex-spouse who had little to no interest in their child's education but who suddenly wanted to play a major role in the college process. Parents (and stepparents) with bitterness about financial obligations related to college costs can start to sabotage the application process by not filling out forms, withdrawing emotional support, and engaging in old battles with each other. Since seniors benefit from family stability during this difficult time, renewed divorce wars over college issues can only add fuel to the fire.

Parents with intense launch anxiety risk telegraphing it to their child, either directly or indirectly. To the extent that these intense feelings are about parental circumstances or "baggage" (parents' own unresolved life disappointments or fears about adjusting to post-launch circumstances), this kind of communication is both unhelpful and potentially destructive, since adolescents almost always sense when they're on the receiving end of emotional reactivity that is about the parents' own issue.

How can parents contain their issues during this vulnerable time? Psychologists speak of the importance of firm parent-child boundaries. The idea of "keeping boundaries" is not synonymous with "setting limits," although it is sometimes used that way. Boundaries demarcate the separations between any two entities, whether it be between an individual self and another person, between the parental unit and children, or between family and the outside world. Boundaries organize how we function. They delineate the emotional distance or closeness we maintain with others—how we relate and what we do and don't share.

When boundaries are firm, we contain our feelings judiciously, without venting extreme feelings that could be destructive and unhelpful to others. Having firm boundaries also means that if we're blasted by others' extreme feelings, we keep a grip on our own reality and assessment of things.

When interpersonal boundaries are rigid, we're not connecting or sharing enough. People with rigid boundaries tend to wall off their own emotions, and others' feelings make little impact. During launching, parents whose boundaries are rigid may, for example, dictate college choice or mandate course selection because they aren't adequately sensitive to their child's world. Alternately, a walled-off child may not share his feelings and ideas related to his future, leaving parents unable to guide and support the launch.

On the other hand, if boundaries are blurry, weak, or too permeable, we can become symbiotic with the other. When parent-child boundaries are weak during launching, the child feels the parent's anxiety, and vice versa. Anxiety becomes magnified, thoughtless remarks ("Keep this up and you'll never get into college!") swarm like flies, and mutual hysteria may mount. Sometimes the senior may need to protect herself from this tumultuousness by avoiding the tasks related to college applications.

Firm boundaries, where parents avoid spilling their fears and disappointments and share a respectful, balanced assessment of their child's situation and decisions, should be the goal. Proper boundaries keep parents accountable for knowing the difference between their children's challenges and their own.

> WHEN PARENTS' BOUNDARIES ARE FIRM, THEY HAVE CLARITY ABOUT THEIR OWN PERSONAL FEELINGS AND DESIRES, WHICH THEY CAN DISTINGUISH FROM THEIR SENIORS'; THIS ALLOWS PARENTS TO RESPOND TO THEIR SENIORS' NEEDS AND TO GUIDE AND SUPPORT THEM APPROPRIATELY DURING LAUNCHING.

WHAT'S NEXT FOR A LATE BLOOMER? FAMILY STORY

Different young people have different timetables for launching, especially those with significant learning differences or conditions such as Attention Deficit Disorder. How do behavioral flare-ups in senior year tie into the picture?

I met the Gibson family through the Adolescent Clinic at the University of Washington in Seattle, where I supervise trainees (graduate students, child psychiatry fellows, child psychology interns) gaining expertise in adolescent psychology and family therapy. Tucker Gibson was 17 when I first saw him. He had been diagnosed with Attention Deficit Disorder (ADD) in fifth grade and had been on medication since the end of eighth grade. Tucker and his family had been followed by their pediatrician regularly and occasionally received counseling for the family turmoil that all too often accompanies ADD—particularly when hyperactivity (ADHD) is part of the package, as it was with Tucker.

When we discussed Tucker's situation at a staff session in the Adolescent Clinic, we all nodded our heads and murmured, sympathetically, "classic" because Tucker typified what happens to some young people with ADD during their senior year. Many seniors with ADD, with their own personal strengths and responsive, consistent parenting, can thrive, head to college on schedule, and succeed; but Tucker's competence level rendered him not ready to leave for college in a number of ways. Mature physically, Tucker looked as if he were a grown man, but having been burned by the consequences of his ADD so many times, he was thrown by the graduation milestone and all that it signified.

Although the Gibsons were familiar with family counseling, the transcript that follows represents my first visit with them. Reading the emotions of the family as they came in, I saw a 17 year old who was seething; he couldn't believe he was being sent back to family therapy, especially after all they'd been through in middle school. The dad appeared reluctant and the mom antsy to proceed.

LK: Tell me about the crisis that brings you in at this time.
TAMARA: Which one? We have a whole odyssey we could tell you about from the last few weeks. (She chuckles, trying to be

pleasant, but as her eyes move from me to her husband and son, she notes that they give her dirty looks.)

LK: Well, you told me something on the phone about the beer cans you found, which led to a blow-up, so why don't we begin there?

TAMARA: (Clearly glad to get started) Well, Tucker was already grounded because he had violated curfew the previous weekend, and then one evening I found beer cans in the back of his car, which I know were newly added because they weren't there the day before. He must have been drinking after school.

TUCKER: Mom, I TOLD YOU, they were THERE from last Saturday night, and they were NOT mine. They were the guys' that I took home, and they were just finishing them when they got in the car. We did NOT drink in the car.

TAMARA: (Smiling to show she has his number) Oh, how ridiculous. (Turning to LK) This isn't one of the more convincing stories as they go. (Turning back to Tucker and saying with sarcasm) The beer cans were from the night you were already punished for, they were not yours, and the beer was, of course, not consumed in the car. Really, Tucker, how naive do you think I am?

I note that Tamara, despite her smiling, rises to the bait. She can't resist calling him on his baloney. Her anger is easily triggered by Tucker's provocative words or actions.

TUCKER: Fine. Don't believe me. You never do. You're always right, and I'm always wrong. Why come here to communicate better, when you will only see it your way!

TAMARA: How am I supposed to listen respectfully when you BS your way through every story?

Judson, the father, has been sitting back, shaking his head occasionally in disdain for this interaction.

LK: Mr. Gibson, what's your take on the beer-can incident?

JUDSON: I don't know when or where the beer was consumed. And at this point, I don't much care. Tucker is almost 18 years old. He's about to graduate, and I'm looking for some peace finally.

LK: What do you mean "finally"?

JUDSON: Well, we've raised three kids—Tucker's our last—and I'm just kind of ready not to make a big deal about every little thing.

TAMARA: You call drinking and driving (she hesitates), I mean possible drinking and driving, a little thing? (Her voice is rising.)

JUDSON: (Sighing, seemingly weary of what is probably a well-worn interaction between them) Tamara, I don't know. I just know I'm tired out from the screaming between you and Tucker.

TAMARA: (Visibly upset) Well, I wouldn't have to be the one to confront him as much if you would help me out more!

JUDSON: What do you mean? I was the one who handled the call from the coach when he got suspended!

TAMARA: Only because I wasn't home. If I had been, that would have landed in my lap, too. And, Judson, how can you criticize me for being the one who screams at him about beer cans, when your fight with him last week led to his leaving home for two days!

I've listened long enough to hear the essence of their dynamic and knew it was time to change directions. I needed to see this interchange to verify that mutual blaming is probably what goes on at home all the time, but letting it go on any longer would have been cruel.

LK: So, I see what you meant by a whole odyssey in two weeks' time. And I get the feeling that this story started a long time ago. Mr. Gibson, would you say that you are usually more tolerant of Tucker's infractions than Mrs. Gibson?

JUDSON: (Uncomfortable with this direct question—he squirms) Well, I wouldn't say "tolerant." It's just that Tamara jumps on everything all the time. With Tucker's ADD, there are a lot of things that stir her up—what with problems with grades, forgetfulness, disorganization—I can let a lot of that go easier than she can. I can identify with those things since I have the same tendencies. I mean, I don't always get my reports in on time at work. But when something happens like this call from the coach last week, I can blow sky-high, too.

TUCKER: You can say that again.

JUDSON: (Cynically) I can blow sky-high (Tucker rolls his eyes.) Basically, what happened is that when I asked Tucker about the fight he had with a teammate, he blew me off, saying it was the other kid's fault and it was no big deal. I knew it was, or the coach wouldn't have called announcing two days' suspension from school. Then we had a big argument, and Tucker went to stay at his girlfriend's house for two days.

LK: What do you think would have happened if Tamara had taken the call?

JUDSON: (Pensively, tentatively) I guess she would have jumped all over Tucker instead of me.

LK: And how would you have reacted to Tamara's jumping on Tucker?

JUDSON: I see where you're going with this. I would have been too busy noticing how upset Tamara was to get around to the real problem, Tucker's fight and the coach's phone call.

LK: Well, it sounds like you both understand the dynamics in your family pretty well actually. Does that sound about right to you too, Tucker?

TUCKER: Yeah, the deal is that someone is always jumping on me.

WHY LAUNCHING UNEARTHS UNDESIRABLE FAMILY DYNAMICS

Only too easily can parents of children with ADD feel as if they have to be their child's brain, memory, secretary, gift finder, counselor, and tutor. To keep these young people on track takes more active and sophisticated parenting than with the average child. There's hardly a mom or dad of a child with this disorder who hasn't racked up a long record of nagging, even though it rarely works and often provokes a backfire effect from the child.

Tucker and his family experienced a great deal of fighting in middle school. Between the biological part of his ADD (inability to retain reminders), the adolescent developmental part (need for autonomy, to become his own person, and act out a little against his parents), and the behavioral part (passive aggressiveness in reaction to the parental onslaught), Tucker started screening out more and more of his parents' directives to keep him on track. Eventually, the family elected to try medication, which helped Tucker.

Although they had to cope with the academic roller-coaster and adjust expectations to a C to C-plus average, high school was smoother going for the Gibsons, who concluded that the worst was behind them. Then came senior year.

Launching often stimulates troublesome relationship dynamics and behavioral patterns, particularly those that families hoped would "just go away." In the abridged interview above with Tamara, Judson, and Tucker, key features of the Gibson's family functioning emerged: Mom was the one who was usually on the front line, receiving the hit whenever Tucker got in trouble. Dad was tired, so he stayed in the background. When Tucker provoked his mother, she reacted like a heat-seeking missile, pursuing her target. Because he wanted peace and saw similarities between himself and Tucker, Judson was willing to overlook a lot, which left Tamara acting on her own. But whenever Tamara wasn't present to handle a problem, there was either a complete vacation from consequences or a crisis in which Judson "blows sky-high."

Family-system psychologists envision the family unit as a network of relationships. Unlike other branches of psychology, which analyze the individual psyche, family systems explores relationships among family members as an *ecosystem*. When problems

OVER THE YEARS, INDIVIDUALS OFTEN BECOME AWARE OF KNEE-JERK REACTIONS AND UNPRODUCTIVE ROLES THEY ASSUME IN FAMILY INTERACTIONS. EVEN IF THEY'VE CURBED SOME OF THEIR INEFFECTIVE WAYS, THE FALL FLURRY OFTEN ACTIVATES SOME OF THESE OLD DYNAMICS.

arise in the family network, everyone is affected or involved in some way, and everyone can be part of the solution.

Patterns of interaction between family members become a primary focus—who is close to whom, who reacts to whom, who has power, whether the parents work together and have an authoritative rank above children, and whether boundaries exist to organize roles and behaviors of family members in healthy, productive ways.

Within the Gibson family system were three related dynamics common to many struggling families, particularly those with children with ADD.

Dynamic 1: *Rising to the bait*. In essence, Tamara's threshold for reacting to Tucker was set way too low, and the consequence of her reactivity was a loss of focus on the problem that needed attention. Notice in the therapy transcript how expertly Tucker avoids his own issues and how easily he pulls his mom into an argument—"Fine. Don't believe me. You never do. You're always right, and I'm always wrong!"—and how effective that was in diverting attention away from the beer-can incident.

While well intended, Tamara's determination to get the story straight aggravated the situation, created a power struggle, and obscured what was really troubling Tucker—his fear of what life held for him after high school.

During times of distress, we need to prioritize and maintain firm boundaries with our children. Parents should ask themselves: Even though a behavior or remark invites a comeback, will my response move things forward? Will my retort help or escalate? Am I inviting further defensiveness?

Dynamic 2: *The family shock absorber*. With Tamara

> WE ALL HAVE TO LEARN ABOUT CENSORING OUR REACTIONS AND RETORTS, BASED ON WHAT WORKS. NO MATTER HOW VALID, IS CRITICISM THE BEST TOOL TO USE?

pursuing Tucker's every infraction, Judson failed to feel the shock of his son's defiance and disobedience, since Tamara was absorbing the shock. It was simple physics: Whenever Tamara was between Tucker and Judson, it would be less intense for Judson. What Judson did feel, however, was the reverberation of Tamara's behavior. His reaction to her anger was to identify with his son and defend him, in a kind of alliance against Tamara.

Judson and Tucker had a natural tendency for a coalition because of the biology and behaviors they had in common, making Tamara the "odd one out" because she isn't forgetful and disorganized like father and son. Notice, however, how over-controlling Judson could be when a problem didn't hit Tamara's threshold first, as with the coach's phone call about the school suspension. Dad's reaction was what we call "over and under," that is, he either overreacted or underreacted. Either way—whether he was quarreling directly with his son or counteracting Tamara's intensity—he was never parenting collaboratively with her.

> **AS DURING ANY "HOT" TIME OF PARENTING, LAUNCHING STRESS CAN TRIGGER A GOOD COP/BAD COP DYNAMIC, WHERE ONE PARENT CARRIES MOST OF THE DISCIPLINING BURDEN AND THE OTHER GETS TO BE THE FRIEND.**

Dynamic 3: *Parent on a limb.* If a parent takes an extreme position without the support of the other parent, she risks going out on a limb. Again and again, parenting books recommend consistent, authoritative parenting for a good reason— it works best. In a two-parent family, the emphasis includes mutual supportiveness and co-parenting. The authoritative parenting style exists at a midpoint between restrictive parenting at one extreme and permissive at the other. It is characterized by the three critical qualities of parental control, warmth, and communication. While the restrictive style is exclusively about parental control and the permissive style lacks control altogether, the authoritative approach emphasizes firm discipline, a supportive relationship, and respect for input from the child. Studies consistently show authoritative parenting to be correlated with the development of competence and self-reliance in children and with positive adjustment.[4]

Parenting a child with a challenging temperament requires even more positivism, consistent discipline, and parental unity, since high stress can split parents in more destructive ways.

> WHEN PARENTS ARE AT ODDS WITH ONE ANOTHER IN THEIR APPROACH TO A PROBLEM, THE CHILD MISSES OUT ON A COHERENT PARENTING RESPONSE, AND THE PARENTS MISS OUT ON SUPPORTIVE TEAMWORK.

Because Tamara was the family taskmaster, she had gradually assumed the lion's share of child-rearing responsibilities, becoming the family's left brain. She needed Judson's help. Instead of just venting her fury, though, she had to ask herself, "What can I do to engage Judson?"

DOING WHAT'S RIGHT FOR THIS SENIOR WITH ADD

The beauty of analyzing troublesome family interactions as a systems dynamic is that no individual is the "bad guy," since each person's behavior is a function of or reaction to the larger network of relationships. Everyone is part of the problem, and everyone is part of the solution.

Even at this late date in child-rearing, the Gibson family could make changes to enhance future relationships. Judson's main job was to become more fully engaged in parenting, while Tamara's was to tone down her emotional volatility so that Judson would have a chance to feel his own reactions to Tucker's acting out. Tamara had to trust that if she reacted less, Judson would react more, and she had to see how much Tucker was suffering from divisive parenting. In truth, Tamara had to live with the reality that Judson would never react enough for her likes, just as Judson had to accept that Tamara's reactions would always be a little over the top for him. Nonetheless, a mutual crimping of their former ways would allow them to parent together, creating more consistent, rational family policies and consequences.

Parenting teamwork is always superior to polarizing and wasting energy on marital resentments, but parenting challenging children can bring out intense beliefs about what's best for the child. Polarizing occurs when individuals with strong beliefs confront each other, moving to more extreme positions by virtue of reacting to one another. Couples can start off in one place, which might not be too far apart from each other, but over time they stake out more exaggerated positions. Because it's a mutual process, each person in the relationship must own up to his own complicity in this destructive two-step.

Tucker's senior-year disruptiveness expressed his trepidation about the future, exposing his fears of adult expectations. Tamara and Judson were so busy dousing the conflagrations lit daily and weekly that they couldn't see that Tucker wasn't ready to head off on the same path as many other seniors. If your child is six feet two, brawny, and masculine (like Tucker), it's harder for him to show—and easier for parents to miss—that he needs more nurturing. How difficult it is to parent a child who is developmentally uneven. Language, sophistication, and ability to obfuscate are at 18, but the senior may still be forgetting chores, blowing his budget, lying, and partying like there's no tomorrow!

For some time the Gibsons had had a question mark in

their minds about Tucker's pace of development, but parents of slow-to-bloom seniors often feel pressure to maintain the timeline and think, "He's 18! He should be doing better than this!" Absolutely, many young people with ADD have the wherewithal to launch straight to college, but Tucker's unique features made it a stretch.

> WHEN EVERYONE AROUND YOU WANTS YOU TO BE FULLY 18—ACROSS ALL DOMAINS OF FUNCTIONING AND RESPONSIBILITY—AND YOU'RE NOT, THAT DIFFERENCE CAN PROVOKE TREMENDOUS FAMILY UPHEAVAL.

Through therapy and in concert with the school, the Gibsons pulled out all stops to help Tucker through his senior year. Dad took over the disciplinary role and met with school counselors to figure out what Tucker needed to do to graduate; Mom's role was more as a consultant to Dad than hands-on with Tucker. A comprehensive structure (for school, extracurricular activities, home life, and social life) was imposed on Tucker to monitor his progress, and his activities were restricted until he met set expectations. Even with this amount of help, though, if a senior really wants to fail, he can still fail.

Tucker squeaked through. He had just enough inner strength to tolerate graduating from high school and facing an uncertain future, but clearly he needed and benefited enormously from more adult oversight. Instead of a full launch in September, Tucker lived at home for the next two years while working part time and attending community college, with mixed results. During this time, Tucker and his parents dealt with a range of challenges, including his problems with budgeting, parking tickets, car repairs, and phone bills. With his partial launch, structured responsibilities, and his parents teaming up around policies, everyone's relationships improved, as did Tucker's maturational rate.

LATE BLOOMERS

Many young people experience complications that hinder their academic performance, making a direct move to college less than sure-fire. These students can be called *late bloomers* because their transition to adulthood and the realization of their potential takes longer than their peers. A list of complications might include poverty, learning differences, Attention Deficit Disorder, a pattern of underachievement, developmental problems, temperament issues, illness in the family, dysfunction in the family (stemming, for example, from an acrid divorce, marital discord, or highly conflictual parenting styles), and personal problems (for instance, chronic illness, mental illness, drug use during adolescence). Often it's possible to pinpoint what interrupted their route, or there may simply be vague perceptions in the teen or the parent that time off for maturation is necessary or holds greater benefits than higher education at this point.

A generation or two ago, young people were either on or off the college track. That's no longer so. America is, after all, a land of second chances. Although students on any trajectory might take a break from school before veering back into higher education, interruptions are common for young people who are slower to bloom. Despite a more circuitous route, an academically slow-to-bloom senior can ultimately be just as successful as others, particularly when emotional intelligence is high. Although the probability of a child's success increases through more education, developmental psychology has debunked the concept of a strict timetable for entry into the adult world.[5] Having a child launch from home at age 18 is not what renders a family "normal" or "successful," since there are many schedules and paths to adulthood in today's world.

On a practical note, if late blooming is creating behavioral uproar, parents need to continue guiding the parts of their high-school senior that behave as if still in middle school, while also treating the child with respect and as an adult in other ways, so he doesn't feel patronized and over-controlled. Despite all of their late bloomers' aggravating behavior, parents who know how to look out for their children become their cheerleaders, reassuring them that they'll find their path. Alternately, if the senior prefers the company of parents, is fearful of independence, and is reluctant to take on increased responsibilities, parents can add incentives to expand the senior's repertoire.

How can parents stay respectful of their slow-to-ripen 18 year old while parenting in a more labor-intensive way than they ever dreamed they'd have to at this stage? The answer: by having empathy for the difficulty of the young person's path.

Keep in mind that many conditions that slow down a young person's development can be as built in and as much a part of the individual's biological predisposition as any physical handicap. But young people with delays, deficits, and problems of temperament are more easily judged than children with more evident conditions. Unfortunately, parents often see the characteristics of late bloomers as character failings and end up judgmental and exasperated rather than motivated to problem-solve, build skills, support every success major or minor, and reach launching goals gradually.

Slow-to-bloom adolescents will continue to mature during the senior year. If you have reasons to believe that a launch to college might be too much of a leap for your senior, instead of narrowing in on college as the only path, widen the possibilities to include other growthful options, like commu-

> IT'S CRUCIAL FOR PARENTS OF SLOW-TO-BLOOM SENIORS TO UNDERSTAND WHO THEIR CHILD IS AND TO SHEPHERD ALONG THE AREAS THAT NEED MORE WORK WHILE ALSO EMPHASIZING STRENGTHS.

nity college, a fifth year of high school, a travel program, military service, or an interim job. Late bloomers are more likely to hit their stride if they can focus their energies on a specific goal and a specific area of strength.

Higher education need not be automatically ruled out, though. A well-chosen small college—one without dog-eat-dog academic competitiveness—may be a chance for a late bloomer to be a big fish in a small pond, be mentored, develop more self-esteem as a learner, and be turned on to something. The key for these seniors is to find an option that will be sure to build competencies and help them feel more capable than they were in high school.

Whatever the path, the priority should be on maximizing maturational gains, while setting up some personal successes that may also help the senior clarify values or discover a career choice.

SURVIVING THE FALL FLURRY

Families have long recognized September as one of the most stressful months of the year, since it hails the beginning of the school year and a marked shift in schedule and routine. With new demands ahead, families take stock and set the stage for the next year of their children's lives. Parents of seniors experience the September milestone in spades.

During senior year's fall flurry, plans are being laid not only for the year ahead but often for launching the following September. During this season, whatever has gone on over the previous 17 years of a child's development comes home to roost, as young people face the inescapable question of what to do next year. Families can be inundated by a cascade of stressors—college entrance exams, maintaining or improving grades, college applications, to name a few. As parents and children alike anticipate loss and change, launch anxiety can reach its zenith, and old power struggles can re-emerge in full force. Central to this time, the college-application process often serves as both a battleground and a "dumping" ground for everyone's stress.

A key task for parents is to assess whether your senior is ready, mature, and motivated to take advantage of college resources next year. Ask yourself, "What will my child benefit most from for the next period of time?" Keep in mind that it is a fallacy to base success as a parent on the caliber of a child's college-admission ticket and that an individual's future is built more on values, drive, and the quality of engagement in school and life than a 4.0 GPA. Make the step to college an informed step, not a lock-step, and create a plan where something wonderful will happen for your child.

The ultimate challenge for many parents during the application process, however, is to establish firm boundaries between the parents' personal feelings and responsibilities and those of the senior. Parents would be wise to deal directly with their own anxiety and to limit the "leaking" that can burden the senior's own load, which is probably overwhelming, although rarely verbalized as such.

Adolescents need calm, steady parenting during the fall of their senior year, whether it is in the form of pure nurturing, limit-setting on various behaviors, or guiding them through their applications. Different seniors need different degrees and types of support, and the magic of good parenting lies in sizing up what the parents' needs are and what the child's needs are and sticking to that business.

Just as seniors gain help on various fronts—from parents, teachers, an objective college counselor, and good friends—parents can benefit from their own trusted support network during the fall shake-up. Emotions of the fall may be a flurry, but if we keep ourselves on track as parents, we help our seniors do the same.

CHAPTER TWO

Winter in Limbo and Spring Flings

Senioritis involves far more than what meets the eye

UNLOOSE THESE CHAINS

The time: Saturday night. The place: the threshold of a home. The people: parents and an 18-year-old son with one foot out the door.

SON: Hey, Dad, gimme the keys.

DAD: They're on the table.

SON: Got 'em. I'm going out.

DAD: Bye.

MOM: Wait! Not so fast. Where are you going? What's up?

SON: Jason and I are meeting some kids at Chelsea's.

MOM: Are her . . . ?

SON: (Interrupts with sarcasm) Yeeees, her parents are there.

MOM: (Firm, respectfully) Watch the attitude. We still have family rules and curfews, you know. I need to know where you'll be, and don't forget to come into our bedroom and let us know when you're home.

SON: (Keeping his cool) Oh, c'mon, Mom, relax. I'm not going to have a curfew in college. No one's going to be checking on me. Look at it this way, if I have more freedom now, then you'll know I can handle it when I'm on my own.

DAD: He does have a point, you know. If we ease up a little more now, he'll get some practice with what's ahead.

MOM: (Glaring at Dad) Once we start "easing up," as you call it, where does it end? No curfew? No accountability? (Turning to son) I don't see what you need to be doing between 1 and 3 in the morning that you couldn't do between 11 and 1. You're still a member of this household. You're not gone—yet. (Dad and son share a glance.)

If all were fair, turmoil in the family would peak once college applications hit the post office, and the rest of the school year would roll easily along. The arduous task of selecting schools and filling in forms complete, families would experience a reprieve while waiting to hear from admissions offices. However, it rarely happens that way. Skirmishes like the one in this family are endemic to senior year, with parents divided over how much freedom to give their seniors, who want to be confident masters of their own universe.

SENIORITIS: WHAT IS IT AND WHY NOW?

As with any transition or life phase, senioritis isn't tidily confined to a single span in time. It peeks through in various ways as early as junior year of high school, pertains to both in and out of school, and extends roughly through the summer after graduation. Although twinges of senioritis surface sporadically over an extended period, it's typically at its worst once applications are finished. Seniors want to kick free. From their perspective, midway through senior year they stand at the gateway to freedom, but we—the parents—continue to see them as our children who need our sane oversight. Even before seniors know where they're headed for college, they move to their next role—college freshman—while we're hanging on to the old model: They're still a member of the family, beholden to our rules and regulations.

What exactly is senioritis? It has three facets.

ONCE COLLEGE APPLICATIONS ARE COMPLETED, SENIORS ARE FREED UP TO EXPRESS DIRECTLY OTHER FEELINGS RELATED TO LAUNCHING THAT HAVE BEEN PUSHED ASIDE. AS ONE PARENT PUT IT, "SENIORITIS MEANS ANTS IN HIS PANTS ABOUT EVERYTHING!"

1. An Academic Slump. Every college counselor and admissions representative warns seniors to keep up their GPAs during winter and spring, but no matter how many times they hear, "Your grades still count," seniors feel battle fatigue for school.

When I ask parents in my launching groups to identify their major concerns after applications are in, slacking grades are a top complaint. Parents observe their seniors becoming indifferent to school or making less effort. There may be some truancy; they may slip up on assignments; or they may plead to drop a course to ease their load. Academic superstars want to keep their high GPAs, but they, too, can start to resent the grinding pace. Academic ennui can shock parents who have taken pride in their child's stellar achievements and drive.

Some seniors' attitudes become more confrontational with teachers. No longer do they want to be accountable to the same set of expectations. At its core, the schoolwork slump of senioritis pertains to how seniors feel about still being in school day after day when they may be elsewhere mentally.

2. "Blahs" to Everything. Senioritis' second aspect is

more elusive than academic indifference, but no less pervasive. A blanket of weariness and ambivalence can descend on their world. Sick of everything and everyone, many disengage. Typically, parents overhear mumblings of boredom like, "There's nothing going on around here." Even their most valued friends are a little annoying, a troubling feeling for most young people. An aspect of seniors' identity shifting, this mood toward friends can be more pronounced for young people who've had a trip or experience away from their peer group. The old *sameness* isn't there because they feel themselves changing. This drifting away resembles what happens between some high-school buddies after their freshman year of college, but during winter of the senior year of high school, the disconnect among some peers is often followed by bonding madly with them around graduation.

3. Power Surges. Think back to the defiance of the "terrible twos" and the bridling behaviors of middle school. Winter of senior year signals another onset of a push for autonomy (the independence to self-govern). Just as a two year old during the first autonomy phase informs her parents, "You're not the boss of me," 18 year olds spar with their parents during the transition to adulthood, as if to say, "I don't want to answer to you anymore."

Evidence for an increased zeal during the senior year can be gleaned from a study of the Class of 2000 by CBS. Between fall and graduation, twice as many seniors reported that independence was what they were most looking forward to—more than their career, starting a family, being successful, or being in college.[1]

At length, seniors in my launching groups tell me how much they want to call their own shots—and how entitled they feel to do so. Bidding for more freedom to run their own lives, most capitalize on their good negotiating position as seniors. Implicitly, their attitude conveys, "I'm way more competent than you give me credit for, but I'm not about to tell you everything I've been through because you'd freak out if you knew—so just trust me."

Some seniors tire of hedging responses and operating behind parents' backs and boldly inform parents that it's time to "get real." Substance use is a prime example: As 18 year olds, most have handled being around alcohol—which will be everywhere on college campuses—so why, they ask, the inquisition about drinking?

Despite their relative maturity, many seniors get way out of line with power surges. Testing their wings too far, some engage in actions like vandalism, reckless driving, binge drinking, or other potentially tragic behaviors. Well-adjusted adolescents survive periodic risk-taking, but this is also a time for parents to keep a watchful eye.

PARENTS CONTRACT SENIORITIS, TOO

Senioritis, as commonly defined, is said to be the senior's condition, but everyone in the family can succumb, contributing to the emotional rollercoaster. No longer can parents escape the stressful realization that it's the beginning of the end of their child-rearing years. Many are dealing with their own midlife issues (jobs, health, loss of youth) and perhaps also with elderly or incapacitated parents. Siblings, who tend to balance a love-hate relationship with older brothers and sisters, may panic at the prospect of being alone at home with a parent or parents.

During this time, many parents pick at their senior's flaws. Whatever they see their child doing or whoever he may be, it's not good enough. Maybe it's the senior's attitude, their boyfriend or girlfriend, their spending habits, wasting of time, or sloppy manners—parents grab at anything as a legitimate basis for tampering with their senior's behavior.

The compulsion is for parents to work overtime to put fin-ishing touches on their children before leaving home. The more their child displays the symptoms of senioritis, the more parents harp, wondering whether their child is ready to leave at all. Observing their seniors revert to middle-school shenanigans and become as temperamental as they were dur-ing puberty, bemused parents ask themselves, "How can this child possibly be mature enough to handle college?"

Most 18 year olds remain ragged around the edges, for no child ever launches from home as a perfect specimen—nor will any of us ever be so. Parents whose seniors are either slumping academi-cally, feeling the "blahs," or surging with power typically endure and maneuver through these behaviors, relying on a grab-bag of parenting tactics such as reminding, ignoring, and intervening with stern rebukes. Only rarely do these first two aspects of senioritis become big-ticket items for parents. Obviously, if the slumps become failing grades or the blahs veer into depression, they've edged beyond senioritis and into the domain where a professional consultation can be of value.

ON THE EVE OF A CHILD'S EXIT, PARENTS WORRY ABOUT THE LOOSE ENDS. WE FIXATE ON WHATEVER ISN'T PERFECT ABOUT OUR CHILDREN, AS IF IT WILL MAKE OR BREAK A SUCCESSFUL LAUNCH FROM HOME. THIS IS A PRIME SYMPTOM OF SENIORITIS IN PARENTS.

Power surges of senioritis, however, more commonly go over the top. A young person who has been basically under control all year might surprise parents with an unsanctioned party or an all-nighter. A student who has always had the highest respect for teachers might be unaccountably rude. To keep from overreacting, parents may need to remind them-selves that power surges belong to this age and stage, but whenever parents have questions about what a behavior signals, a consultation remains an option.

At the very least, parents of seniors want to be smart about maintaining fair and basic family policies that keep emerging adults healthy, safe, and responsible, but it's a rare family that doesn't need to adjust in some way to their 18 year old's push for freedom. In other words, keep your authority and maintain your monitoring and communication, but realize that your senior is training you for another phase of parenting.

HOME ALONE FOR THE FAMILY TRIP?
FAMILY STORY

The perfect place, the perfect family vacation, but this high-school senior has ideas of her own for winter break. What about leaving a nearly grown child home alone? Who has the say about vacations?

The parenting workshops I lead in schools will sometimes be comprised of moms and dads who, knowing each other well, open up and converse freely about their problems, despite the public setting. Often we'll delve into a quintessential senior-year issue like adolescent scams or prom parties.

During one such launching workshop, we discussed a dilemma described by Tricia, a single parent of three children, concerning her oldest daughter, Julia. The all-too-common issue was that of high-schoolers wanting to be left home alone, while the rest of the family heads off on a trip or vacation, and it represents a typical—and relatively benign—power surge of senioritis.

Senior year, families experience many "lasts"—the last soccer game, the last school play, or, as in Tricia's case, the last winter break. Especially over important holidays, parents have pressing expectations for their family, feeling as if time were running out for all that remains to be experienced and accomplished together. Many seniors, however, have different agendas. Parents can be dismayed when their seniors balk ungratefully at an extraordinarily special privilege like a resort trip over a school break. Romanticizing about a full-family vacation, parents think only about how wonderful it will be with everyone together. Not in our senior's shoes, we want it our way.

Seniors, on the other hand, have a heightened awareness of this being their last winter break with high-school friends and, grieving the impending separation, yearn to spend as much time as they can with their best buddies. "How can you try to make me go!" they emote. Not thinking in our shoes, they want it their way.

What a perfect conflict: Parents and seniors are both right from their own perspectives.

Many of the fireworks of senior year happen because parents and their emerging adults hold equally valid yet divergent points of view. What to do? The option of pulling rank as family elder and insisting on the vacation—perhaps putting up with a pouting child the whole time—still exists. On the other hand, should you allow your child to stay home as he pleases, you might spend the trip regretting his absence. Many parents realize that the best way to deal with a conflict involving two reasonable points of view is to walk into negotiations knowing each party will have to give somewhere, which is what Tricia Rosen did.

PARENTS' SENTIMENTAL IDEAS ABOUT HOW TO SPEND VACATIONS CAN OVERSHADOW THEIR SENIOR'S OWN NOTIONS. WHOSE VACATION IS IT ANYWAY? BOTH! THAT'S THE DILEMMA.

WHEN YOU AND YOUR SENIOR ARE AT LOGGERHEADS

In the launching workshop, Tricia explained how she and her three children, along with a group of other families, had a wonderful tradition of skiing during the winter break over President's Weekend. For other school holidays, she alternated having the children with her ex-husband, but she coveted winter break all the more because it was always her time with her kids. To Tricia's disappointment, Julia made a strong case to be left behind, largely because she had been sick, earned an incomplete in history, and had a large research paper to finish.

A hidden motive lurked, however, as Tricia explained to the group, "I realized that what she really wanted to do was to stay home to be with friends, in particular her boyfriend."

Another complicating factor ensued, which Julia seized as a bargaining chip. "We have a big family reunion planned in June, so Julia will be missing a special trip with friends right after graduation. She told me that she would attend the reunion without any complaints but wanted to be let out of the ski trip. She's been such a reasonable kid, as teenagers go."

In the end, Tricia and the two younger children headed off skiing without Julia, who could be at home during the day to work on her paper (friendly neighbors were right across the fence) but had to lock the house up by 9:00 P.M. and spend the nights at a friend's house. Tricia established rules about who could come over and when, strictly limiting who could be at the house at any one time and stating specifically that Julia and her boyfriend weren't allowed to be there alone together. As she presented her dilemma and decision to the group, Tricia reflected aloud, wondering whether she'd given up too much in not only allowing Julia to skip the family ski trip, but also to have access to the house.

Within the parenting group, individuals did, indeed,

speak up to question Tricia's compromise. One parent described family vacations as "the glue that keeps families together," while another objected to the opening this plan created for Julia to be alone with her boyfriend in the home.

Though not 100 percent at ease, Tricia was as resolved as she was ever going to be with the vacation dilemma: "I felt like I was drawing the line on insisting on the June reunion and making her go to a friend's house in the evening. Julia and I have had all those talks about her boyfriend and the emotional entanglements of intimacy and sexual decision-making. I feel like she's very responsible and has her eyes open about the relationship, and, frankly, I didn't want to pick that battle at the moment. I made a direct request that her boyfriend not be there with her alone, but I'm ready to not circle the wagons around it, given what a responsible kid she is. I would never have given her this much latitude junior year, but senior year is different."

What is exemplary about Tricia's story is how clearly she sorted out what mattered most to her (the reunion), where she wasn't willing to budge (no overnights, evenings, or groups of young people in the home), what she was willing to leave a little fuzzy (surreptitiously Julia and her boyfriend could be together), and where she was willing to flex (letting go of the ski trip). Their outcome was a good one, and even though Tricia and Julia each gave up strongly prized plans, the compromise worked for them.

> PARENTS MIGHT FEEL THE SATISFACTION OF HAVING WORKED OUT A REASONABLE COMPROMISE WITH THEIR SENIOR, BUT THEY'RE LIKELY TO STILL BE LEFT WITH WORRIES AND WITH RESERVATIONS ABOUT NOT GETTING EVERYTHING THEY WANTED. HAVING SOME REMAINING UNCERTAINTIES IS OFTEN AS GOOD AS IT GETS AFTER NEGOTIATING.

Another family—because of their values, parenting style, hot buttons, priorities, and, most importantly, who their child is—might not choose Tricia's compromise. Another family might continue to insist on the family trip, or they might enact strict measures to protect against romantic trysts, and these also could turn out okay. In dilemmas like Tricia's, there's no crystal ball—just ideas to weigh, values to consider, and judgments to make.

Research shows that the development of competence during adolescence is correlated with key factors during childhood: good relationships with parents or other caring adults, the ability to self-regulate, social skills, socially appropriate conduct, academic achievement, authoritative parenting, and extracurricular activities.[2] The way Tricia described Julia convinced me that she had adequate reasons to consider Julia competent and capable of handling herself responsibly with the parameters she outlined.

Tricia makes it clear that senior year has prompted a shift in her parenting where she is consciously choosing to give her competent daughter more latitude—a shift many families consider. The questions remains: With what type of senior and under what circumstances might parents reasonably loosen their grip?

SENIOR YEAR IS DIFFERENT: A NEW SLANT ON PARENTING CALLS WITH COMPETENT YOUNG PEOPLE

Parents of mature, competent seniors face a thorny question: How much of a hold do I keep on my emerging adult during this final phase of on-site child-rearing? And if I choose to loosen up, how do I know she can handle the freedom responsibly?

Senior year, parents are on the spot with diverse questions

pertaining to control and freedom: Do I continue to forbid my son from attending a party where I suspect alcohol will be served, or do I save my thunder for drinking and driving? Do I allow my daughter to participate in the senior prank? How deeply do I inquire about the overnight after the dance? Do I let my son cook his own goose when he's slacking off in school?

Speaking as a professional, I've seen families employ contrasting but equally effective tactics around control and freedom. In discussions in my launching workshops, I've noticed roughly three different parental approaches to the question of how tight a tether to keep on a senior. A percentage of parents constitute the "hold the line" group, maintaining control and authority on their side. Calling it as they see it, they remain in charge of their child's behavior until leaving home. In this group, I've observed seniors who are furious because their parents say no to something like a hotel room after the prom, which "everybody is doing," but still proceed through launching without any damage to the relationship. Holding the line can work.

Another percentage make up a "call your own shots" group, openly saying, "You're 18. It's up to you. I trust you." Sometimes this stance is rooted in permissiveness, but other times parents ease up because they have low anxiety personally, high trust in their child, and a high regard for what their child might learn. To their senior's delight, I've been aware of parents who say yes to activities involving amazing risks (non-chaperoned spring break flings), claiming their children benefited from the trust and experience that comes with independence. Maybe they do, but more importantly, everyone is relieved if no fiascoes ensue.

The largest percentage of parents belong to a more ambivalent middle, weighing, evaluating, not comfortable either releasing the tether completely or keeping it reeled in closely. For such parents, maintaining hard-edged family policies no longer feels appropriate, particularly when their 18 year old seems to be handling his life well, but neither does unrestrained freedom. Family policies around curfews and homework still apply, but oversight becomes less intense. Although they stay mostly apprised of what's going on in their child's life and guard against serious risk-taking, they're comfortable not having everything spelled out, depending on the situation. They want to continue influencing their child, but they also see value in letting their soon-to-launch child practice at adulthood and in some circumstances live with the consequences of her own decisions and mistakes.

In many ways, being anything less than front and center with authoritative parental policies goes against the grain of good parenting practices—until emerging adults are on the threshold. Having stayed authoritative up to senior year, parents can begin to weigh in less actively, unless stakes are high. This approach with well-adjusted seniors is often a key feature of a senior's transition out of the home.

MANY PARENTS WHO HAVE HELD A CONSERVATIVE LINE UP TO THIS POINT START TO SEE THE VALUE OF EASING UP SELECTIVELY WITH THEIR COMPETENT CHILD DURING SENIOR YEAR—IN WAYS THEY NEVER WOULD HAVE PREDICTED A FEW YEARS EARLIER.

Although parenting philosophies, belief systems, preferences, and values on negotiation all influence the extent to which parents maintain control, other important determinants are a teen's temperament and track record for handling freedom.

Seniors who have always pushed the limits, have shown problems with decision-making and impulse control, or who have other issues should probably still be given taut parameters, even though it's senior year. It's not in anyone's best interest to offer excessive latitude. For instance, for these young people, parents would be prudent to forbid the overnight-at-home-alone option, or, if leaving the senior behind, to have a house sitter, additional surveillance by neighbors, regular checking in with the senior by phone, and predetermined consequences if rules are violated. The less restrained senior will benefit from a reassertion of where parents stand.

The strategy of allowing a teen more independence should be reserved for mature seniors with good judgment who have proven themselves responsible. These kinds of seniors have their own antennae out, recognizing when they're in over their heads. They've shown themselves capable of pulling back from a bad situation. (Realistically, unbeknown to parents, they've probably been stung by getting in over their heads and learned from it.) On the cusp of moving into a larger world, they already know their way in their current world. Having the self-restrained senior doesn't mean you're obliged to loosen up, though; it means extending more freedom is less chancy, unlike with the wilder senior when a firmer parental hand is well advised.

> GIVING AUTONOMY TO HIGH-SCHOOL SENIORS SHOULD BE INEXTRICABLY LINKED TO THEIR PERSONAL COMPETENCE. COMPETENCE, THAT ALL-IMPORTANT MEASURE, IS AN OUTGROWTH OF A YOUNG PERSON'S MAKEUP AND ALL THAT HAS GONE INTO THE CHILD: TEMPERAMENT, LEARNING EXPERIENCES, FAMILY CIRCUMSTANCES, AND OPPORTUNITIES TO DEVELOP PERSONAL SKILLS.

Although parenting approaches and preferences often hinge on how we were parented, our parenting preferences likewise derive from what's been effective with our children. A parenting style is rooted in who we are, but it has also been influenced by who our child is. Over years of countless bouts of parent-child interaction, we each develop a philosophy for how much control and oversight to extend. Some children are rambunctious and full of opposition to authority; others are adaptable and amenable to the parents' program; still others, regardless of parental restraint, seem endowed with remarkable self-control. To some extent, parents will react differently to these different kinds of children and form parenting styles therein. All in all, parenting can look much easier if you've had the inherently self-restrained child!

During the transition from on-site to off-site child-rearing, the decision to extend trust and loosen the authority strings depends on individual family philosophies, the parents' personal anxiety levels, who the child is, and the accumulation of experiences the senior has managed. Consider also the specifics: How risky is the situation? How much uncertainty can you reasonably endure? What's the worst possible outcome? Extending leeway would be inappropriate with middle-schoolers and with ninth- and tenth-graders, but by the end of junior year and throughout the senior year, parents are in the thick of this quandary.

TWO FAMILIES' APPROACHES FOR TWO DIFFERENT SENIORS' RISKY BUSINESS

From benign to dangerous, power surges are part of senioritis. When parents get wind of risky plans in the making, what's the best approach? In some complex situations, a parent's recourse is to pick your poison.

During the final stretch of their last year of high school, many young people, feeling their oats, devise outrageous schemes. Unlike earlier years, when risky business was more covert, seniors are less inclined to contrive elaborate coverups. I was privy to one of these schemes, related to me by two acquaintances who took different positions with sons bent on pushing the limits. Their different positions offer food for thought on how conscientious parents can make dissimilar judgment calls, depending not just on their values, but also on their child's temperament.

My acquaintances' sons were both skilled rock climbers belonging to a local rock-climbing club. In the fall of senior year, the parents heard that some club members, including their sons, planned just prior to graduation to scale a smokestack near school and, in something of a tradition, to paint their class year on the smokestack, removing a previous year's graffiti. Safety was not foremost in the parents' minds, since their sons had completed more difficult, technical assaults. The problem was—it was patently illegal! As time passed, the parents continued to insist that this was a bad idea they were against, hoping their sons would see it their way, but they didn't give an inch.

WITH SOME PARENTING DILEMMAS, YOU COULD ARGUE ALL DAY ABOUT WHAT'S RIGHT OR WRONG. WHAT'S IMPORTANT IS TO KNOW YOURSELF, KNOW YOUR SENIOR, AND BASE YOUR RESPONSE ON WHAT YOU THINK IS IN YOUR CHILD'S BEST INTEREST FOR HIS GROWTH AND PROTECTION.

The first set of parents who shared their dilemma with me had a son named Buck whom they considered to be a constant sensation-seeker. By nature, Buck was inclined to risk-taking, his actions demonstrating that his exuberance took precedence over carefulness. Throughout high school, the family was up against Buck's substance use, school skipping, and low-average school performance, but—on the plus side—he was popular among peers, socially affable, and excited about his part-time job in a sporting store. To keep their son reined in, the parents had maintained a conservative stance, vetoing co-ed camping trips, enforcing a strict curfew, and participating in parent-organized efforts to curb student alcohol use.

Despite predictable resistance and struggle, Buck had basically tolerated his parents' restrictions—up until now. As a senior, he was unrelenting in his determination to climb the smokestack.

Tenacious though their son was, these parents couldn't get away from the conviction that it was their responsibility to stay consistent and go with a strict position against the smokestack climb. They moved in with direct forbidding. As the mom explained to me, "It's not just that it's against the law. With my son, it's almost a weekly thing that I have to put a lid on his wild-hare ideas. I can't be loose about anything. I need to keep sending clear messages to him about roping in his rashness because he doesn't do it on his own."

LICENSE TO CHOOSE FOR MATURE SENIORS

Another mom and dad with a son named Sean took a different tack, based on their analysis of their son. Well-adjusted and on track, Sean was virtually always responsible and careful. Though they fully disapproved of the climb, his parents were reluctant to lay down the law with their mature young adult.

Sean's parents used a strategy that can be called *license to choose,* an approach that should be reserved for seniors who are mature, grounded, and have their act together, so to speak. Adopting a license-to-choose stance with a responsible young person is germane to many types of parenting decisions.

Neither "hands-off" nor "hands-on," this stance involves weighing in overtly with your concerns, values, and thoughts with your emerging adult before turning the decision over to that child's conscience. It's not granting outright permission, and it's not laissez-faire parenting; it's removing yourself from the yes/no control seat, allowing your senior to ultimately make his own move, in spite of your clearly articulated different view. With license to choose, parents express their strong disapproval but give their senior a choice along with some negotiated parameters, should the senior opt to proceed. What might ensue from the senior's affirmative decision won't be clear, but the parents are willing to take their chances with the level of risk they perceive because they see independent decision-making as a learning opportunity.

Determining that Sean's track record merited a license to choose, his parents insisted on holding a caucus with him on the problems associated with the whole illegal venture. Being the respectful son he was, Sean realized he would have to be attentive to his parents' rundown of their concerns. They looked him in the eye and reminded him that if he were caught and a report of his law-breaking went to his college of choice, his admission might be in jeopardy.

"It seems crazy to us. We're dead set against it, and we disapprove," the parents warned Sean, "but we're not going to tell you what to do. Whatever you decide, know what you're doing when you make that choice. Know what it might mean to your future."

The point of their stories is not that Sean's parents are blurry and permissive, any more than Buck's are strict and consistent. The take-away message is that the parents with the push-the-envelope son realized that they couldn't afford to let him have the decision even at age 18, since it

THE POSITION OF SOME PARENTS OF RESPONSIBLE SENIORS IS: FIRST HEAR ME OUT, THEN ENOUGH CONTROL FROM ME—IT'S YOURS. USEFUL PRELUDES TO TURNING A DECISION OVER INCLUDE EXPRESSIONS LIKE "BE SMART WHEN YOU MAKE THAT DECISION," "I KNOW YOU HAVE A GOOD HEAD ON YOUR SHOULDERS, USE IT," AND "THINK HARD ABOUT THE CONSEQUENCES OF YOUR CHOICE."

could be opening the floodgates. They had a solid rationale for limiting Buck's choices. Sean's parents, on the other hand, believed that they could offer their self-restrained child more options because he wasn't prone to excess.

Another way of viewing this dilemma is that each family had to pick its poison. Sean's parents obviously took a huge risk by not forbidding participation in this law-breaking venture, but there was also a downside to Buck's parents' choice. When parents always have to be strict, like Buck's, they aren't able to allow the autonomy that young people need to become competent at higher levels of decision-making. A parenting approach called *scaffolding* refers to how parents enable a child to function at the edge of his or her capabilities in order to build ever-evolving new competencies. Learning occurs at the fringes of what you already know, so when parents are continually holding the line, learning evolves over a longer span of time.

What happened? Buck, whose parents forbade the climb, was irate, but he nonetheless stayed out of it, telling his friends, "My parents would ground me for life if I did it." On a clear night in May, Sean set out with another member of the climbing club, scaled to the top of the smokestack, and opened the paint. When a police car drove by, the climbers froze in place. Fortunately, the squad car turned the corner without spotting them, but was it safe to proceed? Within a couple of minutes, even though the police failed to return, the boys rappelled down the smokestack without performing the vandalism.

Why did they descend? Something went on in the boys' minds that made them abort their plans. I'm speculating here, and I only know the story of one of the boys clinging to the smokestack, but my guess is that Sean—like many "good kids"—had taken his parents' thoughtfulness and warning along with him. Whether his caution was rooted in his genes or in his *internalized parenting*—the term psychologists use to describe how a parent's influence becomes an integral part of a child's being—Sean had a feeling that directed his decision to come down the smokestack. He recognized, "I don't like the way this is going. I'm getting out of here."

What, however, if Buck had been along on the climb? Again this is speculation, but with his record, maybe—just maybe—he would not have felt similarly inhibited and might have encouraged the group to "go for it." Although he has probably benefited from his parents' hold-the-line stance and internalized some boundaries on his excessive risk-taking, he is still prone by temperament to gun for glory. Although we'll never know exactly what the boys thought or what might have happened, in the end, Sean had a chance to test his own self-restraint, while Buck was protected from a potentially dangerous temptation to go too far with fun.

Increased risk-taking is intrinsic to adolescence because teens want to explore their new physical and emotional selves. Though this normal impulse can be healthy when it's in the form of trying new hobbies or sticking up for causes, teens are notoriously poor in their abilities to assess risks.[3] Fortunately, most improve as they mature. Whatever the parents' inclinations and the child's temperament, parents should be clear about the pros and cons of various approaches to power surges during senior year, since each stance has an upside and a downside to weigh.

APRIL 1: FAT ONES, THIN ONES—THE COLLEGE-ADMISSION LETTERS ARRIVE

Invariably, pleasant surprises and huge disappointments occur with college acceptance and denial. With unprecedented numbers of seniors vying for acceptance into college, many end up receiving the thin letter of denial from the school of their dreams. Because most seniors hedge their bets, they'll probably have other okay choices. Likewise, most seniors enter the application process anticipating the possibility of not being admitted into a school of choice, but that doesn't make it any easier. Many seniors are devastated, and for many it will be their first crushing experience of rejection.

At such a moment, parents tend to experience a rush of empathetic dejection, feeling desperate to do or say something—anything—to help their distressed child feel better. Sometimes parents are able to pull it off, but be aware that even the most well-intentioned gesture—like a warm hug—stands a chance of being rebuffed by a distraught senior. There's virtually nothing that parents can do on the spot to make it all better. Since most parents will feel a dagger in their own heart with their child's rejection, parents may need to put a check on their own reactivity, keeping their boundaries firm and letting this be the senior's loss and not the parent's.

My advice to parents is to avoid holding forth on all your thoughts right off the bat. If you remind them, for example, of their other wonderful choices, it can sound minimizing. If you react with mutual dismay and outrage, they might resent having to deal with your upset on top of their own. If you delve into stories of young people who didn't get their first choice and ended up loving their safety school, they might be annoyed by sap they see as irrelevant. Try not to engage with them too much on the topic if they give you cues they don't want to discuss it.

On the other hand, you don't want to abandon them through silence. Often, the best bet is just to be there with them, a little bit to the background, and say something simple and sincere like, "This is tough news, honey. I'm so sorry it has turned out this way." Follow their lead and use what you know about how your child copes with disappointment.

In the past, what has helped and what hasn't? Ideally, you want nurture them in a way that respects their need to absorb the news. Some seniors will want to talk it out. Others appreciate being distracted, some with a favorite meal or a movie, but most would rather not have parents magnifying their hurt feelings with a lot of focus.

In time, parents can try to facilitate their child's coping. You might ask a question like, "How are you helping yourself get through this?" "What are you telling yourself that helps you feel encouraged?" Let them articulate their own solution, since they're likely to tell you what's appropriate for them. Stay on your senior's side and remind them of the numbers they were up against so they don't take it

> SINCE THERE'S NO MAGIC THAT CAN MAKE REJECTION FROM COLLEGE ALL BETTER, IT'S BEST TO ERR ON THE SIDE OF QUIET SUPPORT INSTEAD OF TALKING TOO MUCH ABOUT IT.

personally. Most seniors bounce back and settle into a new college choice. If, however, your child sinks into a deep pit for weeks, there might be something else going on to warrant professional counseling.

Only rarely do seniors come up completely empty-handed; but, now and then, young people will—against everyone's urging—apply only to one or two highly competitive schools or only to a large state university as a non-resident, or simply have unusually lousy luck. In these extreme situations, college counselors can often pinpoint a college that's a good shot for late applications. Though far from ideal, even in spring, there's still time to scramble for fall entrance.

On the other side of the coin, some seniors find themselves in the enviable position of being accepted into numerous top-tier schools. Justifiably proud of their achievement, seniors might be tempted to crow to their peers. This is an excellent opportunity for parents to reinforce the importance of decorum—the conventions of polite behavior. What could be better than having a senior's efforts in high school pay off in a mailbox full of acceptance letters—but what about the feelings of those who weren't quite so fortunate? Wisely, in today's highly competitive college market, most families contain their celebration appropriately.

SCHOOL CHOICE, WHOSE CHOICE? FAMILY STORY

The Duffys have dedicated themselves to their son's education. Jamal's hard work and his parents' extraordinary support have paid off. One of the Ivys wants him, but much to his father's bitter disappointment, the son doesn't want the Ivy.

Gerald Duffy and his son Jamal had had a huge falling out over which college Jamal should attend. Setting up an appointment for family counseling over the phone, Letitia, the mom, described the headbutting and discord within their household over the last month. With deadlines for responding to college offers now pressing, Gerald and Jamal had each dug in their heels, unwilling to budge from their positions.

"When the letters of acceptance came in April, we all celebrated because of the excellent choices available to Jamal," Letitia explained. "Then the fireworks began. Gerald is practically insisting on a prestigious East-coast university and a law-school track. Jamal wants a less highly ranked school in California that has a strong theater and arts department. My husband believes an African American has a responsibility to do everything he can do to pursue excellence, and that means Ivy League to him."

In an all-too-common predicament for moms, Letitia had been caught in her husband and son's crossfire. Although she and her husband generally agreed as parents, in this instance she saw her son's point of view. Mainly, she wanted the fighting to stop so that a constructive decision could be made, but since everyone in the family was hardheaded, this would be a challenge. One evening, when Letitia tipped her hand to her son's side, Gerald turned on her. A ton of steam behind him, Dad was fuming at both Mom and son. "Look how far we've gotten Jamal," he roared, "putting him through a private school, making sure he stayed on a top academic track, helping him with his courses—and now he wants to do theater arts at his safety school!"

Shortly thereafter, this family reached an impasse and sought help. Midpoint in the consultation, after taking down some family history, we arrived at the crux of the matter.

GERALD: The world will be his oyster—he'll have his pick of the job market if he graduates from a college that's so highly regarded. He should be proud. What an opportunity. Ask anybody, look at the reports, his choice is ranked as a third-tier school.

JAMAL: Ratings are not the point. The school in California gives me what I want. It's where the courses I want are available.

GERALD: You've worked night and day to get your grades. You've gotten into this prestigious university because you have fabulous potential. Why would you throw it all away?

JAMAL: It's not throwing it all away. You don't get it. It's what I want to do. An Ivy-League school is what you've always wanted because of your idea of me. My preference is my idea of me.

GERALD: (Getting very heated) Look, I can't justify spending 30K a year on a loosey-goosey theater program in a place with a dreamy, starry-eyed materialistic culture. It's not a path I can support, and I don't think it's a path you should be on.

At this point, I interrupted the exchange. I had a sense of the dilemma and wanted to summarize. I turned to Jamal, "You feel pretty clearly that the California choice is what you want for college."

Then I spoke to Gerald, "And you don't want it. Theater is where he wants to put his energy the next few years, but it's your money, and your life perspective and experience tell you it's not an optimal choice."

I wanted to hear Letitia, so I drew her into the exchange, "I understand you're torn. Tell me more about your perspective." *I sensed her reluctance to oppose Gerald since they tended to think alike, but it was her turn to weigh in. I could surmise that in private husband-wife conversations, she had taken her son's side more, but in the session, she responded judiciously.*

LETITIA: The problem is, I see it from both sides, and I feel like I'm right in the middle.

GERALD: You're not in the middle. You think he should do whatever he wants!

LETITIA: (Intensely with an air of resentment) That's not fair. Jamal has been a good son. I think we should respect him enough to realize he knows what he's doing with his choice.

GERALD: But isn't that what parents are for? If he's not making good use of those strengths of his and his talents, we should guide him. I know more about life than he does. He needs to take advantage of every opportunity available to build his career path, and those advantages exist by going to a prestigious school. It's so obvious.

JAMAL: There you go again. What's best for me is all according to you.

FINDING COMMON GROUND IN COLLEGE CHOICE

My usual response to a college-choice question is to let a well-adjusted senior make his own decision if he has strong feelings. Without ambivalence, Jamal had informed his parents, "It's my life; trust me with my preferences." For all of the sophisticated rubrics one might invent to decide among colleges, common sense usually rules: Given everything you know about yourself right now—how motivated you are, where your interests lie, where you've succeeded, who you are as a student—make the choice that feels right. Young people will sometimes walk on a campus with their senses alert and proclaim intuitively, "This is it."

Nonetheless, Dad's worries about Jamal's choice were legitimate. Would Jamal's choice be putting him on a less academic track? Would he be seduced by the glamor and glitz of the theater? Was this the best use of his gifts? Personally, I admired Gerald's strong value on education and thought he raised some reasonable issues. The question was: Would insisting work? Was it wise to push an almost grown child this far? There was a risk that if Gerald made Jamal go to a particular college against his will, he could become depressed, perform marginally, or even drop out.

My job as a therapist was to change the playing field so that the terms were not laid out as a win/lose in which: (a) dad wins and son loses if dad gets his choice; or (b) son wins and dad loses if son gets his choice.

JUST AS PARENTS THINK THEY HAVE EVERYTHING LINED UP WITH THEIR SENIOR AROUND A COLLEGE CHOICE, AN UNEXPECTED DIVERGENCE OF OPINION ARISES. THIS PHENOMENON IS FAR MORE COMMON THAN MOST FAMILIES REALIZE.

The current two-against-one dynamic was way too damaging to the Duffy family. The goal was to find common ground among all three family members, moving everyone to collaborate on a school decision that seemed the best, given the circumstances.

Together, we mapped out the situation this way. If Gerald

could have what he wished for his son, what would that be? It was a wish with a condition attached: Not only did he hope that his son would attend the elite institution, he also hoped Jamal would hitch his wagon to that decision enthusiastically, concurring with his father that it's the better choice. Gerald wanted his son to covet the same choice he coveted.

In actuality, Gerald had already lost that option. Even if he were to convince his son to attend the more prestigious college, he would still never get what he really wanted—for Jamal to enroll in that college willingly and eagerly—given how strongly Jamal felt about it being the wrong choice.

We could, however, locate common ground in one circumstance: Everyone wanted Jamal to go off to a college, give it his all, thrive there, and stay open to his future. Once everyone agreed that this was the real objective—one linked to Jamal's specific needs and not to the pedigree of the school per se—we had, indeed, changed the playing field.

A reasonable man at heart and a relentless supporter of his son, Gerald had a big, although somewhat grudging, "Ah ha." Through active parenting, he had guided his son and seen him achieve recognition in school, sports, and extracurricular activities, but if Gerald pushed his program for his son too far, he could lose his influence with him. Once Gerald had these insights, he shifted his perspective. Though he had tremendous disappointment to work through, he began to see his son and his son's choice in a new light. The important thing, Gerald agreed, was to have his son inspired and fired up to do well.

WHEN OUR CHILDREN DEVIATE FROM WHAT WE THINK IS BEST

With rare exception, parents of seniors are no strangers to the turmoil of identity development, having struggled through their child's forging of a separate identity during earlier adolescence. Before children become adolescents, they'll often float along with a parent's program of, for example, taking piano lessons or participating in the church youth group. Eventually, however, if the choice hasn't taken hold as a personal habit and preference, it becomes a hollow choice. Not that children won't comply with their weekly paces—self-discipline or a desire to please parents might keep them doing so—but if they're lukewarm or indifferent, the passion remains the parents', not theirs.

The same idea applies to overt characteristics of identity, when parents want their child to be someone he isn't. Parents might be eager for their son to have a sunny disposition, for example, but he has deep moods; or they hope their daughter will be social, but she is happier as a loner; or they're desperate to have their non-athletic son love sports, but he's lukewarm. Not that families concede to all of their children's ways and choices, but, ideally, parents help their children look within themselves to find what engages them, motivates them, and provides a deep sense of satisfaction.

Parents of high-school seniors experience yet another round of adjusting to their child's identity development, as seniors define themselves through college choice. We may think the world of our children, but we still wince when they're on some kind of beam that doesn't seem optimal to us. We know we can't have everything and that a child needs to be his own person, but that doesn't keep us from wincing.

What about Jamal? His identity had been evolving in a way Gerald had not acknowledged. True, up to a point, Jamal had ridden along with his dad's ideas because that was what he wanted, too. But Gerald neglected to see how turned on his son was to theater, choosing drama instead of basketball, spending his spare time working on stage sets, writing a play for a senior project. Gerald saw theater as a sideline for his son, not a growing passion. Slowly but surely, Jamal had been gravitating toward a different path, which suggested a certain type of college experience.

As close to his son as he was, Gerald was far from oblivious to the shift in Jamal's interests, but he kept pushing away the thoughts tugging at the side of his mind. Because it was easier to keep the peace and not raise his dad's ire, the family never had a discussion about Jamal's keen love of theater or dealt with it in any way. That was the problem, and that was why the upset in the family had mushroomed. All of the repressed and postponed disappointment surfaced as grief and anger.

Although Gerald threatened otherwise, he was reasonable enough to pay for either college. Often, however, money becomes a vehicle to control our seniors' college choices. Financial or other types of showdowns often occur in this context because that's when young people are often ready to declare unequivocally, "This is me. It's what I want."

Whether it's earlier in adolescence or senior year, the win for everyone is to accept a child for who he is and for his differences from his parents. True, we guide, nudge, and encourage our children, but we don't want to be so self-centered as to assume their choices are—or should be—identical to ours. A job we have all the way through child-rearing—and particularly at key transitions such as launching or their marriage—is to face that our children are not our clones.

A PARENT'S STRUGGLE TO ACCEPT A CHILD'S COLLEGE PREFERENCE COMES DOWN TO RESPECT: RESPECT THAT AN 18 YEAR OLD MAY KNOW SOMETHING ABOUT HIMSELF THAT MIGHT HAVE ESCAPED THE PARENT'S RADAR BEAM.

Often, once we move off of our agenda and open our eyes to the growth their affirmative choices lead to, we may see a new kind of win: their drive to establish their own path and achieve their own goals.

CARING TOO MUCH ABOUT COLLEGE CHOICE

Anecdotes exist about parents of kindergartners tied up in knots about their child's college track. Parents are, of course, entitled to their preferences and often play an invaluable role in directing their child's education. But why do some parents become consumed by their child's college choice, as if it will make or break their future? One answer is that we all want the best for our children, but the more telling motivations are usually personal, rooted in a parent's unique background and experience.

Gerald serves as one example of how deep-seated and understandable—albeit misguided—a parent's drive to direct a child's future can be. Over the course of counseling, Gerald spoke eloquently of his own past, describing how his dedication to excellence and his professional path led to a successful career in business and a high standard of living for his family. His thinking was: I see what's good for me; therefore, I see it's good for my son. Most of us cling to our values around achievement, especially if we've been self-starters like Gerald. He was passionate in his convictions. As a black male growing up in the '60s, he attributed his status in life to his academic excellence and resulting career. When he saw his son headed in a direction that was less signed, sealed, and delivered, he felt unnerved.

As an outsider observing Gerald's behavior, it would be easy to judge him as too controlling of Jamal. Controlling can be related to personality, culture, or a belief system. Gerald's controlling ways were all three, but the cultural origins were significant, for he feared that a less traditional path for his son would lose the ground he'd gained for himself, his family, and maybe his ancestors. As is often true, when he believed he was losing control over his son's choice, he became more heated and intense. Exploring his African-American background, Gerald made the point that a black male can't afford second-string anything and get as far in life.

There was a huge rift between father and son in that Jamal hadn't been exposed to as much racism, so he was not figuring it into his decision, while Gerald was. In therapy, Gerald pleaded with his son, "I'm more experienced in matters of race. Don't take the risk of being one-down and throwing away your potential." To hear Gerald talk about his fears for his son softened his intentions, enabling Jamal to see him as less tyrannical.

SOME PARENTS HAVE A LOADED BACKGROUND, FOR EXAMPLE "EVERYONE IN MY FAMILY WENT TO THE IVYS" OR "NO ONE HAS EVER BEEN TO COLLEGE," OR FEELINGS LIKE "I HATE MY LIFE AND YOU NEED TO MAKE UP FOR IT." THIS PREDISPOSES PARENTS TO STRONG COLLEGE-CHOICE BIASES AND A LESS-THAN-OPTIMAL DECISION-MAKING PROCESS WITH A SENIOR.

Family therapy focused on pulling all of the issues together into a multidimensional picture of what was going on and opening up issues beyond the crude question, "What's the best college?" Gerald was stuck in the rut, looking at only one vector of the decision: "This is a no-brainer. The Ivy is a better school. It's obvious." There were, however, more vectors to expose. Gerald's vehemence was about the African-American experience; it was about control due to fears; it was about a child not being a parent's clone; it was about launch anxiety; and it was about a parent's failure to appreciate what a young person was saying and to trust in his wisdom.

The college experience is a process, like adolescence itself.

During senior year, the temptation is to focus on one thing—college choice. As Gerald came to see, what matters in the long run is the development that occurs when competent young people are given a chance to play out their educational passions.

COLLEGE CHOICE: PITFALLS FOR FAMILIES

I've counseled many families with parents and their senior at loggerheads over what's best for the senior. Whatever the specifics of their conflict may be, it's helpful to be aware of the baggage and biases that might be packed into a strong opinion. The following short checklist can clarify whether a parent's needs, vulnerabilities, or dreams are directing the decision. It's followed by a list of common areas of conflict or consternation.

WATCH OUT FOR THESE ISSUES

- Is there anything in your background that makes you care too desperately about a choice?
- How is where you did or didn't go to school affecting your hopes for your child?
- Are you so attached to a choice that you're possibly living through your child?
- Do you see your child as vulnerable in some way (depressed, anxious, has learning differences or previous illness, for example)? Is your preferred college choice "perfect" because of issues related to the vulnerability, but your child wants to take a risk?
- Has your competitiveness blindsided you to your child's needs in any way?
- Are you measuring success in college choice externally, by what others define as success (i.e., solely on college ranking), instead of how a choice might enhance qualities that make for a successful life?

- Are you overreacting? In the scheme of things, will your child's future be truly compromised by attending school X instead of school Y?

HOT SPOTS—UNCERTAINTIES OFTEN ARISE OVER THESE SITUATIONS

- A family is trying to sort out whether a scholarship offer should determine college choice. For example, a young person is debating whether to take out student loans to attend a particular school—and come out owing over $100,000—when he has scholarship opportunities at a college where he could graduate virtually debt-free.
- A senior is leaning toward a choice of a college based on a romantic partner. Unhappily, we all know about the risk of increased intensity in a relationship—like Romeo and Juliet's—when we insist on separating young lovers.
- A young person wants to go to a less prestigious college for a specific reason, perhaps a sports program. Or conversely, parents care intensely about a potential sports scholarship, but a senior is burned out in athletics.
- A family has strong generational family ties to schools. Parents are bent on their child attending their alma mater, but a senior hankers for a new direction.
- Parents and seniors disagree over geographical distance; for example, the student wants new territory, but parents want their child to stay close to home. A related conflict occurs when parents want to ban certain colleges because they believe the urban location is unsafe, but the senior identifies advantages in that locale.
- The type of college is a source of contention; for example, the student wants a large university, but the parents see it as a "party school" and have a strong preference for a small liberal-arts college.

Often, parents and seniors struggle together, assessing perceived future benefits or costs of present decisions. It's hard to underestimate how painfully difficult these situations can be.

Sometimes, seniors are tenacious about "what's right for me," while the parent feels equally tenacious about an opposing position. Ideally, families should have talks early in the process—the summer or fall—to elicit their differences while there's time to work through them and not postpone the decision until it's down to the wire. My general advice is that if it's in any way reasonable—that is, it doesn't involve harm, breaking your bank, or overriding evidence that it's not in the senior's interest—let your child's position weigh in most heavily.

If a nearly grown child has strong and articulate reasons, if these reasons are intellectual and/or passionate, shouldn't we respect that an 18 year old knows himself well enough to merit a try at it? Even if the senior ends up with a regret, won't that be a valuable lesson learned? Can we in our heart of hearts assume we know what's best for a reasonable, well-adjusted young adult?

Not that parents won't have excellent and valid perspectives, not that there won't be conflict as you debate the pros and cons to ensure that your child has her eyes open. The goal is to move seniors to "own" their decision. Parents aren't obliged to rally around all of their offspring's life choices— especially the unhealthy ones—but a college choice can reflect a vital part of an identity, and to say absolutely no to their passionate desire runs a big risk.

RIDING THE FENCE: HANDLING AMBIVALENCE IN COLLEGE CHOICE

From the vantage point of autumn—when everyone's anxiety is centered on the question "Will I be accepted?"—the notion of having too many choices seems unlikely and enviable. It's not uncommon, come April, for students to find themselves agonizing over which college to attend, waffling from school to school, unable to close on a choice.

A particular dilemma unfolds if colleges enter into a bidding war with scholarship offers, especially when sports are part of the equation, and pressure and deadlines are imposed. Although this scenario can be flattering and heady, make sure your senior is receiving support from you and other non-biased, informed adults so that he or she has all the needed information and is not coerced into a decision prematurely.

What's the parents' role when their senior can't make up his mind but they hold definite opinions? It may appear advantageous to have a child who is on the fence because there's an opening for parents to influence, but should you?

Not so fast—not until your senior can go through his own decision-making process. If a parent weighs in too heavily, it might not feel like the young person's decision. Since the child has to live with the choice, it's best sorted out by the senior. Ideally, parents consult rather than dictate on this issue.

NO MATTER HOW TEMPTED PARENTS MIGHT BE TO TELL AN UNDECIDED SENIOR WHERE THEY THINK SHE SHOULD GO, IT'S A RISK. IF IT DOESN'T WORK OUT, IT'S BACK ON THE PARENTS. IT'S WORTH THE UNPLEASANTNESS OF RIDING THE FENCE UNTIL THE SENIOR IDENTIFIES A PREFERENCE.

My advice to parents when their senior is uncertain about a college preference is to let the child hang out with her indecision. No matter how clearly parents see the options, problems could occur down the line if the choice isn't genuinely the senior's. The risk is that the young person will be miserable, dying on the vine in the wrong school.

How might parents facilitate their child's decision-making? In a counseling situation, what I try to do is to keep young people talking, considering different angles, making lists of pros and cons, and gathering their thoughts. Then, I encourage the person to make a best guess, given the various pieces of the puzzle, and to believe in the reflective process that they have undergone. The best decision is often the decision they've made with the information they've had all along.

Emerging adults need to learn that making a choice, de facto, involves loss, whether it's the loss of a college a young person chooses not to attend, a loss in a relationship choice, or the loss of one opportunity for another. Maturation includes facing necessary losses that go along with choices.[4]

When the senior is truly in doubt and needs help with the examination process, parents can rely on the interrogative and ask a variety of questions to elicit the senior's ideas. Instead of stating opinions about whether one choice is superior to another, stay in a Socratic mode, with comments such as "Have you thought about how class size will affect your experience?" "What kinds of learning situations work for you?" "What do you want out of college?"

Often seniors need help articulating their decision. Help them size up why they're drawn to a school and why not. Are they basing their ideas on solid information or hearsay? Ask about programs. What do they want to study? Are they wowed by the facilities and that new athletic complex or by the quality of teaching they observed while touring the school? What did they see in the student body as a whole and not just the personable tour guide? What about the setting? How would it feel to be there? In the end, though, it's amazing how much there is to trust in a senior's simple assertion, "I think I'd feel most comfortable there."

SPRING SPUNK: PROMS, GRADUATION PARTIES, SENIOR SKIP DAY, AND SENIOR TRIPS

Parents' decisions about how strict to be with prom parties, graduation celebrations, and other antics of late senior year will probably match their general parenting philosophy and the level of freedom they believe their child can handle. Nevertheless, so aware have we all become of tragedies on graduation and prom nights that it has become increasingly common for families of seniors to lock arms together and control these evenings. Even parents who lean toward *license to choose* may become more conservative about these evenings. Some school communities, for example, organize a post-graduation activity that's fun and safe. Others find ways to monitor closely, keeping seniors contained in one location and taking away their car keys. These are great ideas.

STATISTICALLY, PROM AND GRADUATION NIGHTS ARE THE MOST DANGEROUS NIGHTS OF THE YEAR FOR SENIORS, WITH INCREASED RISK FOR DRINKING AND DRIVING, UNWANTED SEX, OR SUBSTANCE ABUSE. SENIORS WILL SAY, "OH, COME ON, IT'S GRADUATION NIGHT!" BUT THIS IS NO TIME FOR PARENTS TO SHRINK AWAY.

Even if there's no school-community plan, individual parents should do whatever they need to do to insulate their child from harm. Parents can request check-ins at regular intervals; they can make sure they know where and with whom their child is at all times; or they might set out a written agreement for the evening.

Start early so that you don't have to make a last-minute judgment call based on unclear information. Learn as much as you can about how these events work. Talk it over with your child, with parents of your child's friends, with parents of last year's seniors, with whomever you feel is a trust-worthy source. On these evenings, have more details nailed down with your senior to ensure that there's a safety net. How will they get there? Who is driving? What will they be doing? One of the weakest links for these evenings is a young adult, maybe an older sibling or a family friend, who agrees to buy alcohol for seniors, since it's difficult for young people to be uncool enough to say no to this type of arrangement.

Whether you agree to the limousine, the hotel room, the coed sleepover among friends, or whatever concessions seem necessary to keep your senior alive, it will take thoughtful deliberation on a family's part. Expect to negotiate, but keep in mind that parents who provide some type of structure for these evenings can help limit their senior's risk-taking.

Invariably in my talks to parents of high-school seniors, someone will raise a hand to ask, "What do you think about senior trips?" or "What do you think about senior skip day?" There's no global answer. With any individual child or family, there's a whole story underneath what compels parents to say yes or no, based on who the child is, the values parents hold, and what the specifics of the trip or the sneak entail. One way to deal with these events is to analyze the pros and cons of yes, no, or license to choose, and then set your policy.

Most seniors feel entitled to participate in activities like these and will pressure their parents relentlessly. A whole industry exists, for example, to promote the senior trip to Mexico or Hawaii, with brochures offering package deals mailed to seniors. Particularly if the senior has saved his own money for the trip, parents have a tough time denying their senior this "trip of a lifetime." What if you're a parent who considers it too much of a stretch to consent to a non-chaperoned beach vacation? If you decide you need to take a stand (and many parents do), keep in mind that it's possible to think differently from a hysterical senior who can't believe you're saying no. The risks are legitimate—there's no adult oversight and plenty of temptation—and chances are the senior won't be scarred for life if he doesn't get to attend.

One option for parents desiring to buck a trend is to pull a pre-emptive move by offering an enticing alternative. I'm aware of parents, for example, who were too uncomfortable having their child participate in a senior sneak. Knowing about the sneak ahead of time, they introduced a substitute perk, letting their daughter go on a train trip by herself to a cousin's house instead. Find ways to make the other option look as desirable as the sneak or the trip—or at least a close second.

SUMMING UP THE SHIFTS OF WINTER AND SPRING

Excitement, dread, anticipation of loss, the elation of change—once college applications are wrapped up, parents and seniors alike free up enough mental space to feel more emotions related to launching. Because families are no longer transfixed on the process of applications, the realities of what looms ahead sink in.

If we envision the launching process as a journey, families at this juncture acquire a heightened awareness of moving toward a new destination. This is it, families realize—we're on the train headed toward the station, so to speak. For the moms and dads, the parenting journey as we've come to know it is progressing, too quickly for some. High-school seniors are only too mindful of being thrust toward a new life experience.

How does this awareness of "being on the train" translate into daily life? For one thing, it keeps up the level of tension in the family—the tension everyone hoped would dissipate after the strenuous application period. Second, senioritis, with symptoms ranging from antsy-ness to ennui to high anxiety, takes hold of everyone in the family. Knowing that senioritis is normal helps parents keep a sense of humor and not be so judgmental. Third, because we're more attuned to our seniors' future independence—seniors become legal adults at age 18—it becomes clear that we may want or need to parent differently.

Parents of seniors face as many judgment calls as ever over how much freedom to allow their maturing child. In general, seniors are feeling their oats. It's a time when smart kids might do dumb things. Part of their new confidence is a desire to shed the old rules and restrictions and write their own ticket. Although parents feel chafed by this presumptuous attitude, it's a harbinger of the future.

For seniors who have not yet demonstrated an ability to make reasonably good decisions and keep themselves safe, parents are well advised to maintain a close rein, despite protests from the senior. Danger peaks on occasions like prom and graduation nights, when all parents need to be extra vigilant.

Many adolescents have proven themselves to be competent and responsible, with proven track records by their senior year. With emerging adults like these, parents are likely to engage in more negotiation, more give and take, and more weighing of costs and benefits. Questions involving permission are less answered by "Yes, go ahead" or "No, you can't" than by "What degree of latitude is in my child's best interest for her growth and well-being?"

Decisions around college acceptance create an up-tick in college craziness—the chaos that starts in the fall and resurfaces in the spring. The fall challenge of where to apply is succeeded by the spring challenge of where to enroll. Since most parents are already grappling with control and freedom issues with their seniors, it can help to look at the college decision in the same light. Many parents find themselves stepping aside from an active decision-making role, as it pertains to their competent child's life. With college choice, we're likewise adjusting to parenting emerging adults who have minds of their own and the credibility and confidence to make independent choices. As shifts take place in our parenting dynamic, so too will shifts occur in marital relationships.

By the time our children are 18, we rarely solve their problems for them. We facilitate, we consult, and we support. We give them the respect of having their own complicated lives and of having relationships and choices that may not be ours. Although events and circumstances during the launching years often tilt the balance of authority back to the parents, the second half of senior year can bring a glimpse of the kind of mutuality that will predominate in the parent-child relationship by age 25.

CHAPTER THREE

The Bittersweet Summer

How to manage spoiling the nest, pre-launch jitters, and nagging concerns about readiness to leave home

WHAT'S MY JOB?

Arnie was a devoted single parent who never remarried after his wife died when their daughter, Dacy, was six years old. Recounting his story to me, Arnie seemed at once resigned, consoled, and mindful of a new slant on his parenting role. With only six weeks left until college D-day, Dacy was out with friends until 2:00 A.M.—or later—nearly every night of the summer. Although he no longer waited up, Arnie still felt irritable and sleep-deprived because a part of him listened for Dacy's return. Arnie sympathized with Dacy's urge to squeeze in more time with her high-school buddies, but it was hard enough to deal with the heaviness of his heart without adding fatigue to the emotional brew.

One morning before work, Arnie was downing coffee. Only five hours earlier he'd had been roused by Dacy's padding down the hall, and after that he had tossed and turned until dawn. Running late, as he headed out the door for work, Arnie overheard Dacy phoning a friend to cover for her at her summer lifeguarding job because she was going to call in sick.

Arnie was incensed. At a stoplight, he grabbed his cell phone, leaving a message when Dacy didn't answer, "These late nights out, coming home in the middle of the night, have got to go. As I was leaving this morning, I heard you call Danielle to work for you. You're going to spend the day catching up on sleep while I'm dragging myself into the office."

No sooner had he punched the "end call" button than he redialed Dacy to leave a follow-up message. "Dacy, this was horrendous decision-making. Of course you're going to be too tired to work the next day when you stay out this late. Think about the consequences of your irresponsible actions and your commitment to your job." Click.

Arnie was on a roll. His third and final message took Dacy to task for leaning on Danielle. "It's unfair to call Danielle at 7:30 in the morning to pick up your slack. You put her in a bad position, where she couldn't say no. You're using your friend so you can stay in bed."

Later in the day, Arnie listened to his voice mail, which included Dacy's response to his rapid-fire accusations. Calm and more in control of herself than her father had been, Dacy executed a mature, cogent comeback, "Dad, I'm not saying that what I did was right, but I made my decision, and I'll have to live with it. This is my business, and—right or wrong—these are my choices. I'm prepared to suffer my own consequences. Supervising my every choice isn't your job anymore. It's my job."

Arnie experienced a moment of clarity. His daughter was the voice of reason. Reflecting on the last year, he realized that Dacy was usually responsible, despite the social whirlwind. Although Arnie had every right to disapprove of his daughter's decision, Dacy didn't need him to intervene and micromanage her every mistake, since she was generally squared away and not routinely indulging herself with sick bay.

Where did Arnie's three irate phone calls come from? Superficially, they derived from the frustration of trying to maintain household policies, at a point when seniors are "spoiling the nest" before leaving it. More profoundly, the phone calls came from still wanting to be Daddy. Initially Arnie felt flattened and dispensable: "Dacy is right. I'm not the monitor. If she's responsible for herself, then I feel unnecessary. My job is over."

Reflecting further, Arnie's thinking shifted: "Maybe my job isn't over; it's just changing." He grasped the appropriateness of stepping back and reserving criticism. Suspending judgment would give him more time to enjoy Dacy during her precious remaining weeks at home. Jumping on Dacy like this had been a relapse for Arnie, for until this tiff their relationship had been characterized by humor, closeness, and mutual regard and respect. It was satisfying to be at a point where he no longer had to constantly oversee and discipline.

Arnie's story demonstrates opposing tensions of the bittersweet summer, to be addressed throughout this chapter. On one hand, parents wonder why their child is ruining their last months at home by thoughtless antics. Some parents (secretly) can't wait for their children to leave! How can parents handle this havoc and keep peace? Adding fuel to the fire, our emerging adults minimize our parenting with dismissing messages ("Relax, I don't need your lec-

PARENTS AT THIS JUNCTURE CAN FEEL UNSURE OF WHERE THEY STAND. THERE ARE MOMENTS WHEN THEY'RE PARENTING ACTIVELY, MOMENTS WHEN THEY FEEL LEFT OUT OF PARENTING, AND MOMENTS OF WONDERFUL CAMARADERIE WITH THEIR CHILDREN. IT'S THE BEGINNING OF THE MIXED PARENTING OF THE COLLEGE YEARS.

ture anymore") even as they make life difficult. What is a parent's job as seniors elbow their way out of the home?

On the other hand, parents and their 18 year olds often feel surprisingly in sync. What does this new level of camaraderie say about the parent-child relationship and the evolution of control and authority? How can we handle this transition to ensure the best possible future relationship?

RAPPROCHEMENT: THE BIG REWARD

By spring and summer of senior year, most parents and launching children are feeling—on average—easier and more open with each other. In one survey, 90 percent of seniors reported that their relationships with their parents were good or excellent, compared to high-school freshman, less than half of whom felt comfortable talking to parents about either good things or problems, despite positive relationships.[1]

Not a fluke, stroke of luck, or wishful thinking, this new satisfaction belongs to a developmental stage called *rapprochement*. Rapprochement describes the more comfortable parent-child rapport resulting from achieving a more solid separate identity. Most emerging adults feel safe enough to be close to their parents, sturdy enough for teasing and even negative exchanges (like the one between Dacy and her father), and adaptable enough for flexing in the relationship.

Typically beginning around ages 16 to 17 (but often temporarily subverted by the stresses of applying to college), rapprochement is the big reward for reaching the other side of the tumult of earlier adolescence—the sassing, the mood swings, the limit testing, the cold shoulder, the appearance calculated to say, "I'm a member of my own tribe, not yours."

During middle school and early high school, family conflict temporarily increases, particularly over issues of autonomy and control.[2] Most families experience at least some upheaval as their teens are forming an identity and needing to push away from their parents, sometimes a lot and sometimes very little. Some teens—with milder temperaments, high resilience, strong parent-child boundaries, and advantageous circumstances—separate from their parents quite gradually, their evolution into selfhood unfolding more fluidly. Specialists use the term *individuation* to describe the process whereby adolescents organize cognitively, emotionally, physically, and psychologically into a distinct self, which necessarily involves differentiation from parents.

With maturity comes greater self-awareness. By their late teens, most young people are less egocentric and more cognizant of the impact of their behavior on others. They can hold a mirror up to their behavior and realize they don't want to come across as sassing, ungrateful, and self-centered. Coming more into their own, they would be too embarrassed to behave as before, and they likewise feel less need to lock horns with parents. Whether the process has been smooth or strenuous, individuation is worth the unpleasantness for parents: Research shows that adolescents who have experimented with a range of values and ideas (usually those of peers) and differentiated themselves from parents emerge from their turmoil and confusion as more ethical, empathetic, and well-adjusted than those who stay "foreclosed" with parents, never having challenged family ideologies.[3] Identity achievers are psychologically healthier on a variety of measures, including achievement motivation, moral reasoning, intimacy with peers, reflectiveness, and career maturity.[4]

Once adolescents reach a level of security in who they are, there's a coming back together with parents—a rapprochement. Identity formation evolves at different paces, with some young people basically committed to a self by age 18, but continuing to evaluate and analyze their identities throughout emerging adulthood.

Not that life is easy. Most 18 year olds party, make mistakes and unwise decisions, and still take risks, but the struggles of earlier years are usually diminished. Exceptions exist: Individual differences in teens and families can render the last part of high school stormy and stressful. Nonetheless, most parents find that ages 17 to 18 bring more maturity and easier relating—most of the time.

> WITH RAPPROCHEMENT, YOUNG PEOPLE FEEL MORE RELAXED AROUND THEIR PARENTS. THEY GET THEIR SENSE OF HUMOR BACK. THEY CRITICIZE THEIR PARENTS AND THEIR HABITS LESS AND DON'T MIND SPENDING MORE TIME TOGETHER— THEY MIGHT EVEN INITIATE IT!

As families anticipate launching, the parent-child dynamic moves to new heights of rapprochement. Heartrending though it is to see the child-rearing years slip by, parents often feel great pleasure in being around their more mature children and socializing with them on a level that feels almost adult-to-adult. We begin to appreciate and measure our impact on our children in a more global way instead of on a day-to-day basis. Although it's not uncommon for children to leave for college on a rocky note (often re-bonding with parents like crazy from a distance), many families find the closeness of rapprochement reaches a gratifying peak before departing.

IT'S HANDLED, IT'S NO BIG DEAL, GET REAL—CHALLENGES OF PRE-LAUNCHING

Because so much more is now above board, emerging adults are often back within their parents' radar with their provocative behaviors and attitudes—flippancy, bravado, patronizing—that grate on parents.

No sooner have teens solidified the wobbly self that was

developing during middle school and early high school than they now feel ready to handle anything and everything, as if they had no need for parents at all—unless they need extra cash or help with a traffic accident. In contrast to their earlier insecurity and uncertainty, they now assume, "I'm an adult now, like you." This attitude flourishes the summer after graduation, with seniors basking, as they often do, in the relief of completing high school, the excitement of new ventures ahead, and the intense emotions of leaving friends and family.

By summer of senior year, households buzz with activity. Many young people assume that the old rules are obsolete and that parents should be cool with all the ways they want to extend themselves. For young people who are well grounded and responsible—an important qualification—it becomes another pick-your-battles phase, with individual families determining acceptable limits on household civility and safety. Anticipating that pre-launchers will be pushing hard for autonomy, families devise a modicum of policies everyone can live with, based on principles of mutual respect and well-being.

> EIGHTEEN YEAR OLDS AND PARENTS MUTUALLY PATRONIZE ONE ANOTHER. KIDS SAY, "TRUST ME, I'VE HANDLED MORE SITUATIONS THAN YOU'LL EVER KNOW," AND PARENTS RESPOND, "AS IF I HAVEN'T BEEN THERE AND SEEN IT MYSELF. BELIEVE ME, YOU DON'T KNOW EVERYTHING I KNOW." IT'S A NUISANCE FOR EVERYBODY.

BETTER THAN THREATS AND PUNISHMENTS: THE RELATIONAL APPROACH

Let's assume that up to this point, parents have been operating under a model of authoritative parenting, characterized by support and warmth, judicious control, and open communication. According to this model, the parent (or parents) is the family CEO, setting guidelines for children. Expectations are well defined, and there are fair, consistent consequences when expectations are not met.

As child development unfolds, parenting during late adolescence can feel very different from the usual authoritative model. Once you've been an authoritative parent—sitting on your child for out-of-line behaviors, the messy room, chores, and homework—the payoff emerges: Your child has probably internalized a set of values and developed a capacity to self-impose limits. One standard for readiness to launch is an emerging adult's ability to self-govern, and in the absence of that quality, parents might question whether their child can navigate the hazards of today's college world.

Parents always have the option—or sometimes the obligation—to stay with a hierarchical authoritative framework, since even emerging adults sometimes show poor judgment and slack off on responsibilities. But for well-adjusted young adults, parents often find that a *relational approach,* where parents talk about their own feelings and needs relative to their child's behavior, is more effective than the old model. The relational approach banks on the young adult's need for less parental authority and on the child-parent relationship as a valued resource everyone wants to preserve through positive interactions.

Here's an example. During the summer before launching, children often make plans without cluing in their parents, let alone asking for permission. Telling parents where they are, where they're going, or when they'll be home is a superfluous detail for graduates on the go. An authoritative approach would be to insist on knowing your child's plans up front and to impose punishment like grounding for any lapses.

With a relational model, a parent might say, "I'm not comfortable having your whereabouts up in the air, plus it makes it a lot harder for me to make family plans. I'll do a lot better knowing where you are, so out of consideration for me and the fact that you are still living in this family, would you do this for me?"

As a heads-up, parents might mention the punishments they're *not* imposing with a comment like, "Please be mindful that I appreciate you're growing up. I'd like to think I don't need to do those things."

Some parents adopt a relational approach with younger children, for example, when a parents says to a defiant, cursing grade-school child, "When you talk to me that way, it makes me feel bad and doesn't make me want to go to the park with you." Although this can work, it's usually more effective to impose a salient consequence, since young children tend to be more limited in their self-awareness (that is, they don't "get" how they're behaving). Although they may be able to empathize with the parent's feelings, they can't fully exercise their value on the relationship as a motivation to curb a bad habit.

> RATHER THAN GROUNDING OR RESCINDING PRIVILEGES, REMEMBER THAT MATURE CHILDREN RESPOND BETTER TO A RELATIONAL PARENTING MODEL, EMPHASIZING MUTUAL CONSIDERATION AND GIVE AND TAKE INSTEAD OF RULES AND REGULATIONS. THIS SIMPLE APPROACH CAN MOTIVATE COOPERATION BETTER THAN THREATS OF PUNISHMENT.

Once parents can trust in their nearly grown child's intention to be considerate, fair-minded, and responsible—for its own sake—and not just to comply with rules and avoid punishment, the parenting terrain shifts. This is one of the exciting aspects of emerging adulthood: The mature child in a healthy family is ready for this kind of relationship.

Using a relational model to square away our emerging

adult's behavior is part of our easing out of the role of the family CEO into the role of a valued advisor, an elder with more years of wisdom to offer. Down the road, young people need to be their own CEO, not distracted by directorial parents. Since we never relinquish the role of mother or father, our words will probably always carry weight, our reprimands a sting. That's one of the reasons we need to dole out our judgments judiciously. We might see ourselves as "trying to help" or "trying to keep things organized" or "trying to maintain standards," but this mindset can plant the seeds for becoming the critical or over-controlling parent, a danger to the relationship.

MAKING THE MOST OF DEFERRING

Not many years ago, a senior who wanted to veer off the college track and take a breather between high school and college might have been dropping a bomb on parents. Now, it's a new era. Parents faced with this issue should realize how acceptable deferring has become. Even in a culture as traditional as England's, the *gap year* is commonplace. Many college deans sing praises for deferring because they've seen how students become more focused, confident, and serious about their studies. Getting to know themselves better, young people routinely end up making better use of their college experience.

Colleges also stress that students grow in more productive ways when they have a purpose for deferring and are not drifting in the wind without direction during their time off. To ensure easier reentry into education, many parents wisely insist that their senior apply to college and then defer, instead of not going through the application process at all.

Because most young people will assume they have a good reason for taking time off, the parent's task is to test the validity of that assumption. What would a survey of common reasons for deferring reveal? Some seniors defer as a reaction to the ramped-up intensity and pressure of high-school academics: They're burned out. Typically, parents will respond, "How can you want to leave school? You've worked so hard!" That's exactly some seniors' point. They often know that the only standard they have for themselves is full speed ahead and high marks. They'll do it again in college, but they want to experience more of life than making grades.

> ONE TRUISM OF DEFERRING IS THAT YOUNG PEOPLE GET MORE MILEAGE OUT OF THE EXPERIENCE WHEN THEY HAVE A PLAN WITH AN IDEA OF WHAT THEY STAND TO GAIN. A YEAR OFF SHOULD PROVIDE A TANGIBLE YIELD.

A second common reason is an opportunity or a burning passion. It might be a work, sports, or artistic option, a travel adventure, or some combination of work, study, and service. With all the earnestness of their 18 years, these seniors proclaim to parents, "It's now or never." Whether it's a great chance they can't resist or a fixation on an interest, at this point college feels more like a roadblock than a pathway. The means to their desired end doesn't include more education next year.

A third motivation for deferring is financial. As much as some seniors want to pursue higher education, they also don't want to rack up debt; working and saving up for college is their preferred option.

Legitimate though it may be, the fourth rationale is the hardest to pinpoint and the toughest one for parents to evaluate: Some seniors need time for the sands to shift. Feeling unclear about their future direction, they say, "College would be a waste of money for me now." They believe they'll be more motivated after some time out in the world.

Solid reasons for deferring matter to parents, but usually more critical to their comfort level is the confidence that the child will have a Bachelor's degree in hand eventually. Parents become most alarmed if they believe the time off will steer their child further away from higher education. Soul searching, parents ask themselves, "How much do I trust that it's in my child to want to have this education?" Peers can be a barometer for assessing the desirability of a college education. Not only do children tend to choose friends with similar interests and inclinations, but research shows the similarity among peers with regard to their school achievement.[5]

Although taking time off has become a trend, it's not right for every senior, particularly when parents have grounds to believe their child might never return to the college track. In the end, since deferral decisions are personal and circumstantial, it's out of the richness of every individual and every family that a decision emerges.

Intuition or gut feeling about the deferral option counts, but questions like these can help families sort out the decision:

1. How mindful is your child in expressing what she wants to do? Does it ring true, given what you know about your child?

2. Looking at your child's development over the last 18 years, what do you, as parents, think your child needs, regardless of what makes you feel more comfortable and secure?

3. What does your child's high-school record reveal? Has he shown the baseline characteristics needed for college, like attending classes and completing assignments? If not, could a deferral plan help advance these qualities?

4. Are there opportunities that can't wait and should legitimately tip the balance one way or another?

5. If you made a list of potential gains and losses of a year off, how do gains versus losses compare?

6. If your child wants to defer, has he spelled out a concrete plan for the year and not just "I'm thinking about . . ."?
7. Are there personal issues biasing anyone's judgments?
8. If you and your child disagree, what set of values is driving each person's inclinations?
9. If you're at an impasse, are there ways you can negotiate and amend plans to make it acceptable to everyone?
10. Is there any lurking danger (a peer group, drug use) that makes one decision better than another?
11. Have you given yourself leverage if your child doesn't follow through as planned on the deferral? (Example: your child plans to work but quits the job in a month. What benefits can you revoke to keep your child on task?)
12. Does you child have a way to get back on the college track?

Though the idea of taking a break from school sends many parents into a tailspin, it's risky to fight a tenacious senior tooth and nail. Not only can it hurt the relationship, it can give the young person a cover for not doing well in college, since they didn't want to be there in the first place. Under these circumstances, parents will want to work with their senior to forge a reasonable plan that keeps the college option afloat for the future.

STRAIGHT TO COLLEGE OR NOT? TWO WIN-WIN FAMILY STORIES

The educational script we'd like to write for our children—one with success at each juncture—usually turns out to be very different from the way real life plays out. Nonetheless, parents who stay flexible and work astutely with the "givens" of their child's circumstances can forge a workable plan.

Kristen, a teen I counseled, was a squeaker—a marginal achiever in high school who barely managed to graduate. She, nonetheless, was admitted to a local college and, although vacillating, basically wanted to go.

Kristen's parents, however, saw advantages to her postponing more schooling for a while. Having made peace with their daughter's shaky learning profile, they appreciated that young people like her often take more time to earn a degree. Moreover, they hoped that time off would bring greater social, emotional, and intellectual maturity. Again and again, they had been frustrated by Kristen's goofing off and excuse-making, leaving them every reason to believe she'd do more of the same in college unless she acquired more experience in areas like time management and follow-through. Kristen's "I want to go" had no substance behind it because of the precedent set by her high-school performance.

How could the parents nudge their daughter into postponing college, while allowing her to save face and, likewise, view it as a positive option? Sensitive to the fact that most of Kristen's friends were heading straight to college, Kristen was an example of a student who wanted to pursue higher education as a way of looking as if she were on track like her peers.

Wisely, Kristen's parents steered away from negative statements about Kristen's lack of readiness, like "We don't think you can handle more school right now" or "You haven't shown yourself responsible enough for college, so it would be a waste of our money." Instead, they pointed out how much they wanted her to have time to grow on so that she could eventually continue her education believing in herself.

Kristen became more upbeat about this option once they set to work on a plan involving both a job and travel using money earned at the job. Also—something very exciting to Kristen—she rented an apartment with friends. High-school graduates who hold "treading water" jobs (often the only kind they can land) while continuing to live under their parents' wing usually don't grow as much as those who experience the challenges of living independently.

Under these circumstances, Kristen found herself dealing with one roommate who stole her food and insisted on having late-night parties and another who wouldn't pay her part of the electric bill and refused to do KP in the bathroom. Likewise, through travel and work, Kristen became better able to structure her time, handle responsibilities, and be accountable with money, as she shifted away from a self-image of "flake."

> THE BEST APPROACH FOR PARENTS WHO FEEL THEIR SENIOR SHOULD POSTPONE COLLEGE SHOULD BE AN AFFIRMATIVE STYLE EMPHASIZING HOW THE CHILD DESERVES TO PUT TOGETHER AN EXPERIENCE THAT MAXIMIZES STRENGTHS AND PROVIDES RELIEF FROM TASKS THAT WERE BURDENSOME IN HIGH SCHOOL, BUT MIGHT BE LESS OF A STRUGGLE AFTER A BREATHER.

Expectedly, Kristen bungled—for example, leaving her backpack in an airport, overdrawing her checking account—but her parents saw Kristen's time off as a period during which their daughter developed new competencies, gained new experiences, and became more sure of herself. Not that she would ever breeze through college—higher education was likely to be more hodge-podge for Kristen—but at least she had more problem-solving skills and maturity for the road ahead.

Leo, whose divorced mother shared their story with me, consistently underachieved in high school, despite his high aptitude. Not on the cusp of failure, he was a lackadaisical student who got it together at the last minute. Indifferent about attending college, Leo lived to snowboard: "I'm a ski bum," he'd joke of himself. Witty, social, and fun to be around, he loved to party, and regular marijuana use was a known part of the equation. Given his druthers, Leo would prefer to defer college, work at a ski shop, and enter snowboarding competitions in hopes of gaining a sponsorship. Knowing that Leo could have good times on the side, his mother feared he would drift into a hedonistic and irresponsible lifestyle if he didn't stay on the college track.

Leo's mother was in the same position as other parents whose seniors aspire to follow their bliss with a long shot, whether it be as an actor, a musician, a novelist, a filmmaker, or a professional golfer. Parents—realists who want their children to be secure—tend to be neither comfortable nor dazzled by fields with a lower statistical probability for financial security or a long-term career path. There's something to be said for giving a long shot a go, perhaps failing miserably and figuring out how to pick up the pieces, but maybe not at age 18, maybe not if parents don't trust that their child can get back on a secure path, and especially not when there's concern about a lifestyle involving marijuana use.

The situation was further complicated by Leo's dad, a man who had never made much of his life. He encouraged Leo to follow his bliss, though he did hope that Leo would some day attend college. In counseling, I worked with Leo's mom to help her close ranks with her ex-spouse about Leo's wish to defer.

Leo's mom and dad held a caucus in which they drew up a list of their concerns about each option, trying to predict what was most likely to happen with each scenario. The points emerging most clearly were 1) they both worried about Leo's peers, who seemed lacking in ambition and motivation; 2) they agreed that given Leo's current ways, there was a risk he might never return to the college track once he veered off it; and regrettably 3) he would probably continue slacking in college but was likely to get by as he had in high school. Chances were, Leo's mom conceded, that college tuition would buy neither a career path nor a fund of knowledge, at least in its early stages.

When no clear option crystallized, they agreed to run an experimental year with what appeared to be the least objectionable choice and take a chance on a year of college in which Leo might be only marginally engaged. Leo's mom remained the strongest proponent of the plan. "Go for a year," she urged Leo, "then we'll take another look." On a wing and a prayer, she hoped he might have a great teacher who would influence his studies. She hoped that being around college students—talking about classes, goals, and even their student loans—might be more edifying than peers whose most pressing concern was when the slopes would open up. Maybe, just maybe, he would take to college, and if he could complete his freshman year, he would have that year in higher education as a basis of comparison to taking time off.

PARENTS OF UNMOTI-VATED STUDENTS CAN FEEL AS IF THEY'RE BETWEEN A ROCK AND A HARD PLACE WITH TWO UNHAPPY OPTIONS: GOING ALONG WITH A DEFERRAL THAT MIGHT TAKE THEIR CHILD OFF THE COLLEGE TRACK OR INSISTING ON COLLEGE AND RISKING THAT THEIR CHILD PRETTY MUCH TAKES THE YEAR OFF ANYWAY, DESPITE PARENTS' PAYING TUITION FOR IT.

Not surprisingly, Leo went through the paces of his freshman year, spending time snowboarding. Though Leo's mom knew in her heart that another year's tuition wasn't the best use of her money, she feared that leaving college would lead to a downward spiral. Coloring her thinking even further, she worried her son would wind up drifting like his dad, so she bargained hard to keep Leo in school—a very personal and individual decision.

Fall of sophomore year, Leo's academics improved

slightly. Also, his mom found herself adjusting her expectations and opening up a little more to who her child was. Importantly, she came to terms with the ways in which Leo was not her ex-spouse, realizing that she shouldn't let old marital baggage cripple her decision-making process. Accepting that she couldn't overhaul Leo's personality—he loved to snowboard—she negotiated: In exchange for winter terms off to snowboard and work on the slopes, Leo agreed to make up the terms in summer school. As junior year rolled around, Leo was hooked on a business major and even started his own snowboarding-inspired T-shirt business (with mixed results financially).

This combination of school, work, and sport provided enough real-world relevance for Leo to become invested in school and appreciate his education. By the end of six years, his mom was delighted with the way that the negotiated plan produced a successful college *and* work experience that prepared Leo for young adulthood.

STORMS BEFORE THE CALM: SPOILING THE NEST AND OTHER SUMMER FRAY

Envision an astronaut in a space capsule readying for take-off, experiencing the reverberations of the rocket's forces. At this amazing moment in time—the transition of a lifetime—seniors are feeling the emotional equivalent of that quaking. Launching from home is wonderful and terrifying. Despite the enthralling adventure ahead, there's fear of the unknown, fear that they won't make it, fear about being out of their mind with homesickness, and even buyer's remorse about college choice (some are already thinking about transferring!). Even though rapprochement smoothes out the parent-child relationship, other forces jolt family harmony.

Spoiling the nest takes different forms. Some young people simply need more friction, more chafing, in order to leave. Feeling cozy, close, and comfortable with their parents would make it way too hard to say good-bye. A story of one of my old babysitters typifies this type of pre-launch friction.

Close to his parents throughout high school, this boy usually held up his end of the bargain with household responsibilities; but just before going off to college, he became inordinately messy, leaving dirty dishes and food all over the house, letting his clothes pile up in corners of his room, not cleaning up after himself in the kitchen. He was guilty of another quintessential spoiling-the-nest deed—procrastinating about completing important college registration information for classes.

> SPOILING THE NEST HAS AN UNCANNY WAY OF WORKING: WHEN OUR SENIORS DRIVE US CRAZY, IT SERVES THE SEPARA-TION PROCESS, MAKING THEIR LEAVE-TAKING EASIER. THIS MAY BE NATURE'S WAY OF ENSURING THAT THEY WILL LEAVE AND WE WILL BE LESS DEVASTATED BY THEIR DEPARTURE.

Flash forward a couple of months: By October and parents' weekend, Mom couldn't believe the transformation. Not only was her son's dorm room impeccable, he had carefully lined up his classes. Looking back on his summer "messes," this boy's parents realized he needed more little fights. Upsurge in provocativeness is not conscious on our seniors' part, but it can feel aggressive and personal—a direct rejection of household rules and social graces. Keep it in perspective by remembering that unless there are more serious family problems afoot, it's likely to be about launching and individuation.

Sometimes spoiling the nest takes the form of an incident. All of the spiraling confusion of leaving home becomes organized around an event or a thing to argue about with parents so young people don't have to discuss "I'm nervous about leaving." A common example would be a child who works up a live-or-die emotion around a road trip or a concert, to the point of jeopardizing a summer job. These young people are Mt. St. Helens, with pressure building, about to blow unless they get out of town.

At the same time that a young person is sending signals that he's ready to ship out, he might also be doing the opposite and securing the home anchor. The phenomenon of the torrid summer romance is a typical way to set anchor. The boy or girl who has played it cool all through high school now gets involved romantically. Why? Maybe it's similar to marrying before going off to war and needing the security of a relationship at home; maybe it's because summer relationships have a naturally limited life span and are thereby a light load; or maybe it's just that emerging adults are feeling more confident and energized at the gate. Like fighting with parents, falling madly in love can be part of the emotional churning of this time.

> THE ROAD TRIP, WHICH ROMANTICIZES THE EXPERIENCE OF BEING FOOTLOOSE, HAS BECOME ALMOST A RITE OF PASSAGE OF THE SUMMER BEFORE LAUNCHING. SOME SENIORS NEED TO TEST WHAT IT'S LIKE TO BE UNMOORED AND ON THEIR OWN BEFORE THEY LEAVE HOME. WHEN OUR CHILDREN ARE AWAY THAT SUMMER, IT PREPARES US FOR THEIR ABSENCE.

Sometimes it feels like launching children set minefields to activate family skirmishes. They might party, party, party, then have the audacity to ask you to finish their packing. They might throw a wrench into the last family dinner—a meal that is incredibly special to parents, but maybe not on the top of children's lists compared to a final fling with friends. Many launchers, in a tizzy with their own plans, create a level of chaos that renders parents incapable of orchestrating a smooth send-off.

All this can happen in families with great relationships, but the child needs to create a little more distance and more separate selfhood to make the launch easier. With everyone a little bit irritated at one another, young people feel less vulnerable and less sentimental. What I often hear as a postscript to a scrappy launch is the flood of e-mails throughout the fall from freshmen to parents, to re-bridge the connection. Once gone, it's safe to feel close again.

Nevertheless, as with the following family vignette, pre-launch upset may not be innocuous, but might instead signal a significant problem.

A WOBBLY FOOTING IN THE WORLD
FAMILY STORY

What does it take to raise a daughter who, despite normal insecurities about launching, feels empowered to handle challenges ahead? What sets young women up for the yo-yo dieting, body image obsessions, and eating disorders that are so ubiquitous today?

Most educated American parents have read about the flagging of self-esteem in girls during adolescence. Over the last couple of decades, in the wake of huge societal changes and gender study, parents have been exposed to research and theory about the difficulties of girls trying to grow into a confident, self-reliant individual with a voice of her own.[6] (Recently, we've also focused on the struggles boys have to overcome their own forms of gender stereotyping—but that's a different story.)

Parents have been well advised to encourage their daughters to stand up for their beliefs and venture into areas previously dominated by boys. In a culture overwhelmed by media presence and commercialism, families have searched for strategies to counter messages portraying women in narrow, predictable images. What, though, does the raising of a strong daughter look like in action in the home?

In the spirit of the times, the Sevenis, a family I counseled, were pleased that their daughter Liz played basketball, wrote papers with well-articulated positions, and delved into difficult science and math courses. That she had some trouble speaking up for herself they chalked up to her mildness of temperament. Like most parents, the Sevenis hoped their daughter would leave home feeling sure of herself, but they missed several pieces critical to that end: Although verbally endorsing ideas about raising a strong daughter, they inadvertently put the stamp of "perfect girl" expectations on Liz—being nice, looking good (that is, thin), never being angry, being smart but not too smart, and pleasing others instead of oneself. All of these gender-typed expectations set Liz up for an eating disorder, as they do for any girl because they limit her range of emotional expression, close down permissible realms of identity development, and hamper independence generally.[7] Another difficulty for Liz related to family-system issues—notably a mother to whom Liz was too close and a father who was too distant—all of which played into lags in Liz's identity development.

What didn't happen with Liz—the developmental work she didn't do—tells an all-too-common story of a young woman who learned to be overly preoccupied with her appearance, afraid of conflict, and chronically worried about disapproval. Many girls like Liz that I've counseled launch from home on schedule, do fine in college, and stay connected with their family, but they have a tougher go of it.

WHEN "LETTING LOOSE" SIGNALS A PROBLEM

I met Liz Seveni and her parents, Barbara and Joe, the summer before Liz was going away to college. She had been referred to the Adolescent Clinic as a follow-up to a scary visit to the emergency room. Liz had partied with some high-school friends at a beach house, consumed drink after drink, and blacked out with a dangerously high blood-alcohol level.

A clinician's leading question when evaluating a crisis such as this is, "Why now?" At the initial consultation, wanting to determine what this episode of drinking meant, I asked Liz about her history of alcohol use. I learned that Liz, sweet, attractive, and popular, rarely drank, tending to "just sip on a beer" during high-school parties where alcohol was served. Naive about the toxicity of copious amounts of alcohol, Liz reported that she was unaware of the potency of the drinks that evening.

TO ANY INCIDENT, FAMILIES SHOULD ALWAYS ASK, "WHAT IS THIS ABOUT?" SOME FLARE-UPS ARE BENIGN AND CONTAINED TO LAUNCHING. OTHERS CAN SERVE AS WINDOWS INTO BIGGER ISSUES, REVEALING THAT A SENIOR WHO LOOKS READY SUPERFICIALLY MAY BE ILL-PREPARED FOR AN OPTIMAL LAUNCH FROM HOME.

Ashamed and confounded, Liz explained through tears to me, "Gee, this is what I get. Here I've been so good, never making the trouble that my brother or my friends have made, and I have one big party night and everyone's mad at me."

Barbara, trying to make the best of it, and Joe, saying little, were uncomfortable and baffled. Their older college-age son, Eddie, had created problems, the parents admitted, but Liz had always complied with her parents' wishes. Eddie notwithstanding, the Sevenis projected an image of a model family, everyone knowing his or her place, staying within the borders of a proper and traditional suburban family.

Barbara worked in the office of the elementary school her children had attended, and Joe was a hospital administrator. Together, they controlled the expectations for their children: attend the parochial high school affiliated with their parish, make good grades, and go to a good college. Although on the surface, many families could fit their profile, there was an intensity to Barbara's "we are normal" script that didn't mesh with Liz's streaming tears and Joe's reserve that bordered on stonewalling. Nonetheless, Barbara was sincerely concerned about her daughter and was forthcoming with a review of stressors and upset in their household.

Though it was now mid-summer, Liz and her family were still coping with the disappointment of the various rejection and wait-list letters she'd received last April. Having applied mostly to highly competitive schools, Liz was accepted only at her safety schools.

> WHETHER IT'S COLLEGE ADMISSION OR CAREER CHOICE, FAMILIES WHO STAY RIGIDLY ATTACHED TO A NARROW VIEW OF WHAT'S GOOD AND WHAT'S SUCCESSFUL CAN MAKE A CHILD FEEL "LESS THAN" WHEN HER PATH TAKES ANOTHER COURSE. GOING FOR THE GOLD CAN BE GREAT, BUT ALSO FIND A POSITIVE WAY OF RISING TO THE OCCASION OF WHAT THE OPTIONS TURN OUT TO BE.

"We were all shocked by the letters," said Barbara, turning to Liz as if expressing condolence. Barbara spoke in hushed tones of "poor Lizzy's predicament," as if it were a family tragedy. Why? The whole family had had their sites set on a top-tier college for Liz, who, after Eddie, was supposed to be the solid, problem-free student. Liz was mortified that she was going to her safety school, but Barbara's face was as anguished as her daughter's. Watching them interact in the consultation, I had to wonder, "Was this empathy on Barbara's part or feelings of personal failing?"

Another reason for Liz's upset was Sandra, a classmate whom Liz had hoped to leave behind as a bad memory from high school, but who was following her to her university. Sandra was what I call a "nemesis friend," one of those peers who competes, undermines, takes advantage, and does harm, all with a false smile. Liz had the toughest time in middle school when Sandra engaged in nearly every move in the book that gets girls like Sandra labeled "cruel": snubbing, gossiping, drawing Liz into her sophisticated fold only to control her.

By the end of high school, Liz was able to see through Sandra as manipulative, posturing, and less powerful than she'd once believed. But when she was crossed up by the college-selection process and she and Sandra matriculated to the same college, Liz was devastated. Even worse, at the time of the drinking episode, it looked as if Liz and Sandra—both going through summer sorority rush—might end up pledging the same house. Barbara had her heart set on this sorority for Liz, since Barbara had been a member of this house when she was in college.

Despite Barbara's helpfulness in the family interview, which I appreciated given Liz's gushing tears and Dad's passivity, the evaluation was starting to be limited by Barbara's domination of the family story. I jumped in, asking Liz if she wanted to pledge this particular sorority.

"Yes, sure, I mean, it's one of my choices," Liz responded.

"Of course, Liz will make her own decision. I would never interfere in her final choice," Barbara broke in, smiling, knowing this was the right thing to say.

"Well, maybe they won't choose me. Look at my record with colleges," Liz interrupted with more tears.

Barbara rushed in with effusive compliments and reassurances, which seemed only to upset Liz more. Through her sobs, she retorted, "Oh, Mom, you don't get it!"

"Oh, honey, I do. I do. You've been through so much to end up having Sandra in your life again." I observed how quickly Barbara diverted focus entirely onto Sandra, in order not to focus on Liz's disgust with Mom "not getting it."

As I asked Liz to tell us what Mom didn't get, she kept crying and shaking her head, "It's not just Sandra. It's everything. I don't know."

CAN MOTHERS AND DAUGHTERS BE TOO CLOSE?

The above interview reveals one of the most troubling of parent-child relational dynamics. In a healthy relationship, whether it is a parent and child or a couple, the twosome has a comfortable closeness that includes a tacit understanding: I recognize you as different; I celebrate you as different. I don't know everything you think and feel, and I don't agree with you about everything, and that's okay. You can be very upset, even with me, and I am differentiated enough to not react with mere emotion because I can maintain clarity in my own thoughts and feelings. There is a firm interpersonal boundary between us, not so permeable that we are merged as one (which is *enmeshment,* also known as *symbiosis*) and not so rigid that we don't communicate or can't appreciate one another's feelings and perspectives (which yields isolation, avoidance, and disconnection). True mother-daughter closeness becomes possible when there is healthy differentiation; their interpersonal boundary prevents a circular flooding of emotions.

With enmeshment, there is a fundamental confusion and lack of distinction between two separate selves. Enmeshment has three main sources, and it can exist in other duos (father-daughter, mother-son, father-son) for the same reasons:

1. Family of origin. Parents think, "I didn't have a close relationship with my own parent, so I'm going to make sure my child and I have one," and they carry this impulse to an extreme.
2. Inadequate personal gratification in other adult identity realms. They look to the child to "be something for me," so the parent can "live through" the child, as the phrase goes. Other adult developmental needs are shirked and too many needs become channeled into the child as a project.
3. Temperament and anxiety resulting in over-control and neediness. Anxiety can exist within the child, the parent, or both—after all, they share the same genes. The more a person's natural biochemistry is inclined toward depression and/or anxiety, the greater the likelihood of each person stimulating distress and reactivity in the other. This phenomenon makes it challenging for parents to establish parent-child boundaries and encourage autonomy.

What can come across as intrusive and invasive to teens is often seen by the enmeshed parent as "good parenting": active interest reflected in lots of questions, advice, curiosity, and confiding. To most enmeshed parents, it's all about being close and loving.

Normal adolescent development involves some chafing and cold-shoulder treatment to parents as young people individuate. One interpreta-

DESPERATE FOR INAPPRO-PRIATE AMOUNTS OF INTI-MACY, ENMESHED PARENTS MAKE THEIR CHILD FEEL GUILTY ABOUT NOT SHARING ENOUGH AND NOT WANTING THE SAME THINGS, BE IT CHOICES IN SCHOOLS, ROOM DECOR, BOYFRIENDS, MAKEUP, OR CONFIDING LEVELS. WHETHER THEY FIGHT AND CRY INTENSELY OR AVOID IT ALTOGETHER, THE CORE ISSUE IS THE SAME: LACK OF HEALTHY DIFFEREN-TIATION.

tion of the function of even high levels of mother-daughter conflict is that girls are indeed fighting for acknowledgment and validation of their unique and separate identities—an unpleasant process that ultimately yields a positive outcome.[8] But bids for validation to an enmeshed mom can activate a strong response in her: "Why are you rejecting me?" "Why can't we just be close like we used to be?" The mom thinks that her child's shutting her out is stinginess, rudeness, or a sign of trouble because, after all, she's "just interested." Under these circumstances, instead of eventually achieving the natural rapprochement that follows years of work on individuation, the mother-daughter duo remains locked in emotional impasses, with raw feelings between them.

Usually our children do a good job of training us to give them some space during adolescence. Over time, we figure out when to actively pursue an issue, and we learn to follow our adolescents' leads and stay quiet about their different preferences, different values, and desires for private lives. Watchfulness and good timing become our means of staying connected with our children: We learn to enter on their opens.

LEARNED HELPLESSNESS

When a child has an enmeshed relationship with a parent, stumbling is likely to occur at launching—how can it not? From what I gathered in subsequent sessions, Barbara had a combination of issues that primed her for an enmeshed relationship with Liz: a distant mother; an adequate but not altogether fulfilling relationship with her quiet, introspective spouse; and a tendency to be anxious and perfectionistic and to harbor unrealistic expectations.

With Sandra as a common enemy, Barbara and Liz could be in a tight alliance. They maintained their buddy system as

Liz supported Mom in her struggles with Eddie, when they went on shopping sprees kept secret from Dad, and through the many woes they shouldered together during Liz's middle- and high-school years. As in most enmeshed relationships, Liz's emotions were up and down about the degree of desired closeness she wanted with Mom. Although she'd complain about Mom's hovering, she also wanted her to supply comforts and be by her side in a jam, sending Barbara mixed messages about how responsible she actually wanted to be for herself.

Whenever Liz wasn't in the mood to confide her upset to Barbara, they'd wind up in a tiff. Unlike enmeshed mother-daughter duos who argue noisily for hours, Liz and Barbara would get riled up, but Liz would buckle (as she did in the interview), unable to keep up with her mom's intensity. Liz might react with tears, sadness, anger, and dirty looks, but rarely with an articulation of her feelings because she was too confused, too protective of Mom, and too scared of winding up in more of a processing marathon than she could ever tolerate. The atmosphere in the household was frequently one of bad moods and sullenness, but when Liz's vulnerable nature rendered her hurt, stressed, or overwhelmed, Barbara was there with a rescue.

Instead of reinforcing coping skills and problem-solving with Liz, Barbara was reinforcing the sensitive, passive side of her daughter—the side that felt helpless and needed Mom. From Barbara's perspective, her cushioning was for the good cause of protecting gentle-natured Liz, but sometimes frustrations

WHETHER IT'S COPING WITH A COLLEGE LETTER OF DENIAL, PERSISTING IN A CLASS AFTER A BAD GRADE, OR OVERCOMING THE HUMILIATION OF A SOCIAL SNUB, TEENS WHO STRUGGLE AND RESOLVE THEIR OWN SETBACKS DEVELOP A RESERVOIR OF SELF-RELIANCE AND FEELINGS OF COMPETENCE.

and crushed feelings galvanize young people to rise to a challenge, or at the very least develop a thicker skin. Before they head out into the world, our emerging adults need to feel confident in their abilities to master their problems, whether it's a nemesis friend or some other debacle.

In hundreds of thousands of tiny interactions over the years, Barbara was driven by her anxiety to move in and protect Liz. In large part this is a boundary issue. Though parents never want to abandon or neglect their children in their problems, we sometimes need to contain our mama bear and papa bear rescue impulses and instead endure their hurt feelings, soothe them, then move away and trust that they have it in themselves to deal with their challenges, more and more so as they mature.

THE PROBLEM WITH DISCONNECTED DADS

In a healthy family system, parents look to each other or to other adults for their adult intimacy and friendship needs and not to their children. Establishing a parent-child boundary allows parents to be authoritative with their children, leave them some space for growing, and advocate equally for their children's expanding competencies.

In the Seveni family, mother and daughter were closer to one another than Barbara was to her husband, Joe. Moreover, the children had fixed roles, Eddie as the black sheep and Liz as the good girl. Aware of difficulties with her wilder brother, Liz felt responsible to not give her parents the same trouble; Liz became a pleaser, avoiding arguing and speaking up. Because of her unsatisfying relationships with her son and her husband, Barbara was all the more vulnerable to becoming over-invested in Liz—the daughter, the achiever, and the last to leave home.

Joe, a satellite dad, was in another orbit. Neither sinister nor mean-spirited, he was simply absent—a nice man of few words and very little social cognition or capacity to relate to people. Always at work, he wasn't around to do the schlepping or mundane family interactions that keep parents in proximity to their teens.

Soft-spoken though she was, Liz was unrelenting in her criticism of her dad, frustrated by his lack of interest in a relationship with her. Disconnected dads are often clueless about how they come across, and likewise they often have no idea how powerful they are in the eyes of their adolescents. Having absorbed a script that she wasn't measuring up to the standards that took Dad to his top administrative position at a hospital, Liz believed, "He doesn't care about me as a person. All he does is ask me about school and my activities. Even though I've worked hard, I still know and my college admission record shows—I'm not good enough for him."

Joe, in a sense, took advantage of gender stereotyping. Joe retreated from the constant tension between Mom and daughter, without sharing any of his observations with his wife. For every two-parent family with an enmeshed mother-daughter, there's a father who left them to it. Under guise of "it's between Mom and daughter," Joe could abstain. In any family system, parents ideally hold themselves and each other accountable for their issues and for working on excesses; that way there are fewer unresolved issues drifting down to the children. Barbara found Joe indulgent in his introversion, just as Joe found Barbara indulgent in her emotionality, leaving Liz to deal with her experience of these patterns. In counseling, when a mom and daughter are hooked together in an unhealthy way and the dad, out of befuddlement, begins to withdraw from a relationship with the daughter, I urge these dads to stay in there. Fathers need to pursue their adolescents so there can be no doubt whatsoever that they want a relationship, even if their efforts are messy, confused, and even rejected. The goal for Joe was not to interfere directly with Barbara and Liz's conflict, but rather to be responsible for his own relationship with Liz.

Liz's imbalance—too much from Mom and not enough from Dad—rendered her footing wobbly as she was preparing to leave home. Research has shown that daughters who have connected dads—dads who support them and stay involved with them—have higher levels of achievement and personal security in the world.[9] It logically follows that young women with stronger identities are less likely to lose themselves in a partner or to seek fulfillment in a relationship with an unavailable male.

> **IT'S CLEARLY ADVANTAGEOUS FOR DAUGHTERS TO HAVE A FATHER OR ANOTHER STRONG MALE FIGURE IN THEIR LIVES SO THAT THEY CAN FEEL SECURE AND VALUED BY MEN BEFORE THEY VOYAGE INTO THE REALM OF ROMANTIC ATTACHMENTS AND OTHER RELATIONSHIPS WITH MEN.**

A CLAIM ON SELFHOOD AND RESISTING BULIMIA

In a family without firm parent-child boundaries, where she had never struggled independently with her own challenges, Liz had defaulted to the "perfect girl" stereotype and had not achieved a strong identity by the end of high school. Whether the subject was religion and politics or boyfriends and body image, Liz's notions were fuzzy and unexamined. At a late date, she was doing some of the pushing of the envelope ninth-graders do. The zeal with which Liz went for alcohol on the evening of her binge probably had something to do with her desire to cut loose from her constrained role in her family and school.

Barbara understood the idea of individuation intellectually, having read about girls' needs to find their own voices, but if you'd look at a transcript of their conversations, you'd hear a litany of complaints that Liz was not sharing enough, not wearing "becoming" clothes, not careful enough about her snacking, and not spending her time and money the right way. Barbara, like most moms sharing her proclivity, had no idea that she was undermining her daughter's self-assurance; the comments slipped out because of her concerns and her rigid notions about shaping positive development. The range of what didn't make Barbara anxious was so narrow that she became controlling.

PARENTS NEED TO BE AWARE OF SENDING DOUBLE MESSAGES. WHEN WE SAY, "I WANT YOU TO HAVE YOUR INDEPENDENCE," DO WE FOLLOW THROUGH WITH IT OR DO WE FIND COPIOUS REASONS FOR ACTING MAINLY TO THE CONTRARY? OUR BEHAVIORS REFLECT WHAT'S TRUE.

During therapy sessions that summer, weeping profusely, Liz described how she felt "shallow" for her pursuit of popularity in high school, "like a loser" for ending up at a safety school, and "pathetic" for being so wrapped up in what everyone else thought of her. She confessed to recently getting into dieting and bingeing and purging patterns that met the criteria for bulimia. Bulimia was no surprise, as Liz's family dynamics, gender-typed values, personality characteristics, and lack of coping skills were all classic risk factors.

Liz knew that she was ready to address these issues, and she also knew that instead of blaming Mom for overparenting and Dad for neglect, she wanted to seize control of her life. Even though she had inherited some of her shy and passive temperament from her dad, Liz wanted to choose goals of her own, meet them, and gain the strengths and pride she needed.

Upon entering college, Liz took advantage of group therapy for women with eating disorders available through the college health center. I coordinated her treatment throughout the fall, and Liz improved across the board. She stopped vomiting (luckily, it was short-lived), started communicating with her parents more effectively, dove into her schoolwork, and took an active role in her sorority, which ended up offering Liz an invitation to pledge, but not Sandra.

Liz continued to struggle with assertiveness, body image, and boyfriends. She became involved with a number of "love 'em and leave 'em" types, returning to her obsession with her weight after the boy moved on. Nonetheless, she had progressed a long way from the doe-eyed, confused girl I met who claimed that everything was "fine" in the wake of dangerous alcohol bingeing.

I have to give credit to Liz's supportive parents, who had the courage to open up for their daughter's sake what they felt was a Pandora's box. To me, that is true love—doing what it takes to help your developing child, even if it's very uncomfortable personally and goes against the grain of long-held preferences and assumptions.

PREPARING FRESHMEN FOR COLLEGE WITHOUT THE "LAUNCHING LECTURE"

As children are readying to leave home, parents wonder what specific obstacles their children will face in college and whether they're as wise and ready for these challenges as we'd like them to be. Over the years, I've run workshops for high-school seniors and their parents, separating them into discussion groups. I've found that parents' worries about college life cluster around these general areas:

- Academics/Grades (Will my child make the most of the educational opportunities offered? Is he prepared? Can he handle the academic pressure? Does my child have the self-structure to balance socializing and studying?)
- Money (Can my child handle it responsibly? Are credit cards a good idea? What should I expect her to cover financially? Can she manage a job and school?)
- Sex (How ingrained are the values about sex that I hope I've transmitted to my child? Does he have the wherewithal to avoid unsafe sex and unwanted sex?)
- Substance use (Can my child handle being around lots of drinking and marijuana use? Will drinking impair her judgment?)
- Physical danger and well-being (Will my child be safe on campus? Will she be capable of recognizing a dangerous situation? Can she keep herself healthy?)
- Emotional stability (Can my child handle the experience of college emotionally? Will he be happy? Will he be thrown big-time by something?)
- Friendship issues (Will my child be able to form healthy, supportive friendships? Will she fall into the wrong group? Will she feel left out?)
- The parent-child relationship (Will we maintain closeness? How will I know when my child needs me?)

Most of us would like to have a heart-to-heart talk with our freshmen-to-be, in part to reassure ourselves that they've thought long and hard about the hurdles foremost in our mind. As with the junior-high sex talk and the drug talk, discussions about college life will proceed more smoothly when they're well timed, hinged to their life at the moment, and respectful of information they already have. Though rapprochement makes talking about launching concerns easier, most freshmen-to-be stiffen like a bristle brush if a parent corners them into a preachy discussion on college life.

Most launchers probably won't be warmed up for "the talk," not just due to lecture-phobia, but because they may need to guard their strong-running emotions from parents instead of baring their souls. Nonetheless, it's advantageous for freshmen, especially those who are anxious, to enter college informed about the challenges they might expect in university life. Students with a prepared mindset—that is, freshmen who have been given information and strategies and not simply told "you'll do fine"—tend to do better.[10] Some practical advice gleaned from a college survey of students includes these tips: get to know faculty members; avoid taking an overload of required courses but instead mix in some interesting smaller seminars; structure concentrated study time; and get involved with extracurricular activities that are perhaps connected with your academic, personal, or career interests.[11] College survival guides with concrete advice like this can be a valuable launching present.

> JUST BECAUSE OUR LAUNCHING CHILDREN CLAM UP AT OUR ATTEMPTS TO TALK ABOUT GRADING POLICIES, BINGE DRINKING, DATE RAPE, AND TEMPTATIONS TO OVER-PARTY DOESN'T MEAN WE SHOULDN'T TRY. THOUGH THESE DISCUSSIONS ARE REQUISITE, THEY MAY NOT BE ANY MORE WELCOME THAN ONES WE'VE HAD ABOUT OTHER HOT AND HEAVY TOPICS.

Academics are an area where families would be wise to spell out expectations before their children leave for college. The Family Education and Privacy Act of 1974 established that parents couldn't have access to their college student's transcripts without the student's written consent. The result of this Act, also known as the Buckley Amendment, is that parents may not hear about their child's academic performance from the school directly unless their child is failing. So, to avoid problems, determine policies before they leave: Are they expected to finish in four years, and what will the consequences be if they don't? (Fewer than 40 percent of students finish in four years.) What grades do you consider acceptable? Are they allowed to skip classes, drop courses, or take incompletes? What about course selections or deciding on or changing a major? Is it all up to them? If parents don't tell their freshman that they want to be consulted on such issues, students will consider it their business. The more parents cover beforehand, the better.

From my workshops, I've learned that launching seniors know more about the real problems and concerns of college life than their parents know they do. In the private chambers of their minds or in conversations with friends, many share their parents' concerns, though cast in an 18-year-old version. After all, high-school seniors are more tuned into the information grapevine from students coming back from the trenches of current college life than we are! Out of fear that it might upset or worry their parents or lead to overly long, uncomfortable conversations, young people keep much to themselves.

Here are top issues I hear continuously from young people about to leave home:

- Will I be able to make it academically? (Whether they did well in high school or not doesn't diminish self-doubts.)
- Will I be tempted to party too much? (For young people given to socializing)
- Will I have a social life or will it just be more studying? (For young people who have worked hard in high school to the exclusion of a social life)
- Will I be able to manage my stress level?
- Did I pick the right college?
- I'm the one people always come to: How am I going to set a limit on other people's needs so that I can get my work done? (Particularly girls)
- Will I like my roommate?

- Will I get so homesick that I need to come home?
- I've been with the same people all my life. How am I going to get used to all new people? How am I going to find friends?
- How will I know whom to trust and whether someone's putting on an act?
- Will I be able to find friends who will be there for me if I need help?
- What if I change so much that I don't like any of my old friends anymore?
- I've felt limited by how people pigeon-holed me in high school. I can start all over again and try being someone else, but who do I want to be?
- What's it going to be like for my parents when I'm gone?
- Are my parents going to keep breathing down my neck about grades?
- Are my parents going to call me all the time worrying about me?

TAKING STOCK AS SUMMER DRAWS TO A CLOSE

Like many other species, humans worry about their children as they move out of their proximity. How far can our offspring roam and stay safe? we fret. Too often, parents fixate on dangers, difficulties, negative influences, and all the ways in which their 18 year old is still a work in progress. Sometimes, our parental insecurities lead us to want too much too soon of our children.

Looking ahead, ages 18 to 25 can be years of amazing leaps in development for young people—years when a shy child works up enough assertiveness on her own to approach a college professor about a bad grade, years when a fun-loving one determines to buckle down and work harder because he wants to succeed. Although age 18 is a benchmark, late bloomers can benefit from a plan that allows catch-up time.

Up until the time teens graduate from high school, many

parents are still running interference and looking out for their children, trying to keep their lives as error-free as possible—and if they stayed at home, we'd keep it up. As long as we're actively involved, we maintain our same oversight. As our children mature, our job is twofold: to stay connected while also encouraging them to be in charge of their own lives—a change that necessarily brings less parental intervention and a level of loss.

Even though we know our children are growing up, we can still feel intensely about their decisions, whether it is a relationship choice, a way they use their time, or a plan about deferring from college. How we navigate our ideas versus theirs pertains to a central phenomenon of parenting emerging adults. After years of having a large hand in our children's choices, it would be nearly impossible for us not to have hopes and opinions on decisions that carry life consequences. Since we're still in the territory of adolescent development, we can voice our opinions in important matters, but we should know how big we are in their lives and how constraining our ongoing input can be to their development. Good boundaries between parents and children allow us to listen to our children's different ideas and let these differences work themselves out (perhaps not always to the happiness of the parent).

As children prepare to leave, parents invariably feel tinges of sadness that this is all happening too soon, but most also feel elated that their child is on his way, especially when spoiling the nest occurs. The key to healthy parenting is not to collapse into an exclusive focus on loss, but to maintain optimism about a child's next phase of life and one's own. Like many other junctures in human development, launching is mixed—it's difficult, and it's exciting. Realizing that the parent-child relationship is merely altering and is not lost helps us see that the tumultuous change in family configuration can have positive aspects for everyone.

LAUNCHING
AND THE
FIRST YEAR
OF COLLEGE

Growing Up
Without
Growing
Apart

CHAPTER FOUR

Fall Fledglings

How to parent from afar: From minor
freshman freakouts to significant crises

KISS THEM GOOD-BYE

One of the most emotionally laden moments for any parent—one filled with excitement and anticipation, yet a profound sense of loss—is bidding a child good-bye for college. Although we know intellectually that our children will eventually grow up and be on their own, no one can really prepare us for the feelings of the last few days together, let alone the vulnerable moment when they walk away. Even if the relationship has been rocky and difficult, the last big hug with an entering freshman is among a parent's most emotionally wrenching life experiences.

Parents often wonder how they should orchestrate the send-off and whether they should plan something elaborate to highlight the significance of launching. The more I've talked to parents about the whole experience of leave-taking, the less likely I've become to offer specific advice on how to handle it. As you mull over this momentous change, equate it to any major transition, like adjusting to the first day of kindergarten, or an illness, or getting married or divorced, or a big move. Instead of believing there is one "right way" that will help you and other family members through the transition emotionally, think about your personal circumstances. Ask yourself, "Is this good for me—not just good according to what someone else recommends?"

A useful guideline is to avoid the extremes: During a child's final days at home, parents should, for example, resist possessiveness, refrain from guilt-tripping their child into something they don't want to do, and avoid generating a drawn-out emotive display. If a parent's emotions are running extremely strong, containing some of it can be a real kindness to the child.

Generally speaking, parents tend to confront their child's leave-taking with more awareness and multidimensional thinking about its significance—the end of my active child-rearing years, my own aging, my changing relationship with my child. Children are feeling a lot, too, but their anxiety and anticipation are often more personally targeted at their next step and their free-floating fear of the unknown: Will I like my roommate? Will I make friends? Will the courses be too hard? Compared to parents, teens usually prefer to mark their launching by something that reflects their tastes, something smaller rather than larger, something contained rather than consuming.

ALTHOUGH PARENTS AND THEIR CHILDREN ARE GOING THROUGH LAUNCHING TOGETHER, THERE MAY NOT BE A MEETING OF THE MINDS. PARENTS TEND TO FOCUS ON THE BIG PICTURE OF WHAT LAUNCHING MEANS AND ENTAILS, WHILE FRESHMEN WORRY ABOUT MORE CONCRETE CONCERNS AT COLLEGE.

As for the specifics, one family's feast is another's famine. Even a plan that sounds wonderful and wholesome, like a family hike just prior to leaving, isn't going to work for everyone. One father and son I was counseling, for example, had raw unresolved feelings between them. Had they engaged in an activity providing a great deal of one-on-one time together, too many hot emotions might have spewed out right before the big exit. (Was the divorce fair to Mom? How come Dad spends so much time on his young children and won't contribute more to college?) Everyone will handle leave-taking better if there's peace and kindness instead of clashing. For this dad and son, it was better to plug the dike and know they're going to deal with their issues down the road. What they did was simply go out for pizza and a movie together, and it was perfect for them.

Even though this experience involves the whole family, take care not to place rigid expectations on other family members, and stay sensitive to others' personal styles for coping with change. A common misconception, for example, is for parents to expect siblings of the freshman to have feelings that the siblings may not have. The cursory "see ya" may be as worked up as the brother or sister happens to be at that moment.

Whatever leads up to it, there's a heightened consciousness to the moment of farewell. Once you hug your child good-bye and walk away, do you turn around one last time? One mom described to me how she and her daughter each turned around simultaneously and exchanged a reassuring smile and a wave, creating a moment to treasure. Another mom, upon turning around, saw only fright in her daughter's eyes and had to carry around a freeze-frame of that image in her mind.

How rapidly a freshman adjusts to college life depends on many factors, ranging from global issues—their personality, personal strengths, and general resiliency—to specifics such as the college-student match, class selection, and who the roommate turns out to be. Homesickness, which strikes almost all freshmen, typically abates as students become more involved in rewarding academic, social, or athletic activities. Negative experiences and individual vulnerabilities can aggravate homesickness, even into sophomore year.

The durability of the freshman's personal *infrastructure* and the presence of protective assets (strong moral code, social skills, emotional and physical health, intellectual motivation, adaptable temperament, to name a few) make launching and the transition to college easier; risk factors (neurochemistry imbalance, substance use, dysfunctional family background) can tip the balance and jeopardize the launch.

> WHATEVER HAS MADE GROWING UP HARDER CAN OFTEN MAKE LEAVING HOME HARDER—FOR PARENTS AND FRESHMEN ALIKE.

Over the long haul a young person's independence is indelibly linked to the quality of the connection with parents (or substitute adult support). Freshmen who are securely attached to parents—who feel connected, respected, and accepted by their parents and feel they can talk to them about important issues—adjust to college more easily than young people who are insecurely attached.[1]

What do freshmen say they want of their parents during this transition? College deans have posed this question to entering freshmen. A scaled-down synthesis of what deans have heard from students is a list that starts out warm and fuzzy but ultimately reveals the frame of mind of many college students: First of all, tell me you love me and believe in me; second, don't stand in my way; and third, send money.

A BIT UNHINGED:
A MOM WRITES ABOUT HER DAUGHTER'S DEPARTURE

Between the spring day that Emma turned 18 and the day in late September when she finally left for college, my emotional caul-

dron bubbled and brewed, without a single, identifiable feeling distilling to the top. What I was feeling, I couldn't define. That I was feeling intensely was undeniable.

I worried that something would trip Emma up and she wouldn't leave. My chest swelled with pride at how clearly she had set her sights on what she wanted to do with her life, deciding where she needed to go to learn her trade. Nostalgically, I recalled memories of her as a toddler, her early school years, her tumultuous adolescence, as if to ensure that our life together was indelibly imprinted on my mind for the many years that lay ahead.

I cautiously inventoried myself for regret: Had we seen enough musical theater? Taken enough vacations and trips? Had I done enough to prevent scarring from a divorce—one that was necessary and never regretted from my point of view? Had I imparted my core values? My favorite recipes?

It amazed me that I could know her so well and have only a dim vision of what the next year would hold. I was excited about her beginning her own life, while I fretted over her two younger siblings. How would they weather the loss of their beloved pathfinder? Would they flourish in the space she left available?

My emotions swelled to a crescendo during the last week before her scheduled departure. One evening I entered my 12-year-old son's room for our nightly bedtime read-aloud session. I picked up the book and opened to the page where we'd left off. "I don't want to read tonight," he announced. "I'm feeling a bit unhinged." Well put, I thought.

We ate a succession of last suppers—with friends, grandparents, neighbors. Finally, the day arrived when she would drive with her father, my ex-husband, to college in the neighboring state. I had to work that morning, and before I left I asked Emma who she wanted to be present for final good-byes. Just her brother, sister, and me, she said. When I got home at noon, Emma and her 15-year-old sister were arguing heatedly over a T-shirt. The van was packed, the new computer was purchased, the first quarter tuition was paid—Emma was all set—but there was still *an ax to grind between sisters. Accusations lay hanging in the air between the girls, and I rolled my eyes at Emma's father, "Not exactly the warm farewell I had pictured."*

We stood by the curb waiting for the car to pull away. Then it was over. Emma was gone. I was poised for . . . the rush of tears? exhilaration? misgivings? panic? My 15 year old immediately left for soccer practice. I looked at my son, curious to find that a single, identifiable emotion had, I suspected for all of us, surfaced at last: relief. Relief that the anguishing anticipation of Emma's departure was finally behind us.

MY CHILD IS GONE—NOW WHAT?

Preparing for the birth of a child, many parents educate themselves on the ways their lives must change in order to fold children into the couple's mix. For a positive outcome, parents need to be able to put aside some of their needs as individuals and as couples, have realistic expectations for what good child-rearing truly entails, and derive satisfaction from nurturing and participating in the child's growth. Although prospective research has not been conducted on the launching process, it's clinically well known that it proceeds optimally when parents have gratification in their lives outside the parent-child relationship. First, parents need to make room in their lives for this immensely important addition, but years later they need to fill up the space left by their launching freshmen.

Studies on the psychology of major life transitions describe stages that individuals move through, noting various exceptions to these stages, since life changes happen to different people in different ways. In loose terms, the three phases include a loss phase, followed by a fallow time characterized by some confusion and uncertainty, which is eventually succeeded by a sense of a new beginning.[2]

With launching, some parents feel aimless and fragile, while others become frustrated and impatient. If for years and years your mindset has been on parenting, it's nearly impossible to redistribute those energies overnight. Whenever we're faced with the wide-open spaces of the unknown, it's only natural to feel shaky and insecure. Until we move from the uncertainty to some kind of purpose or direction, we have only ourselves to believe in and rely on. The same shakiness happens to many college freshmen (counselors sometimes call this *freshman existential angst*) and also to many college graduates confronting "What's next?"

OUR ADOLESCENTS' INCREASING INDEPENDENCE, COMPETENCE, AND ABSENCE DURING THEIR BUSY HIGH-SCHOOL YEARS SHOULD PREPARE US FOR THE TASK OF SEEKING FULFILLMENT OUTSIDE THE PARENT-CHILD RELATIONSHIP, BUT THE CULTURE AT LARGE HAS NOT ADDRESSED THE MOMENTOUS DEVELOPMENTAL ISSUE OF LAUNCHING TO NEARLY THE EXTENT AS THE INITIAL TRANSITION TO PARENTHOOD.

It helps to accept that ambiguity and a sense of being in limbo is a natural part of this transition. Midlife itself is a great example: You're letting go of youth, pondering what middle age means, but consolidating a kind of wisdom you'd never have at age 25. When children leave, mothers and fathers can channel their energies into new endeavors, and for parents who have yearned to devote themselves to postponed interest areas, this transition can be a windfall of opportunity.

Although not a hard-and-fast gender distinction, moms seem to spend more time reflecting and emoting prior to launching about "when the kids go" than dads do, perhaps because many moms—usually in the role of primary domestic manager—experience child-rearing on a more immediate level. Because some dads haven't done the mental work that moms have been doing all along—the brooding and bracing themselves for how much they're going to miss their child—fathers are sometimes hit like a ton of bricks by the fallow time, caught up short by the heaviness of their hearts.

> **ADJUSTING TO LAUNCHING IS A DOUBLE-EDGED PROCESS. ALLOW YOURSELF SOME FALLOW TIME FOR VALIDATING YOUR FEELINGS OF LOSS, BUT ALSO START PLANNING WAYS TO REDIRECT YOUR ENERGY TOWARD THE NEXT LIFE CHAPTER.**

Parents who feel extremely rattled by the launch should reflect on previous transitions or losses to determine whether launching is reactivating something from the past. A new loss can rekindle an old one, particularly if it was truncated or unresolved in some way. I counseled one mother, for example, whose brother had died in a motor-vehicle accident involving substance use when he was a freshman in college. As her own son was about to leave, she was suffering from strong waves of anxiety and agitation, even though she was making a deliberate effort to keep the two events separate in her mind. Whether connections are conscious or unconscious, an event that evokes an unhappy parallel is preloaded—a trigger waiting to snap.

Despite steps taken to prepare themselves, parents are often broadsided by something out of the blue that fills them with aching and longing for their child. One mother, for example, told me of her standing in the cereal aisle in the grocery store, about to put her usual five boxes of cereal a week into her cart, before realizing that her son was gone and she wouldn't need such huge quantities. "I just can't be in this aisle right now!" she told herself, choking back tears and hurrying away to regain composure. Another mom described how she was about to grab four dinner plates from the cupboard to set the table, when she stopped midair, realizing her family was down to three at the dinner table. She burst into tears.

SAD SIBLINGS

Siblings who are left behind are a tough group to characterize because their reactions can be all over the map. Some sensitive siblings with special bonds—perhaps a similar temperament or a shared experience—are thrown hard when their good buddy brother or sister leaves. Parents should take care not to minimize what they're going through: This is a shift in an important relationship.

At the same time, parents can take heart in the fact that if their child is secure in his family and has a healthy life, with friends, school, and extracurricular activities, the loss will be reincorporated within a few months, if not within days or weeks. Because launching is momentous to parents, we should take care not to project our own feelings onto children remaining at home. If having a sibling launch does, however, leave an enormous hole for an extended duration, then the problem doesn't pertain strictly to launching, but probably to a bigger issue of why the child has so little else in his life to take up the slack.

If there's any way you can give a truly down-in-the-dumps sibling a visit on his own to see the brother or sister at college, it's probably worth doing to help ease the transition. Do, however, keep in mind that parties will happen and your younger child will be exposed to a whole new world on campus!

Though they may struggle and have some sad times, most siblings remaining at home won't wind up in a truly worrisome situation unless there's already an existing issue, for example, a child with depression; a child who is left as the glue for the parents' bad marriage; or a child whose intense parents focus on children as projects and now have only one project left.

To the great chagrin of parents, siblings' reactions to launching are often about "stuff": the bigger room or the car or phone line that's now available. One tightly knit family with three daughters observed how difficult it was for their two younger children when their oldest, Flora, left for college. With the second about to leave, they readied themselves for a pithy intimate talk with the youngest. "How do you think you'll adjust to being the only child left at home?" they asked her.

> **IN AND OF ITSELF, HAVING A SIBLING LEAVE FOR COLLEGE DOES NOT USUALLY CREATE PROBLEMS FOR THE ONES LEFT AT HOME. UNLESS IT IS COUPLED WITH OTHER SIGNIFICANT ISSUES, SIBLINGS AT HOME ALMOST ALWAYS ADJUST WELL OVER TIME AND EVEN APPRECIATE THE SPACE THEY CAN NOW ABSORB.**

"Well, if it's anything like losing Flora, we should probably get the movie channel," she responded, in all seriousness.

PANGS OF THE ROOMIER NEST: ADJUSTING TO A QUIETER HOUSE

I'm convinced that parents suffer a great disservice with the expression "empty nest." To emphasize emptiness, a word signifying a void or a vacuum, is an unfair way to describe a time when life can be full of growth possibilities. People move through other life phases when they must redirect their energy from one preoccupation to another—without having a troubling adjective like "empty" pinned on them.

The derivation of the term appears to link back to a time when physicians (mostly male) were seeing women suffering from mood dips probably related to menopause, which coincided with their children leaving home. (Nature plays a cruel trick when women go though menopause and launching at the same time!) Instead of supporting women through this natural transition and figuring in hormonal imbalance as a cause for the crying and upset, these women came to be described as suffering from "empty-nest syndrome."

Theorists have debated inconclusively whether the roomier nest has more impact on women when they were not employed outside the home, but they have noted that its interpretation depends upon what's going on in the woman's life generally.[3] What is relatively recent news is that college-educated women born during the baby boom seem to have a positive attitude about their middle-age years and to experience them as providing an increased sense of personal identity and confidence in their personal efficacy.[4]

To the degree that moms or dads have full enough lives and identities outside of parenthood, they usually find ways to fulfill themselves once they remove daily parenting. Refurbishing the roomier nest isn't a small agenda for people with hindrances like low self-esteem or depression because, lacking ego strength, they may be plagued by self-doubt and unable to move forward with some optimism. Or if there are existing problems with a marriage or single parenthood, the nest may truly feel empty. Since launching intensifies issues, people who know they're at a low ebb personally or that their marriage is faltering are well advised to look into these problems before September of their child's college freshman year.

> **WE CAN IGNORE A LOT WHILE PARENTING. WHATEVER ISSUES WE'VE PUSHED ASIDE WHILE PREOCCUPIED BY DAY-TO-DAY CHILD-REARING WILL BE WAITING IN THE WINGS FOR US TO DEAL WITH AFTER OUR CHILDREN LEAVE.**

TRULY A SINGLE NOW

Single parents face some unique issues, since the house will be that much quieter and they can feel truly home alone. Moreover, if there's an absence of sibs, the child will be breaking away from a *dyad,* a relationship of two, which is often tighter and more intimate than a triad of mom, dad, and child, and thereby tougher to leave. Because children of single parents are more prone to worrying that they're abandoning mom or dad when launching, parents will want to assuage feelings of guilt. If single parents behave as if the leave-taking is the natural next step in their child's life, children are less likely to feel personally responsible for "leaving mom or dad alone."

Under the best of circumstances—perhaps because the eventuality of living solo can be so daunting—single parents often get a jump on reorienting their lives prior to fall of their child's freshman year. With a heightened anticipation of how profound this change will be, single parents potentially take the reality of the roomier nest seriously and have made time for adult friends, hobbies, and interests, so that they're set up to enjoy themselves after the launch, as should also be true for their married counterparts.

> CHILDREN SHOULDN'T FEEL GUILTY BECAUSE THEY'RE GROWING UP. WHEN THEY SEE THAT THEIR PARENT, WHETHER SINGLE OR MARRIED, HAS A FULL LIFE, WITH EVENTS ON THE CALENDAR TO REPLACE THE SOCCER GAME OR THE SCHOOL PLAY, THEY LEAVE WITH LESS BAGGAGE.

Issues of marital or partnership status (or lack thereof) can come into stark relief with a child's exit. One mother I counseled, whose daughter was the product of a donor conception, remarked, "The moment has arrived. I've been single since the beginning, but now I'm also alone, which has never been my preference." Another divorced mother commented, "Co-parenting with my ex meant contact, coordination, and compromise with a man I would have liked never to see again. Now I feel truly liberated." A stepfather confessed to me, "I always tried to be a good sport with all the usual stepparenting challenges, like avoiding criticism and feeling like an outsider, but frankly, the launch clears the air of a lot of tension we've had around here."

Whether single or married, by the time children launch, most parents have already been practicing being home alone. As adolescents progress developmentally, they begin to leave their parents in the dust, particularly on weekends, as they pursue activities and social lives of their own. It's like a mini-launch: More and more, they're out and about, readying parents for the roomier nest.

When teens haven't been moving out into the world incrementally—which might be the case with, for example, a shy, dependent child—then the natural consequence of this type of parent-child closeness is a more painful launch. For a single parent and a child with this type of temperament, separation pangs will be intensified, and the family may need coaching in ways to encourage independence for the child and the single parent.

NORMAL SPATS IN GOOD MARRIAGES WHEN THE CHILDREN LEAVE

Roomier-nest couples return to principles of Marriage 101: Having a good time together is what cements a relationship. Although sex is also important, the most satisfied couples are ones who have fun and friendship. Surveys show that the major hurdles for couples after launching are 1) dealing with conflict; 2) communication; and 3) sex. These top issues are one and the same for younger couples, too.[5] Although much changes over the course of a marriage, the fundamentals remain constant.

This is not to say that coming back together into a couple-focused relationship instead of a child-focused one won't involve ironing out wrinkles or even some renegotiating of the terms of their day-to-day interaction. Launching can be a turning point where couples discover that they've grown in different directions and need an overhaul of their relationship. During this major adjustment, it's not unusual for even happily married couples to have fleeting thoughts about whether they still want their spouse—or whether their spouse still wants them—now that they're less needed in their parenting role.

> EVEN IF THEY HAVE HOT ISSUES TO HANDLE, COUPLES WHO CAN RETURN TO THE SPIRIT OF ENJOYING EACH OTHER AND THEIR TIME TOGETHER HAVE WON HALF THE BATTLE OF MAINTAINING A HEALTHY MARRIAGE POST-LAUNCH.

The key for couples is to be patient and gentle with each other, making sure you're tolerant and respectful of your spouse's way of coping with change. One of the biggest challenges in a marriage is to accept a partner's different rhythm and approach to change, looking out for one's self while also for the other. Having a child leave home is a major milestone, and strong emotions are honorable. The three stories below illustrate the kinds of arguments that happen between couples in good marriages.

KNOW THYSELF AND KNOW EACH OTHER
FRANCIS AND STEVE

Over the course of their long marriage, Francis and Steve often reacted differently to experiences, and launching their son was no exception. Of a more resilient and adaptable temperament, Steve missed his son terribly, but he wasn't displaying his feelings as overtly as Francis, the more skeptical, gloomy, and emotional of the two.

Most of the time Francis and Steve were mutually supportive of each other's differences. Francis would be uplifted by Steve's upbeat outlook, while he would find a deeper expression of himself in her sensitivity. With launching, though, they were alienated by each other's reactions. One evening, Steve came home and found Francis crying her eyes out, as she had been doing for days. For 20 years, he'd been dealing with her upset, and this time he cracked.

"Why are you dwelling on it like this?" he snapped.

"Well, how are you feeling? Aren't you sad?" she asked.

"I'm very happy for him, and you should be, too," Steve replied, grabbing the newspaper. Nothing could possibly have felt worse to Francis than having Steve react like this to her despondency. Looking for Steve to validate her sorrow, she felt isolated and abandoned by his chipper outlook.

The problem with this picture is not only that Steve shouldn't snap, but that Francis shouldn't ask a question that sets herself up for a polarized response from Steve. Knowing what she knows about herself and Steve, she shouldn't have necessarily expected him to empathize with her negativity. Steve's "why don't you look on the bright side" felt dismissive and cruel to Francis, but the problem lay not so much in their contrasting sensibilities, but in Francis's miscalculated approach. Better that Francis own her valid grieving, take responsibility for working through the loss, and that Francis and Steve figure out ways to affirm each other's style and find a middle ground where they can work on the marital implications of this transition together.

TAKING IT PERSONALLY
ANGELA AND MARCO

Angela felt as if she were dancing on the head of a pin. Marco, her husband, hadn't been himself since their only daughter, whose lively presence normally filled every corner of the home, left for college. Angela worried about how hard Marco was taking it because, like any good spouse, she didn't like to see him dragging around, but she was also troubled by the way his sadness reflected on her.

Putting on a happy face and trying to be entertaining, Angela cringed at Marco's forlorn remarks, "It's so quiet around here. It's just not the same." To compensate for her daughter's absence, Angela had been working double time to be engaging and fun, as if to fill the shoes of both wife and daughter. Her interpretation of Marco's laments was "Am I not woman enough for Marco? What's wrong with me that he's so lonely?"

This situation was classic. Overfunctioning, Angela felt responsible for her husband's happiness and for smoothing over her daughter's absence, which allowed Marco to mope and underfunction. Angela and Marco both have adjustment issues: If not sufficiently excited about his life—his work, his relationships, hobbies, level of fitness—Marco has work to do to re-energize himself, appreciate his spouse, and get back in the groove. Angela, on the other hand, needs to allow Marco to miss their daughter and grieve the loss without it being about her or their relationship.

THE DANGERS OF DENIAL
JANE AND PATRICK

A busy professional couple, Jane and Patrick hadn't skipped a beat since their youngest child, a daughter, left for college.

At the same time that they were perking along in a life-as-usual mode, they were also becoming more and more irritable and impatient with each other.

Jane was coordinating a large extended-family Thanksgiving celebration and, unbeknownst to Patrick, was waiting for information about her daughter's classes before finalizing plans. Although Patrick had spoken to their daughter earlier in the week, learning about her schedule, he neglected to tell Jane, not realizing its importance.

Discovering Patrick had her long-awaited information, Jane blew up, "I can't believe you didn't tell me! I've been on the edge of my seat to get her schedule. If you knew what I've been through, you'd never be so forgetful. This is one more example of how egocentric and inattentive to my needs you've become. You never tell me about your plans—like last Saturday morning when you waltzed out the door for golf without any notice. With the kids gone, you're a free agent!"

"Well, I can't believe how bitchy and critical you've become of me," Patrick retorted. "Every move I make is subject to your judgments. I can't win! With all the bickering we've been doing, I'd swear you've been picking fights to keep yourself on your toes, since the kids aren't around to spar with anymore."

Not having addressed the big task of becoming a couple again, Jane and Patrick were ignoring too much. Launching is a time for couples to be reflective, thoughtful, and proactive in figuring out new ground rules for communicating and sustaining a healthy relationship. By the way she was anticipating her daughter's call, Jane clearly missed her like crazy, as no doubt Patrick did, too. Instead of denying their loss, Jane and Patrick needed to sift through their feelings. Although their exchange was charged with negative voltage, by removing the negativity and listening to the best part of each other's message, they would discover good ideas for re-tuning their relationship.

A "DUMP" PHONE CALL FROM A DISTRAUGHT FRESHMAN

It can happen with any kind of freshman—a quiet stoic child, a high-energy social child, a spiritual child—not just an excitable, temperamental one. Your phone rings and on the other end is your unglued college student. Maybe the call is about a roommate who drinks too much, or the impossible class, or having no real friends, or the bad performance at a sporting event, and—like many freshmen in a bad moment—she is convinced she has made the wrong school choice.

"Dump" phone calls assume different tones, depending on your child's Achilles' heel. Whatever your child's vulnerability may be—a tendency to worry and whine, to feel envy, to mope like Eyyore, or to complain about other people—the phone call is likely to have a pitch that parents recognize all too well from previous episodes when their child was out of sorts. Distance, isolation, and the phone itself can exacerbate the tone.

How can a parent pick up the pieces of their freshman's distress—or should they? A transcript below shows one parent's efforts:

RACHEL: Mom, I'm so glad I caught you! Where were you? I've been trying for hours!

MOM: Hi, honey, I was at Judy's helping her with—(cut off by Rachel)

RACHEL: Mom, I don't know what I'll do. Everyone here is so much smarter than I am. I'll never catch up with my work. I have hundreds of pages of history to read, and a humanities paper to write, and three lab reports to write up, and that doesn't even include studying for exams that are coming up. I just can't cut it here.

MOM: Well, sweetie, you felt overwhelmed many times during high school, too, and you always seemed to get it done in the long run, and—(cut off again)

RACHEL: Oh, Mom, how can you compare this to high school? That was nothing! I've never been so stressed in my life. I don't see how I can do half of it, and the more I stress out, the more my concentration is shot to hell. And it's impossible to study in my room because Jess either has her music cranked up, or has friends over, or she's on the phone. My room situation is impossible!

MOM: Can't you negotiate with her? After all, you're entitled to study in a room you've paid for, I mean, that your parents have paid for. Have you tried to talk to her about it?

RACHEL: (With a groan) Mo-om, of course I have. She acts like I'm a total whiner and makes fun of me. If I say anything more, she'll make me the joke of the dorm. It's hopeless. It's getting even worse because she's starting to lie around on the bed with her boyfriend. What am I supposed to do while they're going at it? I think she's trying to drive me out of the room, and the bad part is that she's succeeding. I stay out unless I need the phone or to sleep. It's totally depressing.

MOM: Oh, hon, I hate to hear you so discouraged. Don't people go to the R.A. or something in situations like this? What are your options?

RACHEL: The R.A. is worthless. They just do it for the money. Everybody has guys in their rooms, Mom. My situation isn't unique, except that Jess is the biggest bitch in the dorm. Just my luck. I feel like all I do is go to class and study and put up with her and her friends. I really feel like giving up. I mean, like, what's the point?

MOM: Well, you know that you'll study better if you take some time off to socialize and exercise. You've got to have a little fun, see friends, and balance the work out a little bit. Don't you think you might go to one of the parties or something?

RACHEL: Mo-om, I don't have any time! Didn't you hear how much work I have? Aren't you listening?

How well did this mom handle her daughter's call? As well as anyone possibly could have. While this isn't necessarily a transcript for what a parent should do, it shows one way of getting through a call that's probably no-win from the outset.

True, the mom minimizes somewhat ("you always seem to get it done in the long run") and perhaps problem-solves too readily instead of letting Rachel come up with her own solutions ("you'll study better if you take some time off to socialize and exercise"), but she doesn't overreach and likewise tolerates plenty of debris from her daughter. Any realistic depiction of a parent struggling with a dump phone call reveals that parents naturally lean toward these kinds of responses and that young people probably expect no less from their parents, even as they throw their parent's good ideas back in their face.

PHONE CALLS FROM UPSET FRESHMEN CAN BE A MINEFIELD FOR PARENTS TO NEGOTIATE WITH PATIENCE, ASTUTENESS, AND AN OVERRIDING PRIORITY ON LETTING THE FRESHMAN KNOW YOU HAVE FAITH IN THEIR COMPETENCE TO HANDLE THEIR PROBLEMS, WITHOUT MINIMIZING THEM.

Parents should be forewarned: Phone calls like Rachel's do happen. Our freshman's upset can feel like daggers in our hearts as we try to soothe them. Even if we know intellectually that it's normal for children who are flummoxed to unload on their parents, it feels worse from a distance. That college freshmen as a cohort tend to be stressed out and overwhelmed has become fairly well publicized, but how can a parent best respond to these calls? Much depends on the parent-child relationship, of course, but some guidelines can help.

SIX STRATEGIES FOR MAKING IT THROUGH DUMP PHONE CALLS

1. Realize there is no magic technique that will necessarily calm down an overwhelmed freshman.

   Many parents are aware of the technique called *active listening,* where parents make every effort not to engage directly with their child; instead, parents simply reaffirm that they are available and are listening with a comment such as, "Gee, this sounds very stressful." While this useful technique has the advantage of not entangling parents in specifics, it's not a panacea. An overwrought adolescent is likely to rejoin with a one-two punch, "No kidding, Mom!"

   We'd never want to overlook the power of good listening, but parents may still need to do the obligatory dance, as the mother above did, of trying to offer some advice so that the freshman doesn't feel abandoned or cut off. Avoid irritability or impatience ("You always say you're going to flunk"), since that too can come across as rejecting. After the freshman has undergone some catharsis, say something supportive and reassuring like, "I wish I could help you. I feel so helpless this far away, but my only consolation is that you've come through it before and have it within yourself to handle it." Then before your child has a chance to contradict you, add something like, "I know you don't feel like that right now." Your child might remain upset and the phone call may end without resolution, but you've probably helped.

2. Keep your perspective on why your child is calling you and avoid reactivity.

   Whether aware of it or not, college students' goals for these phone calls are to plug themselves emotionally back into their parents, make extreme statements, download on the parent, and thereby purge themselves. The dynamic works: Nine times out of ten, young people hang up the phone feeling better, while parents feel worse.

What, then, should the parent's goal be for the calls? One goal is to understand your freshman's fragility and make a conscious choice not to overreact to what they've laid at your feet. Parents tend to be the designated wastebasket for children to dump their negative emotions. It's a terrible habit and you want your emerging adult to outgrow it, but as unpleasant as it is for parents, it's a surprisingly effective way for freshmen to diffuse emotional overload.

Second, consider it a success if you remain steady, calm, positive, and reassuring because your child will, indirectly if not directly, draw from your well of wisdom. Many parents mistakenly feel they've failed their child after a difficult phone conversation, believing they should have arrived at a solution. Instead, parents can try to keep a philosophical grasp on the purpose of their child's call, recognizing that their freshman looks to them to provide a resource of security.

3. Understand that your child is venting with you because he probably can't express his upset to anyone else.

Although it is a backhanded compliment, parents should appreciate that they are the safe haven to which freshmen can freely expose themselves. Still creating and forming impressions the first semester, college students feel as if they have to keep their cool around others who might judge them, which is all the more reason to share their low functioning side with mom or dad.

TRY TO SEE THE POSITIVE SIDE OF WHY YOUR CHILD IS CALLING YOU: ONLY WITH SOMEONE WHOM THEY CAN UTTERLY TRUST DO THEY FEEL COMFORTABLE ENOUGH TO REGRESS AND RANT LIKE A MIDDLE-SCHOOLER.

Because young people often hide their insecurities from one another, they usually have no idea that their classmates may feel similarly. Encouraging your child to talk to friends may help them see how many others are in the same boat.

4. Keep in mind that you're probably seeing only part of the picture of what your child is experiencing.

More likely than not, what you're hearing with a dump phone call is real at that moment but probably isn't the entire story of a student's college life. It's like the 5 P.M. arsenic hour for parents when everything is easily distorted by a tired and low-blood sugar toddler: Dump phone calls represent a distillation of the worst parts of their experience.

For that reason, a parent's first line of thinking should be to check back later—after your child has caught up on his sleep. When you call back in two days to ask, "What happened with that test?" they might very likely say, "What test? Oh, yeah, that one. . . ." Even if the problem hasn't gone away, it may not be as acute (unless you activate it).

Although an exaggerated example, one family I counseled experienced dump phone calls almost exclusively for two years. The parents were at loose ends because their son called constantly with complaints about his roommate, his classes, and feeling like a loser. On one occasion, after ending a cell-phone conversation with his parents, he accidentally pushed the redial button. His parents couldn't believe what they heard when they picked up their phone! In striking contrast to their immediately preceding miserable phone call, they overheard their son laughing with his roommate, whom he'd maintained he didn't like, telling stories, having a marvelous time.

5. Make an effort to manage future phone calls so that your child doesn't develop a habit of being only negative with you.

Even grounded young people sometimes become conditioned to be emotionally down with their parents: When they hear their parent's voice on the other end of the receiver, they open up the file that says, "I'm overwhelmed. This place is horrible," instead of the file that discloses, "I had a good workout today. My history class is really interesting."

Dependent in an unhealthy way, the freshman may be using parents as a main outlet for relieving stress. Though their world has not fallen apart, they're continuing to put their parents in the role of soother, fixer, and counselor. When this becomes a pattern as opposed to an occasional lapse, parents should ask themselves whether it might be in their children's interest to assume these responsibilities for themselves. Without cutting off from their child, parents can convey their faith that the freshman is the best one to figure out a dilemma.

> FRESHMEN NEED TO BELIEVE THAT THE SAME COMPETENCE THAT GOT THEM TO COLLEGE IN THE FIRST PLACE WILL PULL THEM THROUGH THEIR PROBLEM. COLLEGE STUDENTS WHO USE THEIR PARENTS AS THEIR MOST CONVENIENT AND RELIABLE STRESS VALVE NEED TO BE ENCOURAGED TO TAKE ACTION ON THEIR OWN DILEMMAS.

Consider training your freshman to talk about other things with you. You might, for example, call them earlier in the day, when they may have less need to purge, with a funny story to tell them. Shorter phone calls sometime carry less risk than lingering ones. If phone calls continually degenerate into complaints, resort to other ways of communicating, like e-mail or letters.

Offering too much advice can sometimes inadvertently aggravate a phone call's negative flow. Sometimes children are in the mood to rebuff any idea from parents. Good management of dump phone calls often means not reacting defensively to rebuffs and not weighing in with your ideas until the timing is right. One parent, for example, told me how her daughter called home weekly, feeling homesick and friendless. From the mother's perspective, a problem feeding into the homesickness was her daughter's dogged pursuit of academics, with no time out for fun. Balancing the work-fun equation is a huge struggle for many freshmen, with some going overboard with extracurricular interests and others too tightly wound up in academics. Wise enough not to waste her breath repeating herself, the mom waited for a calm interlude before dropping a broad suggestion, "Have your eyes open for opportunities and students who look like your kind of friends." Shortly thereafter, the daughter decided to go out for intramural lacrosse and bonded with her teammates. The gentleness of the nudge at a propitious moment allowed her good idea to be effective.

6. Recognize when your child needs additional support or counseling.

During their first year of major adjustment, freshmen can routinely be worked up, stressed out, and struggling with everything from homesickness to unsympathetic professors. How can parents know whether their child's phone calls are something more than a normal tendency to complain to parents?

If your freshman won't tell you anything good about his life—he hasn't joined any clubs, made any friends, had any great classes or successes—and it's sustained over many weeks and it's all you tap into, then a visit to the college's counseling service would be advised.

"I'M THINKING ABOUT TRANSFERRING"

Little difference does it make whether a freshman is attending the college of his dreams or his last resort; many first-year students talk about wanting to transfer. Some call home insistently in tears, others write earnest letters or e-mails outlining reasons why this is the wrong college, while still others float vague musings before their parents, like "I wonder if I'd be happier at [some other school]" or "Sometimes I think of joining [a close friend at another school]."

Whatever their style, most freshmen who raise this issue

do so because they're still finding their way in a new setting. Maybe they're missing the deep relationships of old friendships; maybe their identities have shifted to skew the college-student match; or maybe they want a feature their school lacks.

Since your freshman is probably expressing ambivalence rather than clear intentions, a parent's main job is to listen as their child sorts out his feelings. When young people present the idea of transferring, parents can suggest that their student give it some time to improve, asking questions like, "As long as you're there, what strategies do you have to make things better for now?" Because we're parents and want to keep nurturing, we may move too quickly to provide wisdom, answers, or fixes. Sometimes parents wind up defending a school—a tough position since we're not there.

> PARENTS SHOULD KNOW HOW COMMONLY FRESHMEN ENTERTAIN TRANSFERRING, EVEN WHEN THEY'RE ATTENDING THEIR TOP PICK. TAKE CARE NOT TO LOCK IN TOO QUICKLY WITH AN OPINION, SINCE YOUR CHILD MAY JUST NEED TIME.

Some freshmen, however, are unswerving and passionate about their need to transfer. "I don't feel right here," they say persistently. "I can't find a group I belong to, and the professors just aren't my sort." As with any problem that crops up, parents can gauge the problem's significance by its duration and intensity, combined with what you know about your child. Some young people struggle with an ongoing personal issue, shyness, pessimism, or anxiety, for example, and it may be the filter of that issue that's impacting their adjustment and not the school per se. Changing settings may not resolve the problem.

Ultimately, when freshmen determine to transfer, they should bear the burden of going through the entire onerous application process again—this time without mom's or dad's oversight. If they are willing to call admissions departments for catalogs and applications, go through visits and interviews, fill out more forms, write more essays, have records sent, and determine financial aid issues, it speaks to their determination to change.

Some students will go through the whole process but then decide not to transfer at the eleventh hour. That's okay. Sometimes this is what it takes for young people to honor their own reservations about a school choice but come back around to an affirmative position.

LATTES, CELL PHONES, AND DESIGNER LABELS: YOUNG PEOPLE'S EXPECTATIONS FOR A HIGH STANDARD OF LIVING

Many of us can recall our own parents' stories of how they walked ten miles in the snow with holes in their boots to attend school—or some tale of scarcity calculated to make us feel grateful for our relative material well-being. The contrast today is no less glaring, as we shake our heads over how much our children have and how entitled they feel, compared to our own scrounging days of babysitting or raking lawns to save for a secondhand bike. The raised standard of living that parents strive for usually ends up being the same standard their children take for granted.

Unlike our Depression-era parents, who genuinely feared poverty, we've had more disposable income, and our offspring have borne the consequences, for better or worse. Likewise, many families have prioritized extracurricular activities or volunteer work for their children (the college résumé!) over holding down a job. Wishing our emerging adults had a better grasp of the work ethic and the value of an earned dollar, we can look only to ourselves.

When I've questioned and pushed exemplary families on their regrets about child-rearing, better money management is often a weak link where they admit their efforts fell short. One of the most predictable setups for quarrels occurs when parents haven't been able to say no to optional purchases and money-related perks to their children convincingly and effectively. To the degree that college students would like to maintain on their parent's nickel the standard of living they've grown accustomed to, whereas parents want to cut back and set new limits, families end up in a tiff. It's only too easy for college students to spend hundreds of dollars per week on food and clothing, despite parental frustration, but many don't know how to wean themselves from a pattern started years before. After all, who likes to cut back?

The best way to circumvent this predicament is to have a conscious money philosophy and establish budgets for children to live within before it becomes a problem. Before your child leaves for college, determine what allowance you'll provide, how expenses will be covered, and how much money your child needs to earn during breaks. Think through your family's values around money and talk frankly to your children about them—instead of just griping. If, however, you've been remiss, you're not alone: When it comes to discussing topics like budgeting and saving money with children, parents can be every bit as tongue-tied as they are in talking about sex, perhaps because of our own imperfect money management.[6]

Instituting a money diet doesn't become any easier once young people are in college. It makes parents happy to give their children whatever makes them happy—an urge that is as strong with emerging adults as it is for toddlers. What can help young people is a program during the teen years of having a savings account and perhaps a debit card (or a card with prepaid limits instead of a credit card), and sticking to an allowance. Families can determine policies on how much money children have to earn, what they can do with gifts from relatives, how trips or special camp experiences are financed, or what portion of a big-ticket item parents subsidize.

Usually, students who enter college economically responsible are the ones who have been parented toward those expectations all along. They've been trained to live within their means and think twice about spending habits. If parents have been saying, "Of course, you'll work over the holidays," then young adults are prepared to do so. If children have learned over time that their parents can be charmed into caving on money policies, when the proposal surfaces for a spring break jaunt to a tropical island, chances are they will ramp up the charm until the jackpot is delivered, as usual. Conversely, if parents have never handed out money or sponsored trips freely, young people are in a better position to absorb the disappointment of doing without.

Sometimes deleterious money habits take hold because of personality style. Take, for example, a parent who has been a soft touch and a child who has been both a big spender and one of those tenacious "gunners" who is so persistent that he just plain wears his parents down. When this type of child leaves home, parents might want to avoid all sources of credit and dole out allowances weekly, so he can't do too much damage at one time and will be forced to budget.

AS PARENTS, WE STRUGGLE WITH HOW MUCH MONEY TO SPEND ON OUR CHILDREN BECAUSE OF OUR COMPETING IMPULSES. LOVING OUR CHILDREN, WE WANT TO KEEP THEM COMFORTABLE, BUT WE ALSO SEE VALUE IN THEIR LEARNING TO MAKE DO WITH LESS.

Whatever the emerging adult's spending predilections, parents have the same goal: to raise a child to be smart financially and make good choices, paving the way for them to live within their own income. Remember, young people's standards of living are supposed to drop when they leave home. "Weaning" them financially from our pocketbook during the college years prepares them for economic independence. Only under unusual circumstances are recent college graduates able to equal the standard of living they enjoyed under their parents' roof. As their parents, we may want to relieve them of the discomfort of scraping by, so we provide clothes, cars, trips, and dinners out, as a way of showing our love. Part of their competency building, however, is to learn how to be creative and have a good time on a shoestring. What parent would want to rob their child of that character-building opportunity?

BEING A GOOD PARENT TO AN EMERGING ADULT WITH A BIG PROBLEM
FAMILY STORY

Life often confronts us with experiences we never thought we'd have to face. Emergencies involving our children force us to mobilize resources and adapt quickly to a different reality. Whatever the child's setback may be, how can we, as parents, make sure our reaction to the crisis is helping and not making it worse?

Marnie and Rusty Cohen were beside themselves, their world turned upside down by phone calls over the last month from their daughter, Simone, a freshman at a college two states away from their home. Six weeks into the fall term, Simone began calling home hysterically at all hours of the night, not once or twice, but persistently week after week. Although known to be sensitive, high-strung, and often overwrought, this level of upset surpassed anything Simone had ever expressed in high school.

At the Cohen's urging, Marnie's sister, who lived near the college, began checking in on Simone every couple of days, and she, too, was alarmed by Simone's state. "Sometimes she's sobbing so hard that she can't breathe, and her boyfriend has to walk her around the quad to calm her down," the aunt reported.

Distraught and unable to do her school work, Simone went to the college health center and, after a few visits, was referred by the center to an adolescent psychiatrist in the community, who determined that Simone was suffering from depression, the specific form still in question.

As if this diagnosis weren't alarming enough, the Cohens were furious at the college health center, which seemed to be passing their daughter off, and at the adolescent therapist, who refused to discuss their daughter's case with them because of doctor-patient confidentiality practices. As the days passed, signals from Simone became more confusing to read: Still distressed and phoning regularly, she begged her parents to stay away. The Cohens' instincts told them to drive straight to the college and bring their daughter home so they could oversee a course of treatment, but Simone screamed into the phone, "No, don't come down! No, I won't come home!"

In this terrible dilemma, the Cohens arranged a consultation with me to determine how they might best intervene in this crisis to help their daughter. As the couple sat in my office describing Simone's behavior over the last month, I agreed that Simone's symptoms as relayed to me were concerning enough to make a visit to a specialist well advised.

BE IT SUBSTANCE ABUSE, ANTISOCIAL BEHAVIOR, DEPRESSION, ANXIETY, OR OTHER PSYCHIATRIC ILLNESSES, 20 TO 30 PERCENT OF YOUNG PEOPLE WILL DEVELOP SOME KIND OF MENTAL DISORDER. PARTICULARLY WHEN CHILDREN ARE OFF SITE, PARENTS NEED SIGNPOSTS FOR DETERMINING THE SERIOUSNESS OF A CONDITION.

Although college students normally express upset to their parents, Simone's behavior had signs of crossing over into the arena of a mental disorder because it was severe and unrelenting for more than two weeks, and the feelings described were extreme and distorted. Most cases of psychiatric illness will have earlier telltale signs, especially when viewed in retrospect, but mental disorders commonly emerge during the college years, sometimes triggered or intensified by the stresses of college life and launching from home.

From the outset, the Cohens were confident that despite their daughter's extreme anguish, suicide was unlikely. While she had made some veiled comments like "It's all intolerable. If this keeps happening, I just don't know what I'll do," she had no plan and had also directly reassured her parents that she never thought seriously about ending her life. (Any child who makes remarks about suicide should be immediately referred to a specialist for an evaluation; and when someone reveals a plan about how they might carry out a suicide, hospitalization should be seriously considered.)

Much of the Cohens' upset was aimed at Simone's psychiatrist. Simone had complained to her parents that she wasn't sure she liked the therapist, who seemed indifferent and hard to talk to, but who had given her medication. Although I didn't want to be put in the position of defending a specialist about whom I knew nothing, I could report to the Cohens that young people who are as churned up as Simone commonly feel underwhelmed by psychiatric help in their initial visits.

Still, the Cohens were infuriated: "Simone just walked out of the office with a prescription! Everybody and their brother is on Prozac these days, and Simone has always been suggestible. How are we supposed to know whether she really needs medication?" asked Rusty Cohen heatedly. "When you put a child on a drug like this, when do they go off? What are the long-term side effects? I don't want my child to lose her personality to a drug."

In addition to offering the Cohens useful information on depression, the most important goal for the session was to help them move to a calm, problem-solving place so that they could be involved in their daughter's care in a productive way.

All of the strong emotions the Cohens felt were justified. What parent wouldn't be scared by phone calls like Simone's? Simone couldn't help it, but she had put her parents in a terrible bind, simultaneously roping them in with her hysteria, then forbidding their involvement. No wonder the Cohens turned their anguish on the college and a psychiatrist they didn't even know. The problem was that their anxiety had started to match their daughter's. The Cohens' upset wasn't allowing Simone to be comfortable with their support.

IN A CRISIS OF ANY TYPE, FEAR, ANGER, AND ADRENALIN-DRIVEN INTENSITY CAN STEER PARENTS IN THE WRONG DIRECTION. THIS KIND OF UNDERSTANDABLE PANIC WILL NOT HELP PARENTS HELP THE CHILD. KEEP YOURSELF COLLECTED, GET MORE INFORMATION, AND THINK ABOUT WHAT YOU CAN DO TO ENLIST THE TRUST OF YOUR CHILD.

I advised the Cohens absolutely to visit their daughter. "You're right to want to be involved," I reassured them. "You know you need to step in, but not in a way that distresses Simone further."

When a child's mental health is in question and her functioning is compromised, parents should suspend notions about an 18 year old being an adult responsible for herself. But as with any potential rescue maneuver, parents need to understand that they're part of a team and to figure out what their role is within that team.

The Cohens needed a stepwise approach to the problem. First, we sought more information from the psychiatrist. Although clinicians are ethically bound to confidentiality—even with parents—some clinicians are willing to accommodate parents somewhat. If a clinician can get a written consent from a patient for a general appraisal to go to the parents, then parents can hear some of the professional's opinions directly. Not all clinicians will comply, but it's always worth asking, "Can you get my daughter's consent to discuss this with me in general terms?"

PARENTS OF COLLEGE-AGE CHILDREN SHOULD BE SHEPHERDING THEM TOWARD SELF-RELIANCE, BUT WHEN ISSUES LIKE DRUG USE, FAILING GRADES, OR HEALTH PROBLEMS IMPAIR THE CHILD'S ABILITIES, PARENTS CAN BE AN INTEGRAL PART OF THE SUPPORT SYSTEM—BUT IT ALL DEPENDS ON HOW.

In order to get Simone's consent, the parents needed to approach Simone and the doctor in a way that conveyed that they could be calm, supportive, accepting, and patient. They could set up a session with Simone and the psychiatrist in order to form their own impression of her. They could reassure Simone that if there was anything she didn't want to answer in front of them, she could say so, reiterating to her the purpose of their visit: to ask about the diagnosis and treatment recommendations.

Marnie and Rusty Cohen redirected themselves, realizing they had displaced their distress on the psychiatrist, who, as it turned out, was a competent and diligent therapeutic clinician for Simone. Despite the emotionally laden exchanges between Simone and her parents, Simone had moved in the right direction toward clinical care, and her parents felt she would comply with their visit, if presented in a loving, non-threatening context of wanting medical information.

As the Cohens left my office, I felt reasonably optimistic, despite the specter of Simone's serious illness. It has been well documented that young people with psychiatric problems are at risk for failing at adult role expectations (such as college) but that parental and social support can help reduce risks and influence a more favorable outcome.[7] When young people are at war with their parents and refuse to connect with them around their illness, their chances of adjustment are extremely compromised. Given Simone's good relationship with her parents and the absence of overarching family problems, she would have a strong and stable base from which to draw.

MAKING THE BEST OF A DIFFICULT SITUATION

Fast forwarding with the Cohen's story, I consulted with Simone's parents and to a lesser degree with Simone for the next several years. Ultimately, her illness was diagnosed as bipolar disorder type II (also known as manic depression), a disorder characterized by bouts of depression and periods of extreme agitation, anxiety, sleepless nights, and mania. My main role was to coach Marnie and Rusty, directing them on how to work with Simone's psychiatrist and provide support that would leave Simone with as much responsibility for herself as possible.

With cases like Simone's, I usually help families in three broad areas:

Moving beyond the denial, anger, and bargaining stage. Whenever any of us is panicked over a bad situation, we want to bargain with the fates for a way out of the dilemma. It took time for the Cohens to open up to Simone's real illness and need for medication.

In Simone's case, medication was all the more necessary

because she was cutting herself, a sign of how extreme her agitation and distress were. Efforts to intervene on self-cutting, which is always serious, should be initiated as quickly as possible. When suffering from extreme distress, some individuals discover that hurting themselves in a localized way, like self-cutting, serves as a relief, with the physical pain calming the psychic pain. Because it can effectively calm and relieve emotional anguish, self-cutting can become highly addictive and may even require inpatient care.[8] Medication was part of an aggressive plan to help terminate Simone's self-cutting.

Staying focused on the present. Difficult though it always is, families need to devote their energy to the current phase of treatment without gazing into a crystal ball and worrying about eventual outcomes. Even in early phases of treatment, families often hold up the goal of returning their child to "normal," when it would be more helpful to think about day-by-day functioning and striving to cope as well as possible without becoming overwhelmed.

PARENTS WONDER: "HOW CAN PSYCHOLOGICAL PROBLEMS OF THIS MAGNITUDE HAPPEN IN MY FAMILY?" LIKE PHYSICAL ILLNESS, PSYCHIATRIC ILLNESS HAPPENS TO GOOD PEOPLE: IF ONLY OUR CULTURE WOULD UNDERSTAND THIS, THINK HOW MUCH EASIER ADJUSTMENT AND INTER-VENTION WOULD BE FOR THE AFFLICTED.

Whether Simone took her medications, went to classes, handled the stress of a major paper, or made it to the gym for exercise were struggles and hurdles. Only by keeping up with therapy, maintaining realistic expectations, and using support services was Simone's condition able to improve.

Role-modeling an accepting attitude toward the illness. How hard it is for a young person to make peace with a diagnosis of mental illness and all of its unknowns! Parental acceptance can help minimize the shame, guilt, and negative stigma of this disease and can be a crucial step in helping the young person accept herself, her treatment, and her future with hopefulness.

A diagnosis like Simone's often shatters parents' dreams for their child. Disappointed and embarrassed, they struggle with how to tell friends and relatives about this new reality. Once parents realize how much their own process of accepting the illness helps their child, they double their efforts to attend to their own anxiety and overcome negative feelings.

Some general guidelines for communicating with a child about any sensitive problem, including illness, include these:

- Speak openly, directly, and truthfully
- Avoid judgments or disrespectful phrases that can induce shame
- Aim for dialogue, without monopolizing or lecturing
- Avoid dramatic, patronizing, or controlling talk
- Reassure with commitments of your support, not with minimizations of what you might be facing
- Get your own support and take your fears, despair, and panic to other adults so they don't leak over to your struggling child

A huge challenge for families like Simone's is to determine how much the structure of college helps a young person stay on track and how much the expectations that she should be normal, handle the pressure, and control her stress hurt her. Often, as illnesses like Simone's progress, more parental bargaining occurs—if she stays in college, maybe she's not mentally ill—but young people need to be reassured of a safety net and told, "If you need to come home, come home. You can always go back to school later."

Simone was blessed with an excellent lattice of support, including an aunt living near her college, close friends, a top-notch psychiatrist, and a cohesive family with devoted parents who were wise enough to seek consultation on their role in Simone's illness. Still, it was a long haul over six years, which included periods of coming home and doing outpatient therapy, for Simone to complete a B.A.

Parents raised in the '50s and '60s are prone to overlooking emerging psychological problems because we feel shame and were trained to believe that with enough willpower they'll go away on their own. Add to the mix specific personal problems we don't want to face, and we are apt to not get help for children when they need it. Without either overprotecting or overlooking, the Cohens worked with specialists to make well-informed decisions about Simone's care. And in the end, they gave their daughter one of the best gifts parents can give a launching child: acceptance for who she is, support, and unrelenting encouragement.

THE HIGH DEMANDS OF COLLEGE LIFE: SHOULD STUDENTS JUST PULL THEMSELVES UP BY THEIR BOOTSTRAPS?

A glance through college brochures reveals images of expansive green space, academic edifices, and young people milling about, as if to say, these are the best years of your life. The reality is that unprecedented numbers of students are stressed and miserable, particularly in high-powered colleges with high-powered students. Knowing how overwhelming college life can be, most colleges have a range of resources that adequately serve the needs of most students—stress-busting classes, learning resource centers, study-tip seminars, wellness lectures, time-management seminars, and trained resident assistants in dorms.

Typically, heightened stress among college students is linked to increased academic demands, the pressure to succeed in a competitive world, and to fears of inadequacy: "Everyone else seems so smart—I'm an imposter!" Although students readily identify academics as a source of stress, parents should keep in mind that freshmen experience pressure from shifting to a whole new life scheme where it's all on them to manage their day-to-day living: doing their laundry, trudging to the cafeteria, structuring study time, balancing work with extracurricular activities, making the appointment with the professor, and even getting up in the morning for classes! And some 85 percent of college freshmen have never shared a bedroom before.

Rising every year, the numbers of students seeking appointments for counseling and psychological services overloads today's college health centers. Centers try to be responsible about determining what level of care a student needs, but because their resources are limited, they'll generally see a student only five to ten times. Most will do crisis intervention and will monitor at-risk students so they can get what they need, but they generally refer young people with a problem that looks severe or long-term to an area specialist. Families should consider the college's health clinic as their first line of intervention, but since not all young people will get all the services and attention they need from the clinic, parents might be ready to line up services outside the school for extended problems.

Why are record numbers of students seeking counseling?

Most young people eventually adjust to the expectations of college life, learning to self-regulate and self-structure, but when stressors

MOST FRESHMEN ADAPT TO THE DEMANDS OF COLLEGE LIFE, WHICH NECESSITATES SELF-CARE AND EMOTIONAL COPING IN ADDITION TO HANDLING THE ACADEMIC WORKLOAD. IF A FRESHMAN ARRIVES AT COLLEGE WITH A HOST OF PERSONAL PROBLEMS, HIS "GETTING BY" MENTAL HEALTH CAN SWITCH OVER TO SIGNIFICANT PSYCHOLOGICAL DISTRESS FAIRLY EASILY.

and risk factors outweigh protective factors, young people may not be able to hold it together, and their daily regime can deteriorate—always a troubling sign.

Deans of Students report that more young people than ever are arriving at college already overwhelmed, without the internal resources that good parenting and a stable home life provide.[9] In interviews, Deans have commented:

"Students carry more baggage with them to college today."
"We deal with a greater number of dysfunctional students and dysfunctional family situations."
"Students bring more nonacademic-related issues. We are becoming a secondary social-service agency."
"We're dealing with more psychopathology among students of all levels and all backgrounds."

If a college student calls home upset, parents need to be able to differentiate between a dump phone call with problems that will heal themselves over time and disturbances that may be in the troubling range. The four most important criteria are

- Frequency
- Persistency
- Intensity
- Impact on daily living

The more their turmoil limits daily functioning, the greater the possibility that it calls for clinical intervention. Worried parents might raise their concern with a broad comment like "You sound really down a lot lately." Your student will probably reassure you somehow—if you should be reassured—but if their response troubles you, consider monitoring more closely.

Any symptom needs to be put in the context of what par-

ents know about their child and the nature of the parent-child relationship, but in the last analysis, if you have a child on the other end of the receiver who is excessively emotional, cranked up, and making extreme statements, don't assume you can reason with them and fix it, especially at 2:00 in the morning. Parents can't do this. We wouldn't try to fix a cardiac condition ourselves, but sometimes we try to treat a mental disorder over the phone. The most effective counsel for a truly distressed student is to urge them to go immediately to the college's health center or hospital emergency room.

FIRST STEPS IN THE PASSAGE FROM HOME

September of freshman year, many young adults set their bearings and head toward the new life adventure of college. In other families, young people complete a fifth year of high school, defer or postpone college, or proceed with a combination of school and work, depending on circumstances and readiness. Though parents may wrap their arms around their children in a wrenching but exciting farewell hug, it's far more difficult for parents to get their arms around what the momentous experience of launching means for everyone.

Once children leave, parents experience the quieter house and roomier nest, coming together as a twosome in a marriage or, for some, adjusting to single living. Moms and dads need to figure out how to refill the hole left by their children's absence, a process that necessarily takes time, patience, and resourcefulness. As freshmen experience the pangs of homesickness, many parents have their own parallel version of this malady, yearning for their children. A contemplative mood often settles over parents, adjusting to a new life stage. Some parents feel relief, particularly when child-rearing has been challenging. For others, there's a sense of excitement. With

one less person to plan around, take care of, and clean up after, parents have time for themselves and more energy for new endeavors.

When children are off site, parents may have difficulties reading their college student's signals, particularly with dump phone calls, a common freshman-year phenomenon. Emerging adulthood means our children still have many challenges and lessons to learn. Their ache is our ache, even when we have good boundaries and a good attitude toward necessary growth pangs.

No single moment in time determines the success of a child's launch. A cumulative blend of circumstance and child, parent, and family strengths and weaknesses interact over time to shape the complexion of the young person who arrives at school. Launching falters for diverse reasons: A learning-disabled student refuses tutoring from the learning center; a student with a psychiatric disorder is unable to cope with the pressure; a young person from a troubled home fails to receive adequate parental nourishment and support. None of these conditions, however, dooms launching. These students and others can make it through college, depending on their support system, the power of their developmental strengths, and capacity for resiliency to offset their stressors.

Although rarely a perfectly fluid process, leaving home unfolds organically. Preparedness is rooted in who the child is, the development that has occurred during childhood, and the life experiences encountered, all of which enable first-year students to meet the stresses, challenges, and experiences they face when they arrive on campus.

Home Again but Between Two Worlds

Why having your college student back in your home is a mixed blessing

THE REVOLVING DOOR

Off the bus came Alex, fresh-faced, full of life, wearing an endearing impish grin, home from college for a month's winter break. Upon seeing her son, Ingrid, a colleague of mine, couldn't resist remarking to herself how striking and seemingly perfect young adulthood is. Gone was the awkwardness of Alex's adolescence, and in its place was a self-assured young man at ease with himself and the world. It was the happiest of reunions for a mom who adores her son and couldn't have been more excited to see him. Then, out of his backpack, he pulled a floppy-eared, black puppy—an adorable stray he planned on finding a home for—but who was going to take care of him in the meantime?

Not that Ingrid wasn't rattled or peeved, but after nearly two decades of life together, you know your child and his ways. What sprung to her mind was, "It's just so Alex."

A social guy who has always been a bit of a whirling dervish, Alex has a flair for spontaneity. During high school he would arrive home from skiing with four new acquaintances in tow, needing dinner and a place to sleep. The house was constantly filled with activity, like an electrical storm. Bringing home a stray puppy was consistent with who he was and Ingrid's life with him. Parenting Alex was exhausting—no wonder his mother felt a measure of both sadness and relief when he left for college. An upbeat, roll-with-the-punches mom, she realized, "I'm reminded of what comes with this kid. Of course he'd have a puppy in his backpack."

When our children are away, we experience long-distance love, recollecting their finest qualities. Like the romanticized good-bye of September, we idealize this reunion.

ALTHOUGH YOUNG PEOPLE MATURE BY LEAPS AND BOUNDS DURING THEIR COLLEGE YEARS, HABITS DON'T CHANGE OVERNIGHT. ONLY TOO EASILY DO PARENTS OF COLLEGE STUDENTS LAPSE INTO OLD PARENTAL RESPONSES LIKE NAGGING, INTRUSIVE QUESTIONING, OR OVER-CONTROLLING.

Returning children often revert to patterns that yank a parent's chain. If not the puppy, it might be the suitcase dumped in the hall that reminds you of their disorganization, or—unlike Alex—the couch potato who unnerves you with her phlegmatic disposition.

On cue, after dinner Alex gave his mom a quick squeeze on the shoulders and headed out with friends. Ingrid felt "dropped," remarking wistfully to herself that girls wouldn't do this to their mothers (they would and they do). Alex was partying, and in his place was the puppy, becoming less adorable with each successive piddle on the carpet. Parents usually feel somewhat included in the excitement of their child's send-off, but by December, as our college students' social spheres widen, we can feel in a different orbit. Even when young people are nearby geographically or attending the local community college or working and living in an apartment, they may not visit home frequently. What makes winter break so special is that nearly everyone is in town and has been anticipating the moment of all being together again.

Although it may ruffle our feathers, parents should resist feeling offended by their child's easy exiting, since it's largely related to the fact that we are their lifelong family whom they count on always being there. We are, after all, the known quantity and the secure home base from which emerging adults can leave and individuate. What can help parents feel less abandoned by their college student is the realization that we were the secure base when they were two and we usually are when they're 20, and that feelings of security are what allow them to spread their wings.

More so than with friends, parents sometimes resent having to share their child in a divorce situation when the holiday is split between two households. With a pretty small pie to divide among various sets of moms, dads, grandparents, friends, former teachers, and mentors, parents might feel grabby. What's a parent to do when a daughter, for example, is scheduled to spend one week with dad and one with mom, but she wants to go on a trip with a friend for three days on your week, leaving you with a scant four days? There's no easy resolution. In an amicable divorce situation it may be possible to negotiate with the other parent for an extra day, but if there's enmity in the relationship, the ex-spouse is unlikely to budge and may even gloat that it happened on your week. It's certainly not in the interest of the freshman to serve as intermediary between two dueling parents in the middle of the holiday.

To be a big person, the parent who's missing out would be

wise to move beyond wanting *my* time with *my* child because of *my* needs and have some empathy for what the freshman is experiencing. Ask yourself: Do I want my child experiencing stress, worrying how mom or dad will handle their reasonable request to be with a friend? Difficult though it may be, parents should consider showing the same kind of generosity they would have wanted at their age.

BALKING AT CHANGE, TREATING YOUR HOME LIKE A HOTEL, AND OTHER SIGNS OF SELF-ABSORPTION

Arriving back in the nest, many young people have romanticized ideas about home and the Norman Rockwell fantasy of the way things were. Like a dog sniffing their territory, many investigate every corner, noticing whether you've moved the furniture, whether dad has grown a beard or mom has a new haircut, running an inventory and expressing dissatisfaction at whatever is different. Some reveal extraordinary new powers of observation.

Dare a parent appropriate their room for another purpose, trade in the car, or, heaven forbid, sell the family home, brace yourself for ardency. College students have so much ambivalence about change, they can make a parent feel guiltier than a criminal.

Why the intense reaction? One explanation relates to their being between two worlds. In the initial stages of their transition to independence, freshmen are not yet firmly rooted in their next developmental stage. Neither here nor there, they need their home base steady and unmodified so they can use all their energy to become their own person.

Also at play, freshmen are notorious for their self-absorption, which may recall the egocentrism of early adolescence. Though self-absorption tends to be a function of their transition, from a parent's perspective, it can feel like one-way street: "I can leave you," their behavior says, "I can change, I can short-shrift you, but you need to be the Rock of Gibraltar."

Self-centeredness may manifest itself in a different pattern. Instead of tuning in microscopically, another contingent of freshmen come home in their own bubble, oblivious to their surroundings. They wouldn't notice your new hairstyle if it were dyed magenta, not to mention the painstaking effort you may have put into their homecoming.

Another classic, pervasive enough to be a stock parenting grumble, are students who arrive home as if checking into a hotel, coming and going at their leisure, leaving the "maid" to clean up after them. Keep in mind that messiness may not just be a byproduct of egocentrism or the bad habits of dorm living, although they can be part of it. Becoming more lax with household responsibilities may be their way of pulling on their parents' nurturing. After doing their own laundry, being responsible for themselves in ways they hadn't anticipated, college students are relieved to underfunction. They're tired of being an adult, and often parents have missed fussing over their offspring.

Many students arrive home feeling scattered, needing to coalesce, put the pieces of their experience together, and consolidate themselves. Overlooking the old chores may not be intentional, for they may simply be too preoccupied to hang up the clothes they're tripping over. Many are reeling from what they've encountered—the academic pressure cooker, the all nighters for exams, the strains of the social scene and living arrangements, the bulimic roommate, the friend who is wasted half the time, the noisy sex next door while they're trying to sleep. Small wonder they might need to veg out.

One of the big issues of winter break is how difficult it is to be parental and tolerate the tough moments with a remiss or out-of-line freshman, when you want to preserve an image of home as the ideal cocoon to which they can return—plus you relish having them back.

Treating their freshmen gingerly, while freshmen are regressing and wanting to be 100 percent on vacation, parents might feel too sheepish to utter the stern directives that flew out of their mouths during high school. If emerging adults cross a line and it starts to feel like too much take and not any give—videos never returned, dishes left in the sink, wet towels on the floor— you'll have to negotiate your line. Know that there is a piece of this behavior that is normal and they're not just exploiting you, but also know that most freshmen on break will underfunction until you require otherwise.

> INCREASINGLY, YOUNG PEOPLE HAVE OTHER OPTIONS FOR THEIR SCHOOL BREAKS; PARENTS, WANTING TO WOO THEIR COLLEGE STUDENTS HOME AND HAVE EVERYTHING WONDERFUL, FEEL AS IF THEY'RE NOW IN THE MARKETING BUSINESS WITH THEIR OWN CHILDREN!

DO CURFEWS STILL COUNT?

Curfews are an area where parents sometimes need to speak directly before college students comply, since many freshmen come home conditioned to having more freedom. Some parents who sleep well and trust their child and his social circumstances are fine with extending the same "free agent" status to their college student. On average, though, most parents still ask for a level of accountability ("What are your plans? How can I reach you?"), at this point more as a household courtesy and assurance of safety than upholding parental authority per se.

A strategy that can work is to anticipate what you'll want

once your college student is back on your radar screen and communicate it ahead of time, leaning on your relationship with them: "I know you don't have a curfew at school, but I don't sleep as well knowing you're out, so out of consideration for me, would you please be in by 1:00?"

Out of respect for parents, many emerging adults curb their hours, but this can be short-lived, especially if they're home for an extended duration and feel roped in by your rules. As during high school, the more restricted children are relative to their peers, the harder time parents will have enforcing their wishes. Likewise, if you had a high conflict relationship during high school with your teen fighting to get out the door, you may be back to square one, unless patterns have changed.

What becomes clear to most parents over holiday break is how tricky it can be to parent emerging adults, transitioning from being adolescents in our home to adults on their own. We falter in our parenting calls: Am I treating her too much like a child? Too much like an adult? How much leverage and influence do I have at this point? Similar to when they were moving from childhood to adolescence, our children are spanning two developmental stages. Though we may expect more adulthood from them, young people often behave in ways that remind us how half-baked they are! Whether their behaviors are described as regression, underfunctioning, or self-absorption, we're back in the thick of parent-child dynamics. Parents and their freshmen usually haven't made the shift to a mature relationship of give and take—yet—and patterns like these remind everyone of that!

THE NEW ME: IDENTITY SHIFTS

Parents probably won't be able to predict what might cause friction and shatter the image of the picture-perfect holiday they've been envisioning. It could be old havoc or an unanticipated turn of events; for example, they've cast aside a long-cultivated talent, which parents may have encouraged and supported in giving, generous ways. A dramatic identity transformation may be afoot: A homecoming queen turns political radical, or the reticent conservative declares a passion to leave college for a semester to work in a refugee camp. Many educators maintain that the primary learning of these years takes place outside the classroom, but within the environment and culture of college. With campus culture as the impetus to be someone different, many freshmen come home with ideological awakenings or changed interests.

WHEN COLLEGE STUDENTS RETURN, IT'S NOT BACK TO "NORMAL," EXACTLY THE WAY THINGS WERE BEFORE LAUNCHING. THE IDENTITY PROCESS CAN BE LIKENED TO SHIFTING TEMPLATES OF THE OLD, THE NEW, AND AN INTEGRATION OF PIECES OF BOTH, ALL OF WHICH REPRESENT DIFFERENT ASPECTS OF THEIR EVOLVING IDENTITY.

Many parents view college as a holy grail to their child's future but are less attuned to the values exploration that college can provoke as young people are exposed to greater freedom and a new world of different types of people. As college students find themselves and learn to think for themselves in ways outside their family, parents may not be pleased with the outcome. For the most part, parents anticipate only what's positive about a college education, remaining less prepared for impacts on a child's identity development that they may perceive as negative.[1]

During college, it can sometimes feel as if your child has changed by 180 degrees and couldn't be farther from you. The generation gap wasn't just a phenomenon of the '60s. But somewhere between 21 and 25, most young people circle around to a combination of their parents' values and their newly cultivated ones, whether it pertains to religion, occupation, politics, ethics, or life-style choices. Although parents usually make peace with who their child becomes, we'd best prepare ourselves for the monumental impact of the college experience on their identities, occurring outside our purview.

LOSING YOUR CHILD TO A "LOSER" FAMILY STORY

How much influence does Carol have over Tasha's choice of a romantic partner? Feeling as if their mother-daughter relationship is hanging by a string, Carol was agonizing over Tasha's demand to have her boyfriend stay over in her bedroom. Would vetoing this demand sever their already-strained relationship?

Panicked over a recent showdown with her daughter, Carol Sawicki set up a consultation with me. Tasha, her daughter, attended college as a freshman on the opposite coast and was insisting on having her at-home boyfriend sleep over with her during the upcoming holiday break. Despite visible upset, Carol, a single parent, came across as bright, soft-spoken, and gentle with a nice sense of humor. Though Carol was utterly opposed to the idea, there were reasons why a straightforward "Not in my house" was no simple matter.

The background I elicited from Carol spoke to a stormy adolescent period. An alpha-personality, Tasha could be described as smart, creative, and flamboyant with a strong, willful temperament. Reading between the lines of Carol's description of their family life, I could tell that Carol, who had been single parenting Tasha and her sister the last ten years, was a warm, giving mom who had made a secure roost for the girls, despite difficulties with her flaky ex-husband, who was only minimally involved in his daughters' lives.

Although a high achiever who won a full scholarship to a prestigious college, Tasha had pushed the envelope throughout high school—drinking, smoking marijuana, staying out all night, arguing, talking back, and resisting whatever rules Carol tried to impose. Tasha's risk-taking trajectory didn't keep her from juggling more than most grownups do and making exciting things happen for herself.

Once Tasha left for college, their relationship took a positive turn, with Tasha relying more on Carol to steady her through the emotional ups and downs of her first year away. During many intimate conversations and e-mails, Carol lent her sympathetic ear to Tasha's concerns. Their deepest discussions concerned Tasha's unhappiness with the college. "They gave me a full ride here, but do I fit in?" Tasha questioned. "If I didn't have this scholarship, would I choose this college? These kids aren't like me."

After the tumult of high school, Carol was gratified to be allowed into Tasha's world to help her figure out whether her dissatisfaction was just a case of the butterflies.

Then the problem surfaced that brought Carol into my office for a consultation. The summer before leaving for college, Tasha fell in love with an underachieving boy named Boone, who had no plans for his future.

"It's clear to me that Boone isn't going anywhere in life right now, since smoking

> MANY YOUNG PEOPLE DO AN ABOUT-FACE IN COLLEGE. TEENS WHO DISTANCED FROM PARENTS IN AN EXUBERANT WAY IN HIGH SCHOOL MAY SEEK GREATER CLOSENESS; THOSE WHO WERE UNDER THEIR PARENTS' WINGS MAY PUSH AWAY. WHATEVER NEW TREND EMERGES PROBABLY REFLECTS THEIR DEVELOPMENTAL NEEDS, ALONG WITH ISSUES PRESENTED BY THE COLLEGE SETTING.

weed leaves him baked most of the time," Carol explained to me during the consultation.

"I didn't take their relationship seriously," she added. "With all of the drugs, screaming, disrespect, and regretted words between Tasha and me, Boone seemed like the least of my worries. I assumed things would wind down between them once they were apart." Far from fizzling, their relationship had heated up.

One evening, as Carol and Tasha were sending one another instant messages over the Internet, Tasha took her mother by surprise. From her purse, Carol removed a printout of their instant messaging and handed it over to me. True to form, Tasha pulled no punches.

TASHA: I want to be completely honest with you, Mom. You don't know too much about this, but I've grown closer than ever to Boone since we've been apart. You wouldn't believe how caring he is, not like these stuck-up guys at school. He understands me and listens to all my problems. I want him to stay over with me in my room over the holiday break. I hope you're not going to freak out about this. I love him a lot, and you need to accept him as my partner. I'm an adult now, so we should be open with each other about this. Otherwise it's hypocritical. If you don't let him stay over, I guess you won't be seeing me very much over the break because I want to be with him.

CAROL: Honey, this throws me. Why do you have to make an ultimatum like this? You can spend time with Boone during your break, but sleeping with him in our house is too much to ask. It's not okay with me. I'm trying to respect that you have a relationship with him, but think about me and about your little sister. Can't you be reasonable? I'm not at all comfortable with what you propose.

TASHA: Why, Mom, is your comfort more important than mine? I only get two and a half weeks away from this preppy place full of people I can't stand. I've told you how stressed out I am. Why can't you think about me and my winter break? Why are you trying to control me and take us back to all that fighting we did in high school? I was just starting to feel like you understood me and could treat me like an adult. I guess you don't want to see me that much if you're not willing to let Boone stay.

CAROL: You know how much I've been looking forward to having you back home. This isn't about trying to control you, Tasha. How many parents would allow something like you've suggested?

TASHA: I knew you'd be this way. Nothing's changed. If you don't like it, I can spend every night of my break at Boone's. I've already talked to Boone and he has talked to his mother and she's fine with it. I'll stay with him if that's what you want.

Realizing that Tasha was revving up into her old provocative self, Carol had replied they should drop it and sleep on it, since neither of them was doing her best to figure it out.

"What recourse do I have?" Carol asked me plaintively. "You can see from our e-mailing how strong-headed she is. I'm desperate to see her, but I'm against having them sleep together in my home."

So much more was at stake for Carol. During high school, Carol felt as if she would never have the relationship she always wanted with Tasha. Getting a taste during the fall of how wonderful it could be, she worried that with this one incident she could lose the closeness.

Carol's own history played into her desperation, for she

REFLECT ON WHAT YOU WERE GOING THROUGH THE YEAR AFTER YOUR OWN GRADUATION. IS THERE ANYTHING IN YOUR OWN INDIVIDUATING PROCESS THAT MAY BE CAUSING YOU TO OVER-REACT OR MISINTERPRET YOUR CHILD'S VERSION OF INDIVIDUATION, WHICH MAY NOT PARALLEL YOUR OWN?

had broken away from her family during college. Not that her family was overtly unkind, but she had been parented by an aloof mom, who was clueless and ethereal, caring but out of touch. With her mom more attached to her brothers than to Carol, she felt overlooked and disconnected from her parents. College opened up a whole new world for her. Avoiding going home, she had maintained only minimal contact with her parents, who had subsequently divorced and remarried. Her exaggerated separation with her own family scared her to the point that she worried she would lose Tasha to Boone unless she played her cards right.

Moreover, there were echoes from her own relationship with her ex-husband. Sweet and innocent, she, like Tasha, had been drawn to an opposite, having married the "wild guy" herself.

"My worst fear is that if she spends a lot of time at Boone's house with him, she'll drop out of school. She's so unhappy at college. Maybe I should say yes so that I can be around her and influence her. What if she gives everything up for him?"

MOVING OUT OF THE CORNER FOR A WIDER PERSPECTIVE ON A PROBLEM

Carol believed that her whole relationship with Tasha as well as Tasha's future hinged on saying yes or no to Tasha's demand. Whenever you feel hedged in like this, you've probably limited your perspective and need to expand it to include the emotions and issues that are creating the panic.

A bird's-eye view of Carol's problem would include an assessment of Tasha, her developmental process, Carol's background, and her relationship with her daughter. Opening up the process can help Carol figure out what the boyfriend is about.

Many families become entrenched in problems because they fixate on the concrete level: "No sex in my house!" Even when parents believe they have right on their side, if they stay at this level, they risk an emotional tug of war, where the child puts all her energy into being mad at the parent. Anytime a child can make something be about a parent, they get off the hook with their own internal struggle and ambivalence.

In her panic, Carol was not seeing what was apparent to me: Compared to the remote relationship with her own mother, Carol and Tasha are deeply attached. Their situation was distinctly different from the one Carol had growing up, where no one was tuning into her, and she was letting her family-of-origin history distort what she had created in her current family.

Why would I, as a therapist, trust that this mom can trust her foundation with Tasha? Because of what came through in Carol's telling: the love, the fun, the good times and fabulous talks, the connection, the self-awareness, the admiration, how much she has given, the great home she has made. Some parents with a fraction of the turmoil that Carol and Tasha experienced would be seething, critical, and blaming. Despite the drama they'd experienced, Carol never made one resentful, bitter, or malicious comment about Tasha to me. I wouldn't advise all moms, "Feel secure in your relationship and just say no," particularly if there were problems with control, distance, or remoteness, but Carol isn't the type of mother that daughters turn their back on.

I advised Carol to draw on a model that applies broadly to situations when parents need to hold their ground with their emerging adult:

- Affirm aspects of your child's perspective
- Affirm your own point of view
- State your bottom-line decision graciously, with your wisest distillation of it

Whatever Tasha might decide, Carol needed to stay open about her desire to have Tasha in the home: "I love you. I want to spend time with you, but I'm not comfortable having Boone here overnight. I need to honor my desire not to have that happen." Gently saying what she feels and hopes can remove the drama and the confrontational feel from the yes or no: "I value our relationship. This decision shouldn't be a make it or break it. I hope you'll spend as much time at home as possible."

WE CAN FEEL INHIBITED ABOUT EXERTING A PARENTAL CALL THAT MAY TEMPORARILY ERODE THAT RELATIONSHIP. IF THE FOUNDATION IS STRONG, WE CAN TRUST THAT THE RELATIONSHIP IS VALUABLE ENOUGH THAT WE CAN STILL HOLD INFLUENCE OVER OUR EMERGING ADULTS.

Whenever a parent caves in on a strong value, psychological baggage is probably leading the parent to abandon their ideological place. Caving may indicate a lack of confidence in the relationship due to family turmoil; in a divorce situation, it may mean competition for affection with the other parent or a sign of guilt. Like Carol, a particular vulnerability is when parents experienced an early death or a shortcoming of some kind with their own parent. Deficits like these can lead parents to want to make life so good for their children that they are tempted to err on the side of indulgence.

BEWARE OF THE ROMEO-AND-JULIET SYNDROME

Not only the stuff of drama, it's a psychological truism that parental or societal opposition to a boyfriend or girlfriend can make a romance flower; what's forbidden is often what's most attractive. Should Carol take a position against Boone, she runs the risk of making him all the more enticing.

Carol has no guarantee that Tasha and Boone will split up, since opposites often seek each other out. Ramped up, perfectionistic girls who create their own tumultuous waters can be drawn to quiescent, gentle souls like Boone. But if Tasha is a young woman who has her sights set high and is making things happen and he's not—is Boone likely to become her life-long partner?

At some point, compatibility is about matching up. In the best of partnerships, couples admire each other's strengths, including those one person may lack, and they share mutual interests, goals, and life energy. As ironic as it sounds, if Carol truly believes that Boone has little going for him, she might want Tasha to spend more time with him, not less. The more exposed to him she is and the more the relationship plays out, the more likely Tasha might be to become disenchanted with Boone.

PARENTS RARELY GET EVERYTHING THEY WANT IN THE ROMANTIC PARTNERS THEIR CHILDREN CHOOSE. SINCE WE MAKE OUR PARTNERSHIP JUDGMENTS BASED ON OUR PERSONAL TASTES, VALUES, INTERESTS, AND GENERATIONAL INCLINATIONS, AND OUR CHILDREN DO ON THEIRS, WHY WOULD WE EXPECT THEM TO MATCH?

Theoretically, as elders we're wiser and more experienced in how relationships evolve, how people change over time, what needs are satisfied short-term but not for the long haul, but there's often something we don't know—and our children aren't completely able to articulate—about the chemistry of their partnership choices. Parents would do best to stay a little humble about it all.

What happened with

Tasha and Boone? As advised, Carol held her ground in phone conversations in an open, loving way. At a joyful reunion at the airport, everyone avoided the topic. Tasha spent a couple of nights at Boone's home, but without saying much, she started spending less and less time with him, and by the end of the following summer, the romance was over.

When Tasha entered college, Carol was elated that Tasha was on her way, on a full scholarship to a great college, but two months later, Tasha was being lured home by Boone and was considering dropping out. Particularly when the road has been rocky, parents feel reassured when their child launches to college, thinking, "We've turned a corner. The worst is behind us." Each wrinkle may raise the specter of former concerns.

Whether the adolescent years have been smooth or rough, parents still need to expect hurdles along the way. Every emerging adult needs room for developmental fits and starts, without having parents panic. Only through an individual assessment can we know whether a behavior is developmental noise that will clear itself or a deep-seated pattern. Difficulties during freshman year (or whatever the post–high-school year yields) can feel momentous to parents, particularly when we've bought into the "college will be only wonderful" myth.

DO PARENTS HAVE A ROLE WITH AN EMERGING ADULT'S SEXUAL BEHAVIOR?

Having been freed of the taxing job of overseeing our emerging adults' behaviors—and wanting to savor the holiday break—most parents, barring significant problems, ease up on the grab bag of adolescent autonomy issues, which include maintaining curfews, monitoring schoolwork, and overseeing schedules.

The issue of sexuality also comes under the domain of autonomy and control, but unlike a curfew, a college student's sexuality is in the realm of privacy. With, for example, details such as who is sleeping where on a weekend trip away with friends, most parents assume a don't ask/don't tell policy. In the short span of one autumn, asking feels intrusive.

There's much that our parent generation has a hard time relating to. From the possibility of bisexuality to casual sex to sexual practices like cybersex, oral sex, and anal sex purportedly now out there, parents are increasingly unsure of how and when to weigh in with their values. Even well-informed, sophisticated parents may lapse into age-old habits of denial and avoidance with their college student's sexuality. We don't know where to begin, so we sidestep it.

Here's an example of a mom who worked up the courage to discuss a delicate issue with her son over winter break. The mom, Eleanor, with whom I was consulting on a different issue, described to me how she was emptying out her son Sam's pockets for the laundry and found some condoms. Sam, a well-adjusted young man, had previously had a girlfriend, but Eleanor knew he was not currently in a relationship. Eleanor had read articles about the social scene on campuses, where students drink to excess then "hook up" for casual sex. Finding condoms suggested that he was protecting himself and taking responsibility for the sex he was having, which was a plus, but what deeply troubled her was that if he wasn't in an intimate relationship, it could be that he was engaging in casual sex.

In a session, we outlined Eleanor's options:

1. Say nothing, assuming that it's his private life and previous sex education will hold him in good stead.
2. Express disapproval directly. Speak your mind on all the problems involved in casual sex.
3. Devise a middle course where you weigh in with your values in a way

that doesn't alienate him, though it will be awkward and may or may not influence him.

Parents are always entitled to talk about values around sexuality, but should Eleanor decide to pursue that middle course, she needed to be savvy about her approach. For any touchy issue, whenever you want to set it up for success and you think their defensiveness could be high, use a straightforward model: Just say your piece, respectfully and honestly.

A parent's opening comment might resemble this: "I found some packages of condoms in the pocket of your slacks while doing laundry. You're obviously sexually active. You don't have a girlfriend, and this probably means one thing, casual sex. I'd like to talk about that."

The young person's response is likely to be along these lines: "What's there to talk about? If it's what we both want, what's the harm?"

At this point, Eleanor might say: "This could be a difference between us, and I don't want this to break down into your culture is fine with casual sex and I'm old school or against sex. My concern is that if your whole experience of a sex life is in this context, of hooking up with someone for a one-nighter, no strings attached, I think about what you are not doing. Casual sex could exclude the development of a love relationship. It could mean you're not taking the time, the risk, the concern for yourself to be with someone in a more committed way."

WITH EMERGING ADULTS, PARENTS WILL BE MORE EFFECTIVE IF THEY ARE PRO-RELATIONSHIP, PRO-HEALTH, AND PRO-LOVE, AND NOT ANTI-SEX. PARENTS ARE HOPING THAT SOME OF THEIR MESSAGE GETS THROUGH AND WILL SPEAK TO THE PART WITHIN THEIR CHILD THAT AGREES WITH THEM, EVEN IF THEY DON'T ACT ON IT NOW.

By saying your piece about your sexual values, you're hoping to influence your emerging adult by tapping into the part of your values that you believe he has absorbed and integrated into his own.

If Eleanor thinks it's going well or is feeling bold, she might say, "In your heart, doesn't casual sex feel kind of empty or awkward or regrettable the next day?" As she blows on those embers, she might be embedding an idea that might come to Sam's mind later—when hooking up becomes shallower to him, as other campus mayhem will too. In the end, though they may need to play themselves out, behaviors like hooking up—or, equally prevalent on campus, drinking to excess—are not lifetime habits for most people since they increase a sense of isolation and don't yield long-term happiness. You want your college students to grow out of these behaviors, and they mostly do.

Instead of a son and condoms, imagine you've found a daughter's condoms or birth-control pills. Theoretically, our issues should be the same. Over the last decades, as roles have changed, many young women are becoming more openly assertive about their sexual desires, as most men always have been. A generation ago, young women valued being the sweet, demure innocent that a boy would bring home to introduce to mom. The new breed is go-getter girls who don't want to carry the torch as the party responsible for seeking closeness and training men in a relationship. (Many wives are tired of doing the same.) Moving away from gender stereotyping, many young women are less inclined to be the traditional carrier of the relationship values and are now empowered to call a guy or suggest meeting for coffee. Who's left to make sure that dating in the traditional sense happens anymore?

WHAT'S LOST WHEN YOUNG PEOPLE DON'T DATE?

As many Deans of Students and students themselves relate, dating is practically non-existent on many of today's college campuses.[2] Parents may legitimately ask: Why should I care if dating, as we once knew it, has gone the way of the hoop skirt or the top hat? My child engages in extracurricular activities and makes good grades, so why the need for a boy/girlfriend?

One problem with the disappearance of dating is that the college years are a prime stage of life for learning how to be intimate in a mutually caring relationship. Not that young people should attend college to seek mates, but according to classic developmental psychology, one of the tasks of young adulthood involves choices of intimacy versus isolation.[3] At a period in life when biological sex drives are high, how can meaningful relationships be formed if the experiences consist mainly of one-night stands?

Dating during adolescence has been replaced by teens traveling in packs. Many parents approve of their adolescents going out in crowds, assuming that if their sons or daughters aren't dating, it means they aren't having sex (not necessarily so). What has disappeared along with the tradition of dating is an opportunity to practice relationship skills: taking the risk to ask someone out, learning how to say yes or no to an invitation, having conversations, sharing stories, balancing self-interest with the

COMPARED TO TRADITIONAL DATING, HOOKING UP FOR ONE NIGHT OFFERS AN ESCAPE FROM RELATIONSHIP, VULNERABILITY, AND THE AWKWARDNESS OF THE COURTSHIP DANCE, AND THEN YOUNG PEOPLE HAVE THE SEX ANYWAY.

needs of another, and coping with the discomfort of one-to-one while not numbed by drugs or alcohol. Only by being in a relationship do young people develop skills in mutual caring, while simultaneously feeling the anxiety and vulnerability of romantic love and loss.

The secret is that many young adults don't know how to date anymore. It's all anxiety for them, especially the boys. Why date, if they have an easier means for sexual gratification and can avoid the awkwardness of something they don't know how to do? Over time, avoidance builds on itself, and young men in particular end up with a skills deficit in relationships. Many girls aren't much different: A traditional old-fashioned dinner and movie might be way too much commitment. Some girls, however, do want to date, but not enough to admit it, and not enough to risk having their invitation turned down.

We all know how complex marriage is and how extensive the skills required are, once the first flush of romance subsides: sharing power, knowing how to talk about hurt feelings, compromising, being patient, learning how to listen and resolve a conflict, respecting differences. Ideally, we want a relationship not at the expense of a self and a self not at the expense of the relationship. Navigating these difficult waters calls for a skill base that takes years to develop.

AIDS, STD'S AND UNWANTED SEX: WHY A SEX-ED REFRESHER WITH YOUR COLLEGE STUDENT IS MORE IMPORTANT THAN EVER

Given the preponderance of sexual activity on today's campuses, parents should not be naive about practices that put college students at risk. With AIDS being lethal and other sexually transmitted diseases carrying life-long consequences, even if it's off-putting, parents are well advised to step up to the plate and make sure their emerging adults are informed and protected. As "un–with it" as we may be, making an effort at discussion in a respectful way at least shows we care.

Despite all the "yes, buts" that may explain why we're not speaking up ("It always falls on deaf ears." "He ridicules me." "She resents it as part of my preaching." "I think we should trust our college kids by now."), parents should air their values, which may be the only conventional ones college students hear.

Parents probably covered many issues related to sexual activity—or at least tried to—pre-college, but perhaps only now are these issues germane. As we've always known about any sex-ed discussion, the best talks are ones that are salient to a person's life at the moment. Winter break may be especially relevant timing, since our emerging adults are now in the thick of the actual social scene, with 75 percent of girls and at least 80 percent of boys sexually active by college freshman year.[4] Another incentive for mothers talking to their daughters is increasing evidence that a mother's attitudes toward sexuality, acceptance of one's own sexuality, self-esteem, and gender-role identity are transmitted intergenerationally.[5] It's hard to imagine that it would be any different for sons and their fathers, but male sexuality has been vastly understudied (perhaps because males don't get pregnant?).

Along with the critical topics of AIDS and other STD's, parents should consider broaching the issue of alcohol and sex, since unwanted sex associated with alcohol is rife on today's campuses and freshmen are a group at particular risk. Some statistics drive home the point that alcohol underlies most of the problems associated with sex on campus:

- 60 percent of college women diagnosed last year with an STD were drunk at the time of infection;

- Alcohol was involved in 90 percent of campus rapes (as it also is with 80 percent of campus vandalism and 95 percent of violent crimes on campus);
- Alcohol with the date rape drug, Rohypnol, creates high-risk situations for women at parties.[6]

ON TODAY'S CAMPUS, A LOT OF SEX HAPPENS FOR ALL THE WRONG REASONS, UNDER ALL THE WRONG CIRCUMSTANCES. STUDENTS ARE OVER-WORKED, STRESSED OUT, UNCOMMITTED IN RELA-TIONSHIPS, USING ALCOHOL TO UNWIND AND BECOME UNINHIBITED ABOUT SEX. INURED TO THESE CONDITIONS AS A NORM, COLLEGE STUDENTS MAY NEED A PARENT'S SANE VOICE AS A COUNTERPOINT.

Parents can be part of the wake-up call for their emerging adult to realize "These things could happen to me." Anything parents can do to increase consciousness and pull their college student out of denial without triggering their automatic shutdown is worth the effort; if the worst thing that happens is that they shut us down, it's still worth it.

Young people are susceptible to harm because of their "myth of immunity"—an apt term from adolescent development theory that describes a mindset of denial and invincibility. Though college students swear that they can handle alcohol, bad things like alcohol poisoning, accidents, aggression, and vandalism suggest otherwise.

Parents sometimes muse, "What good will it do to wade into these murky waters if I'm not likely to change their behavior?" My response is: Don't assume something won't seep in. Moreover, you need to be able to answer to yourself and know that you've done the one thing you can do, which is to speak up about your concerns.

Traditionally, parents felt greater anxiety about sex and daughters because of the risks of unwanted pregnancies, but AIDS and STD's infect across gender lines. Of particular concern with sons is the potential for date rape and allegations of date rape. Young men need to understand that "no" means "no"—a point that can be difficult to grasp, since movies routinely portray girls feigning "no" when they apparently mean otherwise. Alarmingly, in one large research study, a majority of adolescent boys felt it was acceptable for a boy to hold a girl down and force her to have sex.[7] How complex the thicket of sexual consent is, and while under the influence of drugs or alcohol, it's all the harder to judge.

One way crucial information reaches college students is through workshops, talks, and a variety of campus educational programs, some of them excellent. Administrators, however, are caught between two consumer groups: upset parents who urge, "Do something!" and outraged students who rail, "You can't do away with the legacy of our annual Bacchanalia or our traditions in the Greeks!" In the end, a question for parents is this: How else will you know someone is going to talk with your child about complex issues like date rape unless it's you?

Like earlier years, success with sex-ed talks depends on the timing, how open emerging adults are, their mood, what they think your agenda is, and whether they think you've been intrusive or judgmental in the past. With the majority of college students sexually active, we need to face the facts: Just as leaving home and attending college are a rite of passage for most emerging adults, so too is their transition to more autonomous lives, which includes sexuality and all the issues that accompany it.[8] As inextricably as sex is related to health, parents should include discussion of this topic as part of maintaining a close and supportive relationship.

BEING AN ACCEPTING PARENT TO YOUR CHILD
FAMILY STORY

With each child, parents will be tested in unique ways. How can parents gracefully handle a turn of circumstances they dread, particularly if it has life-long consequences? Being a decent parent may not be enough. Rising to a challenge can bring out the best in all of us.

Popular, outgoing, and best friends with many girls, Travis never had a girlfriend during high school, though he did have a date for every prom and homecoming. His parents, Joanne and David Erickson, were mystified, wondering what was holding back their attractive, well-liked son from developing crushes.

After each formal event attended, they'd inquire, "Well, are you going to ask her out again?" receiving the reply they became tired of hearing, "No. We're just friends." At one point they worked up the courage to ask Travis whether he ever had any feelings for boys. When he said no, they readily accepted his response, but between themselves they raised the possibility of a gay sexual identity once or twice.

Three months into college, Travis sent Joanne and David a long, emotional letter, explaining how he'd been attending a gay men's alliance group and what a wonderful and accepting experience it was. At last, he realized he was gay. To his mind, he was absolutely sure and was soaring emotionally, freed of the burden of uncertainty and confusion.

Setting up a consultation for Joanne and himself, David explained to me over the phone, "We're trying to be respectful of Travis's news, but both of us were taken aback by how certain he is about such a huge thing so suddenly, Joanne even more than I. Travis is overjoyed, but my wife is crying and confused and can't even talk to him about *it*."

I'm always impressed by people who are wise enough to

seek help in a situation they find challenging, hoping to avert a blowup instead of waiting until one occurs. Unsettled by Travis's news but eager for his impending homecoming in December, the Ericksons felt as if a dark cloud had descended on the holidays.

With the consultation under way, the Ericksons appeared to me as sincere, loving parents trying to handle their son's coming-out in a civilized way. They were, however, over-whelmed with reservations, not ready to take their son at his word. I also noticed how each parent filled a different role based on temperament. David seemed even-keel and concili-atory, while Joanne was reserved, conservative, and deliber-ate to the point of prickliness. Clearly, she was the parent who butted heads with the children, managing the home and schedules.

Joanne forthrightly expressed a concern that inevitably arises when young people come out in college: "Might this just be a phase with Travis?" she asked me. "It's almost trendy to be alternative these days, it seems, even with sexual choices."

"You're right," I responded. "It's wide open on the cam-puses. The acronym GLOW ("Gay, lesbian, or whatever") says it all. A lot of young people want to keep it open and not be defined as anything specific."

"That sounds better than what Travis has told us," Joanne swiftly retorted. "He's thrilled. Keeping it open would be welcome compared to what he's stuck us with. He says he knows what he is. Couldn't the college scene be influ-encing him?"

"The open-mindedness of the milieu allows for explo-ration," I responded. "The fading away of taboos of the past invites individuals to explore areas like bisexuality, which some theorists believe is a possibility for many people. The openness of his campus, with organizations and talks and group houses, may have made it more possible for him to raise questions about his sexual preference and find things out about himself, but it probably wouldn't be enough to convert him to the kind of certainty he's expressing."

"That's the problem," Joanne said. "How can he know for sure in just three months? I'm dubious. Shouldn't he take more time to sort it out?"

Upon hearing a strong revelation like Travis's, many parents hold back on 100 percent acceptance, tacitly hoping that their pullback may help shift their child away from this identity. If they're too quickly accepting, they reason fallaciously, might they be tipping the balance to create a sexual identity that's still in process? Might it even be reversible?

This is a problematic stance. As elated as Travis was, he wasn't going to be open to questioning his position. Weighing in with hesitations and challenges wasn't likely to stimulate the kind of re-analysis that his parents wanted to see. Given his resounding, "Yes, I am gay," he wasn't going to reconsider; it was unlikely he'd say, "Good point, maybe I should hold off on the feelings I'm having."

My recommendation to the Ericksons was to be respectful about what Travis had said. In his letter he wrote that he knew his parents were going to have doubts, but he implored them to believe him. With strong statements like his, you're walking on thin ice to question the integrity of whatever process Travis went through on campus to reach his decision. Moreover, studies show that parents who support their gay and lesbian children can make a difference in their child's overall self-esteem.[9]

Parents would have a different role if their child had ambivalent beliefs about his gay identity and was upset, suicidal, and not believing he could possibly have a good future ahead. If, for example, a high-schooler came to his parents confused and self-loathing, parents should tailor their response to where he is in the coming-out process, conveying to him, "You don't have to make any decision. This process takes a lot of time. You can stay in limbo as long as you want." Everything depends on where your child is: If he's on the fence, be with him there. To heap more negativity on top of a child's own self-critical attitude runs a big risk.

My advice to the Ericksons in our session emphasized these points: Given his position, don't try to talk him out of this. Do a lot of listening. Be humble. Say and mean it that you have much to learn. If he gives you grief about not being more enthusiastic or not being excited about meeting a new boyfriend, know that you're on safe ground when you ask for time to adjust. But be aware than any chilliness on the topic is likely to be interpreted as a withdrawal of love, and you'll have a setback. The Ericksons had a wonderful base in their relationship with Travis and didn't want to risk losing the rapport that is so precious to parents.

Still, winter break didn't go perfectly, as became clear in our next session.

"AS IF" ACCEPTING

Shortly after Travis arrived home from college for winter break, Travis, Joanne, and David arrived in my office, bringing with them a small crisis, made visible by the obligatory and awkward smiles all around and the cool demeanor between Joanne and Travis.

David explained the falling out that had recently occurred when they were gathered round the dinner table at his sister Robin's home. Sitting next to Travis, Robin had inquired whether Travis was dating anyone. "Yeah, I am," he had replied. Because Travis had not up to this point dated any-one, everyone's attention at the table turned, and he went on to say, "And his name is Tony." Robin didn't miss a beat. She simply kept asking questions about where Tony was from and what was his major.

On the ride home, Joanne reacted. "Did you *have* to bring it up at the first family dinner home?" she'd asked Travis, adding that it was a bit of a conversation stopper.

Travis was furious, "If this is who I am and this is a good thing in my life that I have a relationship with Tony, why would you want me to hide it?" Zeroing in on what he saw as hypocrisy, he retorted, "If this were a girlfriend, Mom, you wouldn't want me to hide it!" He went on to describe how appreciative he'd been of Aunt Robin's generous reply, compared to his own mother's response.

MANY PEOPLE ARE WELL INFORMED, OPEN-MINDED, AND CAN BE INFINITELY ACCEPTING OF CHALLENGES PRESENTED BY OTHER PEOPLE'S CHILDREN. THE BIGGER TEST IS ALWAYS THE CHALLENGE FROM OUR CHILD: WHATEVER IT MAY BE, A CURVE BALL SENT TO US BY THEIR UNEXPECTED DIFFERENCE MAY THROW US FOR A LOOP, BUT IT ALSO SHOWS US THE STUFF WE'RE MADE OF.

This incident typifies the confusion, hurt, and misunderstanding that often accompanies the coming-out process.

In the Erickson family, the challenge related to their son's sexual identity, but their story relates to any parent disappointed by who their child is: the academic whose child is a lackluster student, the sports enthusiast with the unathletic child, the small-statured fitness fanatic with a chubby child. Overcoming resistance always involves some grieving of the loss of the picture of the ideal you've always had. Down the road, you can learn that something else can be just as good as that original vision, but until you've had time to reconstitute your picture, you can feel at a loss.

The many emotions hanging in the air could be distilled into a central problem: Travis was further along in accepting his gay identity than his parents. Although he was not "out" in high school, invariably parts of his mind had been adjusting for years to the possibility, which came into focus with an experience in college. What happened at Aunt Robin's illustrated a classic disconnect: Joanne had in her mind that Travis's coming out would be more gradually orchestrated. Although she was a mom with a good heart and good intentions, it was nonetheless all coming too fast for her.

Why, though, should Travis have held back? Sick of covering up his feelings, he had every right to feel relieved of the burden of uncertainty. Coming out is an apt metaphor because it expresses a blossoming of something that has been suppressed. Telling Aunt Robin about his boyfriend—particularly because she handled it like a pro—was an affirming, uplifting moment.

Under circumstances like those Travis experienced in college, among an accepting peer group with whom he could identify, coming out can happen fast and furiously. Almost euphoric with love, Travis wanted his parents to flip a switch to total support, but his parents couldn't possibly have shifted as rapidly as he would have liked. This is a paramount difference between high school and college: Joanne and David hadn't been around Travis to absorb the week-by-week transformation, so they could only experience it as a massive change.

No matter how insistent Joanne and David were about accepting Travis's sexual identity, he was able to supply examples of what he resented as double messages. Many parents are educated enough not to directly oppose their child's sexual preference. Most of the time they say the right thing, but their subtext might express reservations, and side statements can slip out that amount to "as if" accepting. A typical remark might be, "I accept that you're lesbian, but I don't see why you have to advertise it by wearing your hair so short or dressing that way." An even more seemingly benign remark would be, "I know being gay is a normal variant, but I'm still sad about not being a grandparent."

What young people hear in these remarks are all the ways parents don't accept what they desperately and passionately want parents to respect. To a young person who says, "I'm out," any nuance of parental grieving, uncertainty, reluctance, or any leanings that look uninformed or homophobic are offensive. Having gone through a great deal of internal processing before coming out, they don't want to be pulled back into confusion or self-rejection.

A psychological process explains their intensity: By reacting with hostility to parental reservations, they're reacting to something within themselves. Even when a son, for example, has made up his mind that he's gay, a part of him may still be worried, since it's very difficult to purge entirely the cultural messages that this is an evil, bad, or abnormal choice. When he detects ambivalence in parents, he'll flare up at them, dealing with his own reserve of negative or scared feelings about himself by spurning what he hears in his parents.

A critical pointer is for parents to be conscious of their unresolved issues. When a conflict surfaces, parents can reply honestly and ask for time to adjust to something they're just beginning to understand: "I know I don't have it right yet. You've been dealing with this intimately on some level within yourself for years, and I need to go through my own adjustment. I hope we can keep talking, and you'll let me know when I've stepped on your toes, and we can be patient with each other."

Because it quickens parents' learning curve, going to PFLAG (Parents and Friends of Lesbians and Gays) group sessions is enormously helpful. Necessarily, parents have to go through their own acceptance process. If you want to be the best parent you can to a child with a gay or lesbian identity, why not pick the path that widens the most efficiently and join PFLAG? Books and the Internet are also sources, but PFLAG group meetings not only provide information, they also introduce parents to others who went through similar confusion and distress and can lend some unique support and guidance.

Though young people, lightened by coming out, have every right to be excited about their new horizons, parents have an understandable position, too. Down the line, Joanne's, David's, and Travis's perspectives would probably merge, perhaps to the degree that they could go happily on vacations together with Travis and a boyfriend in a couple of years. In the meantime, families like theirs will experience phases in their acceptance process, particularly as they hit a bend that swerves them from their known terrain.

OTHER CHALLENGES TO THE WINTER-BREAK DYNAMIC: GRADES, NEW DIRECTIONS, AND ISSUES AROUND ACADEMIC EXPECTATIONS

One overriding theme of winter break is the difficulty of dealing with glitches when everyone has been anticipating fabulous family togetherness. Below are issues that have thrown even the most astute of parents:

- Summer expectations (whether young people need a paid job, whether they're expected to live at home)
- Spring break plans (Can they drive to a party scene with their college friends instead of coming home?)
- Levels of financial support (whether it needs to be adjusted based on a misunderstanding or how fast they went through their allowance!)
- Grades and other academic issues
- Transferring or taking time off
- Freedom during the holidays (family responsibilities and household courtesies and new habits)

- Expectations about next year (Can they live off campus? Do they get a car?)

Of these areas, academics bubble to the top of many families' concerns to become the dreaded topic of contention. Much like the grade dip that occurs between junior high and high school, freshmen are in a whole new environment, with more cognitive stress and strife and new friends and freedoms to negotiate.

WHAT ADMINISTRATORS TELL NINTH-GRADE PARENTS APPLIES TO COLLEGE FRESHMEN: GIVE THEM SOME ROOM TO FIGURE THINGS OUT. THOUGH GRADES MAY SLIDE FROM THOSE EARNED IN HIGH SCHOOL, MOST RECOVER BY SOPHOMORE YEAR.

If parents haven't already clarified expectations for various facets of academic performance—discussing issues such as dropping courses, changing majors, taking incompletes—they may find themselves picking up the pieces after grades come in.

If academic performance is borderline, families will need to investigate the college's policies for academic probation or taking time off. Ideally, when grades are a problem, parents can use their retained leverage. As an incentive to improve a GPA, what I see most frequently is a change in permission to take a car to college or less leeway about living circumstances. Usually, these changes are presented as logical consequences: For example, before parents say yes to the apartment, the student needs to demonstrate that he can handle the autonomy without impacting study habits.

Parents who have trusted their freshman's performance, leaving standards and expectations unspoken, may be caught unaware when, for example, their student switches from a pre-med to a religion major or perhaps didn't attend biology lectures after all, but only downloaded notes off the Internet.

The freshman probably thought she had the autonomy to make those decisions without consulting parents.

Based on the parents' knowledge of their child—whether she's wise and reflective or dreamy and impulsive and whether her judgments tend to be sound—families tend to handle these predicaments in individual ways. The process will be a reflection of temperaments, values, and precedents set in the dance of decision-making. Whether it involves an academic issue like dropping a course or another arena like plans for the summer, the goal of the parent is to make sure it's a well-informed choice, which conforms to the goals you and your freshman have for evolving adulthood.

If the issue relates to a switch of major with, for example, a son who is typically random in his decision-making, a parent might ask him to take another class or two in this new academic area before making the change. The parent might encourage the son to talk to professors in the department to find out exactly what the new major entails. Usually, today's parents don't mandate their child's direction, though most of us feel more secure if academic decisions suggest a career direction.

Parents of procrastinators—and you know if you have one!—need to be especially alert to the temptations of grade incompletes. By nature, procrastinators tend to wait until the last possible moment and then leap to short-term solutions: "I'm in this box, how do I get out of it?" When procrastinators are up against the wall, they can further postpone an assignment by taking an incomplete, without thinking about how it might jam them up later. Parents would be wise to discourage incompletes, but if students default to this option, be clear about a timeline for making the course up and have consequences in place if they don't comply.

Whatever the dilemma may be, from the student who switches majors four times to the one who doggedly pursues academics to the exclusion of any social life, parents would be wise to express their hopes and expectations directly, continuing to listen and, if need be, negotiate with their emerging adult's position.

BACK THEY GO!

Whether young people are home for two weeks or a month, much happens over school breaks that can throw parents for a loop! Parents may be dreaming of a cozy, convivial holiday—and often it is—but then there are grades, identity shifts, the social whirlwind, the tug of war for their time, regressive behaviors, and the need to parent on touchy or difficult topics. Through it all, parents will want to keep the relational piece going to assure their children are growing up without growing apart.

What's terrific about the holiday visit is that we have our children back with us in flesh and blood, and there's nothing like it. Most parents revel in pampering their child a little and in supplying them with their favorite traditions; the rosy moments are almost always worth the hard parts.

Nonetheless, parents should have empathy for themselves—and their children—during a college student's first extended stint back in the nest, since in many ways the holiday break holds a condensed version of the entire two-year launching transition. As one parent put it, "I love it when they come home, and I love it when they get back on the bus."

One of my friends told of hearing her younger child crying upstairs once her oldest daughter, Laura, returned to college after her first winter break. Asking her child what was wrong, she replied, "When Laura first left, I didn't know what to think, but now I know how hard it is when she's away." After winter break, gone is the first flush of excitement that accompanied fall departure, and we now know more of what loss feels like.

What can mitigate the intensity of our child's absence is that the break itself can be exhausting. Some parents derive comfort in "out of sight, out of mind," feeling relieved that they aren't tracking their child daily and looking forward to more peace.

Our children are off to new waters, and everyone's sights are set high! Often, there's backwash: She wants to transfer; she doesn't like her roommate; the classes are terrible; she's partying every night; she's totally self-absorbed. Parents can be caught off guard by the ongoing need to problem-solve, negotiate, and even set limits.

After the fretting of senior year—Where will they be accepted to college? Where do they go? Can they get a scholarship?—parents experience a sense of completion and accomplishment in their child's launch. What we discover after the first semester is that there are more hoops to jump through. Winter of freshman year, many families are still soul searching; perhaps their academic superstar is listing or their once-focused student seems directionless. With reality setting in, parents may question what this highly prized college education is all about. One thing we know for sure about the college experience is that it is tied into our children finding their way into the bigger world. Who said that was supposed to be easy?

CHAPTER SIX

Fine-Tuning

Staying connected while letting go,
knowing when to parent actively, and
attending to qualities young adults need
to thrive

FREEDOM FROM CHILD-REARING: BONUS PRIZE OR CURSE?

With the second half of the freshman year under-
way, parents typically find themselves reflecting on how well their children are doing, not only
academically but also with the myriad challenges presented by greater independence. Many parents are
gratified by the way their freshmen are settling in and
adapting to college life, though some will still be
struggling through this transition. Likewise, we take
stock of ourselves. Many parents miss not only their
own children but also their children's friends and the
liveliness of having teenagers around. With less hub-
bub and youthful energy in the home, parents' moods
may drift downward. Like any other phase of life,
instead of being "home free," we'll encounter hills
and valleys. Whether we're feeling encouraged

may be related to our freshmen's circumstances—remember the adage, "A mother is only as happy as her least happy child"? Or some personal issues may be at play.

Midlife is associated with our children going to college, our youth fleeting, our bodies aging, and maybe even our health declining. No wonder the launching stage can be so hairy: Given the other life events co-existing with launching, it's difficult to tease out a clean causal link between launching and any particular feelings we may have. Our lives are half over, our babies are leaving, and our parents are faltering or dying. These are losses—grievous losses—but there are positive features of the next half for most people. We stand a better chance of seeing them if we've been attending to the challenges of our own adult development—tasks related to finding meaning and generativity in our lives.

Week by week, as you think about not having children at home and life ahead for you, what are your associations? Even a 50-50 balance of negative and positive musings can be okay, particularly since the whole first year after their leave-taking is a transitional year. If associations are mainly negative, it probably has to do with absences in your life. Freedom from child-rearing can feel like a "curse" when having to face new enterprises and experiences elicits anxiety and fear, instead of enthusiasm for opportunities ahead.

Can you conjure up images that are positive and exciting? Do ideas come to mind that make you look forward with delight to the post-launch phase of life? Although middle age is worrisome for many, others feel invigorated, less shackled by children's needs, and buoyed by the wisdom and experience they now possess. At midlife, people tend to feel less directed by externals and are more inclined to focus on their own choices rather than others' "shoulds"—sometimes for the first time in their lives!

Life experience between 20 and 50 helps us know not to sweat the small stuff. Minor reversals of fortune can be better coped with because we've bounced back before. Our own experience and wisdom can guide us, reassure us, and keep us centered in a way that's not possible when we're young. Many of us would never trade this kind of security for the vulnerability of youth.

REMIND YOURSELF OF SOME OF THE ADVANTAGES OF THE ROOMIER AND CALMER NEST: THINGS STAY WHERE YOU PUT THEM; YOU DON'T HAVE TO PLAN YOUR LIFE AROUND CHILDREN'S SCHEDULES; YOUR SLEEP IS LESS INTERRUPTED; AND THE DOG NEVER TALKS BACK TO YOU.

Looking at the big life picture, what's ahead for parents once their children leave home? That depends on how you've lived your life and whether you have realistic expectations for challenges that might be presented by this next life phase. Here are portraits of two moms, Jill and Jackie, who have conducted their lives under two different sets of assumptions.

GETTING BY

Adhering to an identity that is 100-percent parent, Jill feels without question that the best years of her life are over with launching. From the day her children were born, she assumed that her active child-rearing years were destined to be the most fulfilling. Not compelled to do anything about this feeling, Jill let the next phase of life remain a blank page.

Her steady and unrewarding job with the State is the proverbial set of golden handcuffs—a secure job she must keep for its health insurance and retirement benefits. Afraid to go after things for herself, she has less gusto in her life generally. She married a decent, loving guy, had babies, put up appearances, and assumed that having a good family would be the reward. At this juncture, Jill isn't in dramatically difficult straits, but there's not much she's looking forward to, as she recalls her days of active child-rearing instead of envisioning an equally satisfying future.

THRIVING

Jackie has been the most devoted and child-oriented mother you could ever find, throwing herself enthusiastically into parenting and the accompanying volunteer activities. At nearly every one of her children's sporting or school events, Jackie was there. Not that she's perfect—she can be impatient and judgmental, and she has a huge clutter problem—but she knows her flaws and works on them. Although Jackie flirted with the idea of paid employment, she liked the mom-at-home role and the latitude it gave her, so the family made ends meet on one salary.

Open, spontaneous, and social, Jackie makes an effort to build relationships with many types of people. Between her friendships, her hobbies, and her involvement in her synagogue, she has a full calendar outside her "parent life." At age 35, she went completely gray but didn't give a hoot. Both Jackie and her husband work at maintaining good health, staying active in sports as recreation.

When it turned out that the family needed additional income to help with college expenses, Jackie was adaptable. Out of the work force for so long, she could only find low-wage options, but she made sure she went for a job she'd enjoy and landed a job in a bookstore that suited her perfectly. Jackie exudes a sense of someone moving on, making the most of her life.

> A FATALISTIC ATTITUDE—WHERE AN INDIVIDUAL TAKES NO ACTION TO RESIST HIGHLY LIMITING LIFE BELIEFS AND EXPECTATIONS—IS ONE OF THE HALLMARKS OF A LIMP-ALONG APPROACH TO LIFE WHERE ONE AT BEST GETS BY.

From these two stories, we can calculate the life potential for Jackie and Jill. These two moms look different on a group of qualities that represent the keystones to a successful post-launch phase of life. Important questions to ask are these:

- *Outlook:* Are you primarily looking to the past or forward to what might lie ahead?
- *Making life meaningful:* Are you able to find satisfaction and bring good things into your life, whatever the life stage?
- *Marital status:* Whether married or not, are you okay with how things are?
- *Life without children in the home:* Are you dreading a roomier nest because you can't find other parts of your identity and life to develop?
- *Emphasis on the losses of launching:* Are you preoccupied with the negative aspects of launching and finding it extremely hard to identify advantages?
- *Transition in parent-child relationship:* Can you identify pleasures associated with the next phase of parenting?
- *Employment or other work in the world:* Are you satisfied and happily enough engaged in some kind of work or activity?
- *Social relationships:* Does your life include friendships and social activities?
- *Aging:* Can you accept your own aging process without undue distress?
- *Well-being:* Are you taking care of yourself physically, emotionally, spiritually?

BUNGLING YOUR RELATIONSHIP WITH YOUR CHILD

Only too easily can parents' personal problems be played out in the parent-child relationship and throw a wrench into both launching and future dynamics. Between our children's individual challenges and the hardships life thrusts on them, why would we become their stumbling block—or the kind of parent that young adults dread visiting?

Described with the broadest brushstroke, one common pattern for parents whose own development is faltering is to have a tougher time loosening their hold and respecting their child's need to individuate. Alternately—although parents who care enough about their launchers to read this book aren't likely to be among them—some moms and dads are so preoccupied and narcissistically involved in their own lives that they don't give their children adequate support, guidance, and focused energy. Like children whose parents cling too much, young people with self-absorbed parents still aren't given the adequate context for individuation. Individuation is transacted optimally when there's room to be independent with one's own identity achievement while also staying connected. It's the blend of letting go and staying connected that works the magic in the individuation process.

What follows are two examples of families with whom I consulted. Though details of each case differ, the common thread is that a parent's problem affected their handling of their child's need for more autonomy.

DEFINING LOVE IN YOUR OWN NARROW TERMS
FAMILY STORY: THE KING LEAR DYNAMIC

Fran Mason was caught in a triangle, trying to explain her daughter to her husband and her husband to her daughter. "The issue sounds silly," she explained to me, "but it has caused a huge fracas in our home, and Edgar is sulking like a child." Fran's husband, Edgar, a conservative, formal man, requested that his daughter call home from college weekly, every Sunday evening. The daughter, who caused hardly a bump in the family throughout her adolescence, dutifully complied with her father's wishes all the way into the spring, but then she balked at this obligation, explaining that she wished to phone less frequently and on her own timetable.

Up to now, they'd had a close, charming father-daughter relationship that Fran had encouraged. Father and daughter were intellectually well suited and shared many interests, which had contributed to the daughter's high achievement. Fran, proper and traditional herself, tolerated Edgar's brisk inflexibility, but his reaction seemed excessive. Edgar truly believed and had arranged the whole saga into "If she loved me, she would. These are my terms, and it's not too much to ask." The daughter's unwillingness to call on a schedule legitimized his shunning of her, as he saw it, and he became frostier, more distant, and stubbornly refused to go on a spring visit to her campus they had planned since fall—a truly passive-aggressive move. For the daughter, it wasn't about phone calling, but that this was her line in the sand. Until age 19, she had conformed to his terms of endearment, but this became a sticking point.

What we dealt with in the consultation was not just this incident but the circumstances driving Edgar's intensity. Having just retired—with his wife still working and at the pinnacle of her career—he felt as if he were losing his grip in this different stage of life. It was classic: If his child's life was expanding as his was getting smaller and his wife's was bigger than ever, where did that leave Edgar? Without a lot of friends and hobbies, Edgar didn't have plans in place to ease himself into retirement. Instead of dealing with it directly, he became petulant with his daughter and put his wife in a triangle, his own developmental deficits dovetailing with his daughter's need to individuate.

I said to Edgar, who knew Shakespeare better than I, "It's King Lear." Edgar immediately made the connection, recognizing how hubris can provoke an unnecessary ultimatum and challenge to "Prove your love this way." Any observer of this daughter would say, you're in the 98th percentile of what any parent would be satisfied with in a father-daughter relationship: You love her, she loves you, and you're willing to squander it for the principle of not getting exactly what you want?

A question for parents to ask themselves is this: Are you insisting on rules for maintaining your relationship with your emerging adult without consulting with them about what works for them? Conflict inevitably occurs when parents assert, "Here's my idea of what's good and healthy and loving," and children rejoin, "Here's my selfhood, my identity, my rights, and my life."

College life often accelerates young people's autonomy-seeking, which can be a jolt for parents who, for whatever reason, have been even mildly needy in the parent-child relationship. In Edgar's case, the coinciding of his retirement with his daughter's launching contributed to this.

IT'S ALWAYS PROBLEMATIC WHEN PARENTS DEFINE LOVE NARROWLY, PARTICULARLY WHEN CHILDREN ARE STILL INDIVIDUATING. WHAT IF YOU HAD YOUR HEART SET ON A MOTHER'S DAY GIFT OR THE SPRING BREAK AT HOME, BUT YOUR CHILD DOESN'T COMPLY? AS YOUNG PEOPLE CARVE OUT THEIR OWN WAYS, DON'T ASSUME IT MEANS THEY LOVE YOU ANY LESS.

When our young adults are living full and independent lives, they might be fine telephoning haphazardly—missing weeks and then calling in a flurry for a specific reason. Less communication or a thoughtless oversight from a child in a loving, connected relationship doesn't add up to a diminished bond. As our children grow up, they carry a part of us within them, just as we have a part of them within us. For secure emerging adults, we're there—why go out of their way to contact us if we're already inside them?

LOYALTY TO LAUNCH OR LOYALTY TO FAMILY NEEDS? A CHILD'S AGE-OLD DILEMMA

Starting at age 11 when Allison started to want her own way, she and her mom Sue Li began warring regularly about how she should dress, how much time she should spend with friends, and particularly about ice skating, a sport Sue was adamant Allison continue, though her interest was on the wane. The parents in this family had a fine relationship, with the dad acting as a peacemaker for both mother and daughter. There was a younger son in the family, but the largeness of Allison's personality and the intensity of the mother-daughter interaction took up enough space to allow him room to grow up independently.

Despite the tough adolescence, Allison launched successfully. Still, not having staked out a sufficient claim to selfhood, her individuation from Mom was tentative. Spring of freshman year, the family suffered a tragedy when Allison's father died suddenly of a heart attack and her mother subsequently developed depression and an anxiety disorder. Without a question, the mother expected her daughter to leave college, and the daughter expected this, too, especially since finances were tight.

Sue and Allison lived together and, without Father to calm them, reverted to more fighting, as the mother-daughter relationship sank to a new low. Two years after Mr. Li's death, with Allison still on leave from school and working locally, the son left for college on schedule, though he seemed to repress his feelings as much as the women in the family emoted. As the only Chinese son, Allison's brother had, according to Allison, a "ticket to ride" out of the family, while she had the traditional responsibility to care for her mother. A struggle all the way, it took years for Allison to re-launch from home.

Many families would agree that of course Allison should come home from college for her mother. Some children would do as Allison did; others would remain actively enrolled and resolve the loss gradually over time; and still others would remain at school, not grieve sufficiently, and struggle later. Whether it's a parent who becomes ill, loses a job, or goes through a difficult divorce, the complicated question remains the same: When a parent suffers a blow, how much should they depend on a child in a crisis? At what point does the situation verge on the child becoming a parent to the parent?

Balancing the needs of the parent, the child, and the family unit is an age-old phenomenon, ultimately determined by the values, culture, and personalities of the particular family unit. Not to minimize the crucial role of family in a time of suffering and grieving, but after a period, might Sue have also looked to friends or relatives as adult support? How appropriate was it for her to take this amount of energy away from her daughter's independent life? Under the guise of "we're family," parents may use an incident or a condition to pull a child back from launching because they're not able to handle their own adult issue.

CRISES GIVE RISE TO SOUL-SEARCHING QUESTIONS: HOW DO WE DECIDE WHEN TO PRIORITIZE THE NEEDS OF THE LAUNCHING ADOLESCENT AND WHEN TO PRIORITIZE THE NEEDS OF THE FAMILY? WHEN IS THE PARENT LEANING UNNECESSARILY ON THE ADOLESCENT IN A WAY THAT ISN'T OPTIMAL FOR THE CHILD MOVING ALONG IN THE LAUNCH PROCESS?

Resolving questions of the individual versus the family boils down to the fact that we all have to live with the results of our actions and decisions, so we'd best know what the stakes are, what our motivations are and the nature of the forces that may influence or bias us—ways we may regret later if we haven't examined them deeply enough. The Lis Chinese culture probably played into Allison's coming home. Unrelated to culture, Sue's anxiety disorder made her needy. Throughout adolescence, Sue's messages conveyed to Allison, "Be loyal to me. Be sensitive to my feelings." Dad was the major buffer between Mom and daughter, and when he died, with anxiety and grief sky-high, nothing stood between Sue and her need to cling to Allison.

In each of these stories, bungling can be traced back to the nature of the parent-child relationship. Edgar's rigidity and need for control led him to start a feud with his daughter, who wanted to flex her independence. In Allison's case, launching triggered stress that, in conjunction with other life events, threw her off track for years. Not strictly a freshman-year event, launching happens in the context of a life. Existing dynamics, whether helpful or harmful, are waiting in the wings to come center stage.

HOW MUCH SHOULD PARENTS TELL COLLEGE STUDENTS ABOUT PROBLEMS AT HOME?

Never underestimate the degree to which launched children can worry about conditions on the home front. Invariably, life marches on in our children's absence—the dog may die, Granddad's health may fade, a parent may receive a worrisome diagnosis, or a parent's job may be in jeopardy. Just as we struggle to get an accurate view of our children's hardships and delights, most young people worry about what's happening with their family.

When problems arise, parents wonder how to impart the news to their children. The reasons for breaking difficult news to children are to keep the connection and maintain intimacy and trust—your trust in them that they can cope, and their trust in you that you'll be honest, rely on their maturity to handle it, and be willing to keep them apprised of news good and bad. The reasons not to disclose problems are to spare them worry and to not take mind share from their schoolwork.

To some extent, different responses can be appropriate. A marital struggle is a case in point. One line of thinking some parents follow is, why bring it up unless they'll benefit? Why draw them into your problems and create anxiety while you and your spouse are hashing out a conflict still unresolved? Another line of thinking is to consider that they're already privy. Many young people in discordant homes live in absolute fear that their parents will divorce the minute they walk out the door and will be made more nervous by the coverup than the truth. Instead of trying to hide marital storms, tell your young adult that you're working on it. You might say, "We used to circle our lives around you. You probably saw our differences and disagreements. We're proud we're in therapy and are working on it. We'll let you know what we think you need to know."

A divorce during the first year of college can be a significant stressor for young people. A generation ago, parents often "stuck it out for the sake of the children," divorcing once their children left home. This can, however, make the secure base from which to launch very insecure. Although not as common, still today some couples stay together until their children leave, usually depending on how deteriorated the marriage is. Divorce is always a personal decision, and though some will conjecture, there's no ideal time for it, especially once children are part of the equation. We have clinical recommendations for "how" best to divorce, but not "when" or "whether," since any time is likely to be highly stressful and upsetting to children.[1]

Whatever the nature of the difficulty may be, the decision

of what and how much to disclose depends on children's temperaments, how fragile they are, and what you think they can manage. The more prone they are to upset and anxiety, the more conservative you'll need to be about what to divulge from a distance. Timing also matters—whether they're in the middle of midterms or finals and whether it's elective and can wait until you're face to face. Whatever the information or timing may be, you're still weighing the values of connection, honesty, and trust versus their potential distress. Sometimes when parents withhold news, young people feel deceived. Then again, others will appreciate why you chose to hold off, if you put it in the context of, "We wanted you to know about this, but we didn't want to burden you. We were concerned that this diagnosis would be harder for you to hear from a distance, and we felt it could wait until you were home and we could discuss it more fully."

WITH BAD NEWS, CONSIDER AN EDITED SUMMARY THAT CONVEYS NECESSARY INFORMATION, CONFIDENCE, AND OPTIMISM. THE BOUNDARY CONTAINING YOUR ANXIETY PROTECTS THEM FROM UNNECESSARY WORRY, AND IN RESPONSE TO THEIR ANXIETY, YOU CAN REASSURE THEM THAT THEY CAN COUNT ON YOU TO HANDLE WHAT NEEDS TO BE HANDLED.

That said, parents can steer a middle course since telling them too much or nothing at all can be problematic. A concrete protocol is to present a "bounded version" of the truth about stressors at home, not filling them in on everything but providing enough of the fuller picture to satisfy them and to role-model how to cope.

Incrementally over the next five years, more mutuality will enter into the parent-child relationship. For still a while though, our children may not always be as empathetic as we'd like, since many still dwell in a little bubble of egocentrism.

As mutuality becomes more the norm than the exception, our children become increasingly capable of absorbing the lesson that life goes on with its inevitable obstacles. The greater their maturity, the more able we are to trust them to be conscious of life's quirky mixture of happiness and sorrow.

TWO FRESHMAN-YEAR FIXES
A TWO-PART FAMILY STORY

Although their two sons launched on schedule, the Simons were soon pulled back into the thick of parenting challenges. Spring of freshman year, their oldest son, Aden, was embroiled in a drinking and vandalism fiasco. A couple of years later, Jacob boomeranged back home. Making the most of these challenges, the Simons cultivated essential attributes in their children and through it all embraced that ever-vital quality—resilience.

ADEN'S DRINKING DEBACLE

Disaster had struck, Rita Simon believed, reeling from a phone call from her son, Aden, a freshman at a state university. During a beer and bonfire rally for one of the university's athletic teams, Aden and his fraternity brothers became rip-roaring drunk and started a brawl with a rival fraternity. To make matters worse, in their alcohol craze, Aden and his brothers had shoved their way into the rival fraternity's house, damaging and vandalizing property. The ceiling was punctured by flying objects, light fixtures were ripped from walls, windows were shattered, and furniture was broken to bits. Fortunately, despite fractured bones and multiple lacerations, no one was badly injured, though the threat of legal prosecution hung in the air. Scheduled to appear before the university's judicial council, Aden feared expulsion.

As if the incident itself weren't bad enough, what contributed to Rita's despair was a sense of *déjà vu*. Hadn't they already been through this with Aden's Minor in Possession citation freshman year of high school? Had the huge effort and the resources they'd rallied to curb his drinking been all for naught? Because I had worked with the Simons during high school (Aden at that time was 15, and a younger son, Jacob, was 10), they called me again for advice in this crisis.

To recap Aden's earlier run-in with alcohol, he was a "big man on campus" in high school. Voted "most popular boy" by his high-school classmates, he was also a party guy, a prankster, and a student who didn't uniformly apply himself. When he received the MIP citation in ninth grade, Rita was all over him, gathering brochures and information on drug-abuse programs for teens. Temperamentally, Rita, a fifth-grade teacher, had her feet solidly on the ground, describing herself as a "sensible Swede," but substance use was a hot button. Not only had she engaged in some significant drinking and drugging when younger, but she also identified several family members as active alcoholics. Recognizing that drinking could easily progress into addiction for those with the "alcoholic gene," Rita was adamant about coming down hard on 15-year-old Aden. Moreover, her own bout with depression—which she valiantly faced and sought help for—led her to worry even more about her son's biological vulnerability to using substances to self-medicate against uncomfortable feelings or mild depression, should he develop it.

Compared to Rita, Harvey wore rose-colored glasses and was only temporarily rattled when Aden received his MIP. Affable and easy-going, Harvey believed that boys will be boys, saying, "Rita and I both drank and partied, and we turned out okay." Smart and successful in business, he, like Aden, had been an enthusiastic social animal and a lackadaisical student. More optimistic about Aden's prognosis for alcohol use, Harvey felt that Aden would be sufficiently punished by the MIP's obligatory drug class and community service.

Gender typing being what it is, there's implicit support for boys who rev up and want to have a good time. Peer buy-in and other cultural influences sanction it, and by the time that young adults launch, many parents are turning a blind eye to boys' rabble-rousing. Just as we've become more sensitive to cultural pressures for girls to be nice, thin, and accommodating, we've recently become more attuned to messages to boys that they must be tough, cool, and cover up their vulnerable feelings, which can lead to substance use.[2] Rita leaned on Harvey with her concerns about Aden, risk-taking, and alcoholism, but was she overreacting? How can parents know what their child's substance use means and what kind of response is most appropriate?

HOW MUCH DRINKING IS TOO MUCH DRINKING?

When working with the Simons initially, I introduced the concept of the drug-use continuum, which evaluates use according to when, where, how much, and type of substance. In addition to the personal lenses through which a parent views substance use, response to an alcohol incident should depend on where the child is on the continuum and what else might be pushing it along.

Stage one on the substance-use continuum involves experimentation. These young people, driven mostly by curiosity, have a limited exposure to alcohol or marijuana. Most parents of college students usually expect that if their children haven't experimented by high school, they will by college. Though discouraging substance use is prudent, an important longitudinal study indicates that young people who merely experiment with substances turn out to be psychologically healthier than abstainers or frequent users.[3]

Stage two involves recreational use of alcohol or drugs while socializing. These young people don't use drugs on every social occasion, and they don't go out of their way to make sure it's always available. Illegal though it may be for underage students, recreational use has become part of the fabric of many college students' lives.

Stage three involves regular use of substances and active seeking of them in order to have a good time. Partying with alcohol and/or marijuana is routine, and experimentation with harder substances may occur. Regular users may experience some negative impacts on school, social life, and family life.

At stage four, substance use occurs daily (or almost daily) in order to have a sense of well-being. Drug abusers seek a drug-induced state and are often indiscriminate in drug choices and in mixing drugs. They almost always have problems with school, social life, and family life, although they are likely to deny it and claim they could stop if they wanted to. For anyone at this stage to curb use, they almost always need a program.

In stage five, alcoholics and addicts are both physiologically and psychologically addicted. Desperate to use substances, they require significant intervention for recovery.

At the time of his MIP at age 15, Aden used substances recreationally. Had his parents not intervened, he most likely would have become a regular user in high school. Research has documented that parent monitoring can deter heavier future drinking among adolescents, even if their closest friends drink.[4] This shouldn't be a surprise; after all, if early and frequent use can be abated, there's less likelihood of progressing along the drug-use continuum. The longer use can be postponed, the greater the likelihood that cognitive and emotional maturity can play a role in healthy decision-making.

Young people who carry more risk factors—starting use early, family alcoholism, a risk-taking temperament, family problems, neurochemistry issues like depression or ADHD—advance more readily along the drug-use continuum; whether they're high-schoolers, college students or adults, there's more to worry about. My initial consultation with the Simons during high school focused on pulling Rita and Harvey together into a united front with policies about Aden's grades and alcohol use that they could each live with and enforce, despite their different inclinations.

WITH ANY CHALLENGING CHILD, PARENTS EXPERIENCE AN INCREASED LIKELIHOOD OF MODERATE DIFFERENCES BEING TEASED OUT INTO POLARIZATION. WITH ANXIETY AND WORRY ON BOARD, EVEN SMALL STRESSORS CAN BECOME AMPLIFIED.

Through counseling, the Simons figured out a system for increased monitoring of Aden and strict, consistent consequences for any use. Likewise, for schoolwork, the parents imposed a mandatory study period each night. The Simons did a great job of working together to become more authoritative with Aden, risking rapport with him to keep a firm rein on his socializing, while still maintaining warmth, flexibility in other matters, and clear communication. Not that high school was a cakewalk, for Aden gave his parents lots of grief about being overly supervised compared to his friends. But by the end of high school, the Simons experienced smoother sailing. Aden's grades improved somewhat, and his social life seemed to revolve less around alcohol and more around his athletics. With friction eased, Rita and Harvey's marriage was more stable, and family life was more enjoyable. Everyone was delighted when Aden was accepted into the university—though concerns about the "alcoholic gene" lingered in Rita's mind as she launched her son into an environment where

adult eyes are considerably less vigilant about freely flowing
alcohol.

DOES JOINING A FRATERNITY UP THE ANTE IN ALCOHOL USE?

"We're having a meltdown," Harvey explained to me, when
he again contacted me to consult about Aden's bingeing and
college vandalism incident. "Of course I'm as concerned as
Rita is, and we're going to do whatever we can do to discourage prosecution and keep Aden enrolled in college. If he does
get out of this jam, though, Rita is insisting he quit his fraternity. The articles she has read about drinking in the
Greeks have her totally up in arms."

One of my first questions to Rita, as the Simons sat with
me in counseling, was for her to describe Aden's response to
the trauma. She granted that he was full of remorse and desperate to stay in his fraternity. Realizing that Aden was doing
some of his own appropriate self-prosecuting, Rita backed
off on her indictments, acknowledging that Aden was seriously chastened, crying, swearing off drinking, and believing
his future to be on the line. Nonetheless, Rita despaired that
they were back where they were in high school—another terrible drinking incident just like before. Aden's humility, however, stood in vivid contrast to his earlier recalcitrance.
Though it might look as if he'd slid to the same baseline, we
could capitalize on Harvey and Rita's earlier work to regain
ground lost in this setback. This could be a real wake-up call
for Aden—at last—and similar reining in could again contain
his drinking.

Nonetheless, family system problems were back in force,
with Rita over-reacting to the crisis and Harvey under-
reacting. Harvey spiritedly defended fraternities: Even

though sororities and fraternities are hotbeds of copious drinking (he knew this firsthand!), Aden's brothers were a great bunch of guys whose friendships could last a lifetime. Rita's one-sided view of fraternities failed to acknowledge the many qualities that Harvey valued, like camaraderie around studying and dedication to service projects and leadership. Harvey didn't see that yanking Aden out of his fraternity would necessarily translate into decreased alcohol use.

Articles on fraternities and drinking and on college life were fueling some of Rita's upset. What's a parent to think when you're relinquishing your child and, like Rita, you're reading nail-biting statistics like these:

- Studies generally concur that both fraternity and sorority members are more likely to binge drink than other students. One study, for example, found that a staggering four out of five residents of fraternity houses binge drink and that 50 percent binge frequently—bingeing defined as 5 or more drinks in a row for males and 4 or more for females.[5]
- For college students at large, a 1996 Harvard School of Public Health survey revealed that 44 percent of students who drink have binged in the previous two weeks. Even more alarming, the survey revealed that nearly one-fifth of college students (19 percent) are frequent binge drinkers, meaning that they binged three or more times in the previous two weeks.[6]

Predicting exactly who is prone to big boozing in college is inexact. An insular young person without much drinking experience can get loosened up in the college setting and match rounds with the most experienced drinking extrovert. A grounded one who normally shows restraint and discipline may be just the type to party hard when out of the box of schoolwork and adult expectations.

Survey results of why college students imbibe are almost identical to why adults do. Students and adults alike drink in order to relax, to cut loose, as a social lubricant, to escape problems, and to deal with stress.[7] Reasons for drinking have remained constant over time, but what has changed is the booming of bingeing, a practice far more lethal than social consumption. Because students believe that bingeing is normal, it has become more acceptable within college culture.

> ONE OF THE SCARIEST ASPECTS OF COLLEGE BINGEING IS THAT THE MORE NORMATIVE A BEHAVIOR BECOMES STATISTICALLY, THE MORE LEEWAY A YOUNG PERSON GIVES HIMSELF TO JOIN IN: "IT'S OKAY FOR ME TO GET TANKED BECAUSE EVERYONE IS." THIS ATTITUDE COULDN'T BE MORE DANGEROUS AND SELF-DESTRUCTIVE.

The Drug-Free Schools and Community Act makes it incumbent upon schools of higher education to certify that they have a program to prevent illicit use of drugs and abuse of alcohol. The problem is, what works to diminish use on campus? And given the huge resistance from the college population—who insist that they WILL drink—who can take effective action?

Many colleges have concluded that it's unrealistic—and could be more hazardous—to switch to a dry campus, since students will go off campus, risking drinking and driving. To forbid drinking at parties may increase the likelihood of students retreating to private settings—with fewer pairs of eyes on guard—to get smashed. Some colleges are making an effort to insulate students from risk somewhat by banning hard alcohol and kegs on campus and by creating social alternatives to drinking. Likewise, other institutions are spreading information about the numbers of students who don't drink in order to establish a social norm of not drinking. In the end, however, many university administrators and parents feel caught in the cross winds and live with cloudy policies. While the debate around student alcohol use takes place in the public forum, parents also need to think long and hard about issues to address with our own children and in our own families.

How can parents know what's going on with their college student? When children come home and their social life is within a parent's view, parents can stand by to see what it looks like. College students are often more open about their drinking with their parents than they were in high school—if they don't feel threatened and their habits aren't ones they want to conceal from mom and dad. A good heart-to-heart conversation at a well-chosen moment, where you mostly listen but let your concerns and values be known, is always worth a try.

Conceivably, our college students could be drinking heavily for years without our knowing. Many college students go in and out of regular alcohol use, and many who drink to excess can also maintain good grades. Another common pattern is the celebratory binge after major papers and tests are complete. Parents hope these behaviors are only part of a developmental learning curve, and thankfully they often are; eventually, most young people are able to look out over the horizon of their life and see habit-forming substance use as an undesirable pattern they don't want to get started.

For the Simon family, however, the questions remained: Would Rita's ideas of dramatic intervention and pulling him out of the fraternity be effective? Most important, how can Aden's parents use this incident to help him?

As during high school, Aden needed to have his feet to the fire. Drinking had to run a precarious course before it became bad enough to pull in his parents to provide the external boundaries he needed to restrict alcohol use. In high school, parental intervention kept him from becoming a regular user, though that didn't stop him from enjoying the party life in college. Given Aden's drinking fiasco, his parents returned to a more active parenting role because that's what he needed.

The Simons' roles were primarily twofold: first, to support Aden in this crisis as he responded to any legal action and went through the university's judiciary system; and second, to make the most of the incident, using the summer to impose necessary structure on Aden.

As it turned out, rival fraternity members were rattling swords about legal charges, and the incident was handled primarily within the university's judicial council, which placed Aden and his brothers on social probation. Property destruction was turned over to the fraternity, which assessed Aden $1,500 for his share of the damages. Chastened by the ignominy of going before the judicial committee, Aden was quiet, reflective, and worried—showing all the right mature attitudes. The college's judicial system was working with the Simons, and this combination was critical. Across the board, from parents and college, Aden was receiving the same message: A different approach to his life was now required.

Rita didn't need to play the parent-coercion card and pull Aden from his fraternity because she was able to get to her goal of decreased consumption by tightening down on Aden in the summer—in a way he would tolerate because of his contrition. Ironically, this horrendous incident had side benefits because it allowed the Simons to reinforce the admonition of the judicial committee and move in with conservative policies that would help Aden approach life more responsibly.

For Aden to remain in the fraternity, his parents set forth these strict terms. First, they worked out a structure for paying off the vandalism. Although Aden had a job lined up at a local fun coffee spot, Harvey helped Aden land a position with a well-paying janitorial service. Rita and Harvey insisted on the janitorial job because its higher wages made it possible for Aden to pay for damages and also earn spending money.

Second, they rescinded use of the car for the summer because they didn't trust him to stay abstinent and they worried about drinking and driving. Wanting to offer a carrot as well as a stick, they stayed open to giving him car use for the last few weeks of summer, contingent upon compliance with a summer contract that required abstinence, curfews for weeknights, and a collaborative attitude around the household. Any violations would result in no car, shortened curfews, and reconsideration of fraternity membership.

I also worked with the Simons on how to communicate with Aden around this incident. Only too easily, in the aftermath of an experience like Aden's, do parents shame, lecture, and interrogate: "Are you partying?" "Are you drinking on weekends?" "Well, you'd better get yourself to the library." Although this kind of exhortation is tempting, it closes down communication and makes college students want to get off the phone. The only thing it stimulates is their withdrawing or stonewalling.

When young people stray from the right path, despite our all-too-human anger, upset, and frustration, staying connected with our emerging adults should be the priority. Experienced parents looking back on the college years often advise that "just listening" was the most important part of their phone calls with their students. The better the relationship we can maintain with them, the more we're able to influence them and make a difference.

ANY OLD SUMMER JOB MIGHT NOT DO: USING SCHOOL BREAKS TO ENGAGE EMERGING ADULTS, HELP THEM FIND THEIR INTERESTS, AND REFINE WHO THEY ARE

Unlike the more family-oriented Thanksgiving and December holidays, spring break of freshman year may be the first time parents face the possibility of their child not coming home during a break. Compared to summer, spring break is a peer-culture phenomenon. College students will push to make their own plans, but parents can provide input and steer their child in a direction that will benefit their growth. For example, with a son or daughter who traveled last summer, parents may not want to fund another adventure; on the other hand, an introverted freshman who studied like a hermit may actually need the spring fling to enhance her social development! Trips are options for the privileged college crowd, so parents need to be ready to deal with a student's wanderlust. Even young people from humbler roots can shock their parents with fantasy ideas picked up from friends.

> SPRING BREAKS INVOLVE A SLEW OF POSSIBILITIES, FROM A HOME VISIT AND HOMEWORK, TO BACCHANALIA AND INDULGENCE, TO VOLUNTEER WORK IN A NEEDY COMMUNITY. KNOW THE CHOICES AND BE READY TO NEGOTIATE AND GUIDE YOUR YOUNG ADULT ACCORDING TO YOUR VALUES.

Too often, families take a one-size-fits-all approach to summers—just come home and get a job. One quarter of a year, summer break is too fertile a time to let youthful energy lie fallow, even if they do arrive at your doorstep exhausted from finals (most students rebound fast!). Although finances are likely to dominate any decision about summer, parents can still be strategic about what they insist upon, agree to, or encourage.

Bureau of Labor Statistics indicate that summer employment for both high-school and college students is down, as more young people attend summer school, take internships, volunteer, or travel. It used to be a rite of passage for young people on the college track to hold down a paid summer job involving some drudgery, as a way of rounding out their experience, acquiring an understanding of the value of a dollar, and developing character. This time-tested formula still has merit, but other options exist. Gaining exposure to a specific employment setting may shed light on a career choice.

Assisting with the family business may fulfill a crucial obligation. Making top dollar may be necessary for college expenditure. A travel or foreign-study program may enhance personal development.

Keep in mind that young people often promote cushier options for themselves, while a parent's role is to consider the big picture, weighing possibilities and values. Random samplings of youth reveal high rates of malaise and disconnection; it's striking how bored many young people are much of the time, without structured opportunities to develop initiative.[8] Particularly in today's world, initiative—the capacity for independent action, motivated from within—is a core requirement for success. Unless young people are stretched to new domains, they may lapse into what's easiest.

In large part, planning for breaks means parents have a schema about what they want to support, what they want to build in their child, and what will develop initiative. For this potentially fruitful span of time, parents should challenge their young adults to discover what engrosses them. Many adults hearken back to summer jobs and other opportunities as being what awakened a future career interest and path.

THINKING STRATEGICALLY ABOUT THE BIG TEN: A GAUGE TO MOVING INTO THE WORLD SUCCESSFULLY

At any moment of parenting, interacting with children with an eye to qualities that young people need to be up and running can help promote these all-important features. What are your child's strengths and weaknesses? What area of their development is a little soft? What sensibility do you want to awaken? What existing strengths might you exploit?

The list below of ten key attributes roughly corresponds to the "Readiness for Launching" survey in chapter one. The

Big Ten also includes concepts from research on social and emotional competence, which was synthesized by Daniel Goleman in his work on emotional intelligence.[9]

This group of attributes forms the backbone of what young people need to have to leave home with sound bearings. For optimal child development and launching, parents have been working toward these qualities during their child's first 18 years.

> EXTERNAL CRISES NOT WITHSTANDING, DEFICITS IN THE BIG TEN VIRTUALLY ALWAYS EXPLAIN WHY YOUNG PEOPLE FAIL TO LAUNCH SUCCESSFULLY FROM HOME.

Guiding their children through the young adulthood years, parents can try to enhance these qualities. Whether it pertains to a summer job choice or to the way your child is handling a dilemma, parents can run an overview and pinpoint an area where they think their child stands to grow. What a tall order it would be to achieve perfection in any of these areas; rather, we hope that our emerging adults demonstrate some level of competency in each area.

1. **Motivation and drive.** People with this quality have zest and zeal for life, pursuing that which ignites their interests. They take initiative and look for opportunities to engage fully in activities. Realizing that "natural talents" aren't necessarily enough to take them where they want to go, they have ideas of how to go about accomplishing their goals.

2. **Practical reasoning and judgment.** These individuals use problem-solving skills and good judgment to think through a situation or manage a problem. Whether it's tackling a school assignment or planning a trip, they can devise an approach or organizational scheme, responding with flexibility and adaptability to wrenches that may be thrown into plans.

3. **Moral attentiveness and character.** People who are morally alert

have integrity and a conscience, operating with a sense of responsibility and an awareness of consequences of behavior. They follow through on commitments, are conscientious about obligations, and act with consideration for the greater good. They're compelled to stand up for what's right and fair and to care about those who are less fortunate.

4. **Emotional awareness.** This quality means you are attuned to your own feelings and motivations, have a vocabulary for expressing your feelings, and have empathy and insight into others' concerns, perspectives, and motivations. It involves intuitive skills for understanding dilemmas, people, and life issues.

5. **Healthy habits.** This attribute requires an awareness of what behaviors and habits contribute to physical well-being. People who exhibit healthiness use good judgment to limit risk-taking, have a value on wellness and the discipline to do what's needed to maintain it.

6. **Self-control and affective regulation.** These individuals can delay gratification, whether it pertains to spending money or sacrificing an immediate pleasure to stay on track. In the face of difficulties, they show persistency and are resilient in the face of difficult emotional setbacks. They're able to self-soothe, cope with problems, and control impulses.

7. **Social skills.** People with social skills have the ability to size up social situations and plan appropriate actions. Good at developing friendships, they're willing to cooperate, are interpersonally effective, and know how to make people feel comfortable.

8. **Communication skills.** Having skills in this area means you're a good listener and question-asker. You can interpret others' communications accurately and know how to send "I" messages instead of blaming. Those high in communication skills are not only able to articulate their own ideas, but can also function well in a group and facilitate group consensus.

9. **Intellectual interests and abilities.** This quality involves a demonstrated interest in a life of the mind and the pursuit of skills needed to wrestle productively with ideas, concepts, and difficult sets of information and data. People with an intellectual bent hold the value

that education will be of benefit and that learning is a key to life fulfillment.

10. **Spiritual awareness.** What characterizes people who are spiritually aware is their connection with a force of strength and goodness beyond the self. Centered in life, they can accept what "is" and that life is complex and presents difficulties and challenges for everyone.

AVOIDING THE "MOTIVATED BUT DIRECTIONLESS" TRAP

Many of today's young people dream big goals with little practical knowledge of how to achieve them. In a study of 7,000 adolescents, researchers reported in their book *The Ambitious Generation: America's Teenagers, Motivated but Directionless* that young people—far from seeing themselves as the slackers they're often portrayed to be—have more ambitious goals than 20 to 30 years ago, but they are not reaching them.[10] Too often, they choose the wrong courses and wrong colleges and remain clueless and naively oblivious to the idea of formulating some type of career path, albeit a flexible one at this stage. Particularly in an era when getting into the "best" college has become an obsessive focus, young people fail to cast their gaze beyond college acceptance to form a life plan (one that can be altered) with priorities and small specific goals and plans along the way.

Why, the researchers asked, do some young people reach their ambitious goals while others don't? Or, to cite a specific instance: According to projections, five times as many young people want to be lawyers and judges than needed. Which ones will achieve their dreams? Those who get where they aspire to go are more qualified and knowledgeable, having made strategic choices about how to use their time to gain experience in the field of their dreams. They've aligned their ambitions with practical application and know-how, having laid a path of stepping stones to move themselves forward.

Studies show that the more parents and mentors assist and support young people in aligning their activities with their goals, the better they do with goal attainment. Before college students decide on a major, they should try some coursework. Within their field, students should make sure they have an advisor behind them, directing not only their coursework but also counseling them on how different combinations of majors and minors yield different career options.

Summers are pivotal. Whether their goal is to be an astronomer or an architect, young people who pinpoint a specific career need to get a taste of it to see if they like the reality of this career in practice. Even if it doesn't earn money, if young people have a unique opportunity that builds who they are or provides experience in a future career function, parents may decide to take on the financial hardship to give their child that opportunity. Summers can also lead to some rule-outs, as young people discover they don't enjoy business, or healthcare, or working with children after all.

TESTING OUT IDEAS, GAINING EXPOSURE TO SETTINGS TO HONE THEIR CAREER PLANS, AND EVEN EXPERIMENTING WITH FAR-FETCHED MONEY-MAKING SCHEMES CAN BE BUILDING BLOCKS TO HELP YOUNG PEOPLE DEVELOP SUCCESSFUL WORK LIVES. SUMMERS ARE A PRIME TIME FOR YOUNG PEOPLE TO ADVANCE WHAT THEY KNOW ABOUT THEM-SELVES.

Likewise, part-time jobs on campus can yield practical experience: A job at the computer center may allow a student to have the wonderful liberal-arts major, while simultaneously acquiring employment skills. Working during college is an individual option. Sometimes it's necessary financially; sometimes it helps students who study compulsively to balance their lives; sometimes it presents an opportunity to work with a professor who will provide a valuable graduate school recommendation; and sometimes it's an overwhelming burden. During high school working more than 12 hours a week can drain valuable time from young people's intellectual and social development.[11] Despite the impacts, mature college students can and do juggle work and school.

The point is that parents should start having conversations with their college students about the fact that they need to prepare for financial independence—how much and how soon is a family's own decision. Not that every summer, school break, job on campus, or course taken has to help crystallize their future, but just as we don't want our children to graduate without the character qualities and personal strengths of the Big Ten, we likewise don't want them leave school without an iota of information about the working world.

BOOMERANG KIDS AND THE LAND OF THE LOTUS FLOWER
FAMILY STORY CONTINUED

For the Simons, dealing with their second launcher was easier, but not because launching their son Jacob was glitch-free. Having risen to the occasion of their personal, marital, and child-rearing challenges, Rita and Harvey knew how to handle it when Jacob declared intentions to leave college after his freshman year, live at home, and attend school locally.

Having shared in many highs and lows of the Simon's child-rearing experiences over the years, I received each winter a holiday card updating me on how family members were doing. The December after Jacob's freshman year, their card contained a long note filling me in on Aden, a college graduate working for a large manufacturer of athletic shoes and apparel, and Jacob, whose path had taken an unexpected turn. What Rita explained of Jacob's situation went something like this:

Believe it or not, we had a boomerang kid, and Harvey and I handled this one all by ourselves! If this had happened with our first child, we would have been in your office like lightning. By spring of his first year, Jacob was convinced he didn't like Southern California—and we thought he'd love going to college where there are beaches close by. But you know Jacob. He likes the comforts of home, maybe a little too much. Jacob wanted to take some time off, get a job, and move back into his basement apartment. Lots of his friends go to the local community college, and he asked us to trust that he would earn a college degree one way or another.

Harvey and I didn't mind if he took a year off. Not that we were entirely pleased about it, but the idea of having him return home made us worry. We always knew we'd babied Jacob and were a little looser with him—or maybe we were just a little lazier! Jacob needed the wolf at the door before he was ever going to get motivated. If he lived at home, it would be too easy for him to live off the fat of the land, so we told him that he needed to find his own apartment by September. It was very difficult for us, but it turned out to be the best idea ever! What a learning curve these last three months have been for him. I wouldn't be surprised if he was back in school in Southern California soon!

Reading their holiday card, I couldn't have been more impressed with Rita and Harvey's confident leap of faith to go against the grain of Jacob's comfort zone. With just the right blend of loving care and level-headed problem-solving, the Simons determined that Jacob needed to test the waters of a more independent life style, whether he was in college or not.

In consulting with Rita and Harvey during Aden's mishaps, I had developed an impression of Jacob based on their colorful narratives. Jacob appeared to be a nice young man—morally sound, not into drinking, and a charming guy whom everyone loves. If there was a consistent theme in the parents' concerns about Jacob, it was that he was almost too content and even phlegmatic, without the fire in his belly. Sizing up his development relative to some of the Big Ten qualities, his parents would evaluate him as low in sustained interests (he started a lot of things but didn't follow through); exceedingly disorganized; generally responsible about things that affected other people in a hurtful way, but loose about debts and a chronic procrastinator; high in social skills (he could use those skills to ply teachers, parents, and friends alike with excuses); high in emotional awareness, but a big dreamer without the steps in between to make it happen. Even as a high-school student, he didn't come across as a true believer in education as the best path to success and learning. Jacob was an enthusiast for life.

IF THINGS PROCEED AS THEY OFTEN DO WHEN YOUNG PEOPLE BOOMERANG HOME, MOM WILL SOON BE DOING HIS LAUNDRY AGAIN, THE PARENTS WILL BE WORRYING ABOUT HOW MUCH TV HE'S WATCHING, HOW HE'S SPENDING HIS MONEY, AND WHETHER HE'S LATE FOR SCHOOL OR WORK AGAIN. IT'S THE LAND OF THE LOTUS FLOWERS FOR KIDS.

Assessing their son's development astutely, the Simons questioned the way Jacob came home. Was the college's region the problem or was that just a cover for a "return to the womb" where it was safer and cushier and there would be less accountability to step into the big scary world? At a time in their lives (ages 18 to 25) when most young people should be on a large growth curve, Jacob could only too easily coast at home.

Sometimes it makes sense for a child to return from college to live at home. Finances alone can be the card that determines where a child resides. A young person who is pursuing a special interest instead of college and whose Big Ten qualities are up to par would probably do fine at home without much backsliding. Illnesses (anxiety, depression, drug dependency, eating disorder) commonly hurl young people back where they started, for in many cases they weren't ready to launch in the first place. Many young people with a temperament issue, a learning disorder, or a developmental delay can benefit from an additional year or two of hands-on parenting. Or, for some not-quite-identifiable reason, some young people need to marinate a little longer in the security of the home. Whatever the case, parents can set up a structure with mandatory household responsibilities and obligations to ensure ongoing maturation.

Statistically, fewer than 40 percent of young people who start college will finish their undergraduate program in four years, which means that the better half of them are juggling decisions about where and when to attend school, how to pay for it, and where to live in the meantime.[12] To have a child boomerang back to the nest is in no way a parenting failure, since it may be that the young person needs to regroup, rethink goals, and can benefit from mom's or dad's support in that process—particularly if parents have a plan for how they're boosting the Big Ten.

Ultimately, the question for parents to pose to themselves is this: When my child is living at home, am I supporting new growth or are we all falling into old patterns that stymie development? One of the biggest reasons young people return home is that, lacking the infrastructure of the Big Ten and all the coping skills they entail, they're still highly dependent on their parents. If parents want to "keep their job" as parents—instead of stressing the value of independence and deriving some pleasure from their child's maturation—they might unconsciously favor having a child back in the nest. Believing that they are helping the child while he gets back on his feet, they might instead be retarding the launcher's growth. If having an emerging adult in the home reinforces an "adolescent personality" because he is not assuming responsibilities and parents are footing the bill and doing little to encourage a turnaround, parents would best do some soul searching about living quarters.

Good launching is like good parenting: There are thousands of judgment calls about when and how to support and challenge. The dynamics are such that we support our children as they experience challenges from biological, social, cultural, and environmental sources. And then sometimes for their growth and development, we're the ones who impose challenges on them. We do this in many contexts, whether it's insisting that our children delay immediate gratification for a long-term reward, or not rescuing them in a hardship so they can wrestle with it themselves, or asking boomerang kids to live in their own apartment. What matters most of all, however, is that we impose those challenges in a caring spirit of optimism, continued attachment, clear communication, and respect for who the child is.

LET LAUNCHING INSPIRE YOU

As a life event, launching a child from home is as big as birth. If you do it well, with an ingenious mix of staying connected and letting go, it can inspire you. How we go about launching our children can make a difference in all the rest, as we come to appreciate that there will be more life ahead, more close relationships with others—and maybe even the possibility of grandchildren down the line.

Most of us start out naively as parents, with a cookie-cutter mentality of hopes, dreams, and promises for our children. From family to family, in vacation photos of youths lined up and smiling, children from different families can look almost interchangeable, particularly in the early years of elementary school. Had someone interviewed any of us at that point about what we thought our children would do by age 18, our answers would overlap, "Well, they'll graduate from high school and go to college. . . ." And then the surprises come, as those children who once looked similar develop distinctly, launch in different ways, and forge different life paths.

One thing we can know for sure is that our children nudge us along in our development. As one parent put it, "I had one way of thinking about things. My kids have shaken that up and challenged me and given me a new way of thinking. Not that any of it has been easy, but without that, I think I'd be a pretty rigid thinker." The problems and complexities of raising children can humble us, as we're presented with obstacles we never thought we'd have to face. What we make of them can build us up or take us down. But whenever we rise to the challenges, we'll evolve and grow in new ways.

Launching, like child-rearing, can also bring moments of awe. One insight that dawns on us—usually by the end of the freshman year—is that being physically away from us and productively engaged contributes to an emerging adult's successful transition to adulthood. Research shows that having a young adult in the home or geographically close to parents does not correlate with emotional closeness, since feelings of strong attachment are what allow young people to spread their wings securely.[13] What delight we feel when our children return home with an air of new confidence, knowing how integral we've been to their blossoming! We can be as enchanted by them as we were when they were babies— but now it's even better because of the budding mutual appreciation.

We may have our own resistance to the roomier nest and the diminishing of our active parenting role, but we begin to want the experience of the big world so much for our children that we can prioritize it over our own desire to have them back in their own bedrooms. Awakened to a new admiration for how much they've grown, we're better able to let them go. And likewise mindful of how much we are and will always be a part of them, we treasure our enduring bond.

Notes

INTRODUCTION

1. Jeffrey J. Arnett, "Emerging Adulthood: A Theory of Development from the Late Teens Through the Twenties," *American Psychologist* 55 (5) (2000): 469–80.
2. Terri Apter, *The Myth of Maturity: What Teenagers Need from Parents to Become Adults* (New York: W. W. Norton, 2001).
3. R. Cairns and B. Cairns, *Lifelines and Risks: Pathways of Youth in Our Time* (New York: Harvester Wheatsheaf, 1994).
4. Robert Keegan, *In Over Our Heads: The Mental Demands of Modern Life* (Cambridge, Mass: Harvard University Press, 1994).
5. Robert Arnstein, "The Student, the Family, the University and Transition to Adulthood," *Adolescent Psychiatry* 8 (1980): 160–72.

CHAPTER ONE

1. R.R. Koback and Screery, "Attachment in Late Adolescence: Working Models, Affect Regulation and Representations of Self and Others," *Child Development* 59 (1988): 135–46.
2. Thomas Hayden, *Handbook of College Admissions* (Lawrenceville, N.J.: Peterson's, 1995).
3. J. Garbino and C. Asp, *Successful Schools and Competent Students* (Lexington, Mass: Lexington Books, 1981).
4. L. Steinberg, S. Lamborn, N. Darling, N. Mounts, and S. Dornbusch, "Over-Time Changes in Adjustment and Competence Among Adolescents from Authoritative, Authoritarian, Indulgent and Neglectful Families," *Child Development* 65 (1994): 754–70.
5. Apter, *The Myth of Maturity*.

CHAPTER TWO

1. CBS and C. Macker, *The Class of 2000: A Definitive Survey of the New Generation* (New York: Simon and Schuster, 2000).
2. A.S. Masten, J.D. Coatsworth, J. Neeman, S.D. Gest, A. Tellegen, and N. Garmezy, "The Structure and Coherence of Competence from Childhood Through Adolescence," *Child Development* 66 (1995) 1635–59.

3. Lynn Ponton, *The Romance of Risk: Why Teenagers Do the Things They Do* (New York: Basic Books, 1998).

4. Robert Arnstein, "The Student, the Family, the University and Transition to Adulthood," *Adolescent Psychiatry* 8 (1980): 160–72.

CHAPTER THREE

1. CBS and C. Macker, *The Class of 2000*.

2. Laurence Steinberg, "Independence in the Family: Autonomy, Conflict and Harmony in the Parent-Adolescent Relationship," in *At the Threshold: The Developing Adolescent*, S.S. Feldman and G.R. Elliot, eds. (Cambridge, Mass: Harvard University Press, 1990).

3. J.E. Marcia, "Identity in Adolescence," in *Handbook of Adolescent Psychology*, J. Adelson, ed. (New York: John Wiley & Sons, 1980).

4. G. Adams, T. Gullotta, and R. Montemayor, eds., *Adolescent Identity Formation* (Newbury Park, CA: Sage Publication, 1992).

5. T.J. Bernt, J.A. Hawkins, and Z. Jiao, "Influence of Friends and Friendships on Adjustment to Junior High," *Merrill-Palmer Quarterly* 45 (1999): 13–41; J.L. Epstein, "The Influence of Friends on Achievement and Affective Outcomes," in J.L. Epstein and N. Karweit, eds., *Friends in School* (New York: Academic Press, 1983): 177–200.

6. Lynn Mikel Brown and Carol Gilligan, *Meeting at the Crossroads: Women's Psychology and Girl's Development* (Cambridge, Mass: Harvard University Press, 1994).

7. P. Fallon, M. Katzman, and S. Wooley, eds., *Feminist Perspectives on Eating Disorders* (New York: Guilford Press, 1994).

8. Terri Apter, *Altered Loves: Mothers and Daughters During Adolescence* (New York: St. Martin's Press, 1990).

9. John R. Snarey, *How Fathers Care for the Next Generation: A Four Decade Study* (Cambridge, Mass: Harvard University Press, 1993).

10. Sanford Dornbusch, "Transitions from Adolescence: A Discussion of Seven Articles," *Journal of Adolescent Research* 15 (1) (2000): 173–77.

11. Richard Light, *Making the Most of College: Students Speak Their Minds* (Cambridge, Mass.: Harvard University Press, 2001).

CHAPTER FOUR

1. Maureen Kenny and Kenneth Rice, "Attachment to Parents and Adjustment in Late Adolescent College Students: Current Status, Applications, and Future Considerations," *Counseling Psychologist* 23 (3) (1995): 433–56.

2. W. Bridges, *Transitions: Making Sense of Life's Changes* (Reading, Mass: Addison-Wesley, 1980).

3. P.K. Adelmann, T.C. Antonucci, S.E. Crohan, and L.M. Coleman, "Empty-Nest, Cohort, and Employment in the Well-Being of Midlife Women," *Sex Roles* 20 (1989): 173–89.

4. Abigail Steward and Joan Ostrove, "Women's Personality in Middle Age: Gender, History and Midcourse Corrections," *American Psychologist* 53 (11) (1998): 1185–94.

5. David Arp, Claudia Arp, Scott Stanley, Howard Markman, and Susan Blumberg, *Fighting for Your Empty Nest Marriage* (San Francisco: Jossey-Bass Publishers, 2000).

6. Gallop survey, commissioned by Lutheran Brotherhood and Search Institute, 2000.

7. Ann Vander Stoep, S. Beresford, B. McKnight, A. Cauce, and P. Cohen, "Community Based Study of the Transition to Adulthood for Adolescents with Psychiatric Disorder," *American Journal of Epidemiology* 152 (4) (1999): 352–62.

8. K.L. Suyemoto, "The Functions of Self-Mutilation," *Clinical Psychology Review* 18 (1998): 531–54.

9. Arthur Levine and Jeanette S. Cureton, *When Hope and Fear Collide: A Portrait of Today's College Student* (San Francisco: Jossey-Bass Publishers, 1998). Quotations from Deans are also from this source.

CHAPTER FIVE

1. Robert Arnstein, "The Student, the Family, the University and Transition to Adulthood," *Adolescent Psychiatry* 8 (1980): 160–72.

2. Arthur Levine and Jeanette S. Cureton, *When Hope and Fear Collide: A Portrait of Today's College Student* (San Francisco: Jossey-Bass Publishers, 1998).

3. E. Erikson, *Childhood and Society,* Second Edition (New York: W.W. Norton & Company, 1963).

4. B. Benda and F. DiBlasio, "An Integration of Theory: Adolescent Sexual Contact," *Journal of Youth and Adolescence* 23 (1) (1994): 403–20.

5. P. Moen, M.A. Erikson, and D. Dempster-McClain, "Their Mothers' Daughters? The Intergenerational Transmission of Gender Attitudes in a World of Changing Roles," *Journal of Marriage and the Family* 59 (1997): 281–93; S. Usmiana and J.C. Daniluk, "Mothers and Their Adolescent Daughters: Relationship Between Self-Esteem, Gender-Role Identity, and Body Image," *Journal of Youth and Adolescence* 26 (1997): 45–55.

6. Levine and Cureton, pp. 106–7.

7. J. Goodchilds and G. Zellman, "Sexual Signaling and Sexual Aggression in Adolescent Relationships," in *Porn and Sexual*

Aggression, N.M. Malamuth and E. Donnerstein, eds. (Orlando, Fla.: Academic Press, 1984): 233–43.

8. Lynn Ponton, *The Sex Lives of Teenagers: Revealing the Secret World of Adolescent Boys and Girls* (New York: E.P. Dutton, 2000).

9. Ritch Savin-Williams, "Parental Influences on the Self-Esteem of Gay and Lesbian Youths: A Reflected Appraisals Model," in G. Herdt, ed., *Gay and Lesbian Youth* (New York: Haworth Press, 1989): 93–109.

CHAPTER SIX

1. C. Ahrons, *The Good Divorce: Keeping Your Family Together When Your Marriage Comes Apart* (New York: HarperCollins, 1994).

2. William Pollock, *Real Boys: Rescuing Our Sons from the Myths of Boyhood* (New York: Random House, 1998).

3. Jonathan Shedler and Jack Block, "Adolescent Drug Use and Psychological Health: A Longitudinal Inquiry," *American Psychologist* 45 (5) (May 1990): 612–30.

4. Alan Reifman, G.M. Barnes, B.A. Dintcheff, M.P. Farrell, and L. Uhteg, *Journal of Studies on Alcohol* 59 (1998): 311–17.

5. J. Cashin, C. Presley, and P. Meilman, "Alcohol Use in the Greek System; Follow the Leader?" *Journal of Studies on Alcohol* (1998): 3–70.

6. H. Wechsler, "Alcohol and the American College Campus: A Report from the Harvard School of Public Health," *Change* 28 (4) (July–Aug., 1996): 20.

7. J. Nowinski, *Substance Abuse in Adolescents and Young Adults* (New York: W.W. Norton, 1990).

8. Reed Larson, "Toward a Psychology of Positive Youth Development," *American Psychology* 55 (1) (2000): 170–83.

9. Daniel Goleman, *Emotional Intelligence: Why It Can Matter More Than IQ* (New York: Bantam Books, 1995).

10. Barbara Schneider and David Stevenson, *The Ambitious Generation: America's Teenagers, Motivated but Directionless* (New Haven, Conn.: Yale University Press, 1999).

11. E. Greenberger and L. Steinberg, *When Teenagers Work: The Psychological and Social Costs of Adolescent Employment* (New York: Basic Books, 1986).

12. CBS and C. Macker. *The Class of 2000.* Over the last decade and a half, the statistic of 40 percent has been documented.

13. Lonnie R. Sherrod, "Leaving Home: The Role of Individual and Familial Factors," *New Directions for Child Development* No 71 (1996), San Francisco: Jossey-Bass Publishers.

Resources

ADD/ADHD

Alexander-Roberts, Colleen. *ADHD and Teens: Proven Techniques for Handling Emotional, Academic and Behavioral Problems*. Dallas: Taylor Publishing, 1995.

ADOLESCENT DEVELOPMENT

Apter, Terri. *The Myth of Maturity: What Teens Need from Parents to Become Adults*. New York: W.W. Norton, 2001.

Csikszentmihalyi, M, K. Rathunde, and M. Wong. *Talented Teenagers: The Roots of Success and Failure*. New York: Cambridge University Press, 2000.

Gardner, Howard. *Intelligences Reframed: Multiple Intelligences for the 21st Century*. New York: Basic Books, 2000.

Goleman, Daniel. *Emotional Intelligence*. New York: Bantam Books, 1995.

Kastner, Laura and Jennifer Wyatt. *The Seven-Year Stretch: How Families Work Together to Grow Through Adolescence*. New York: Houghton Mifflin, 1997.

Kegan, Robert. *In Over Our Heads: The Mental Demands of Modern Life*. Cambridge, MA: Harvard University Press, 1994.

Ponton, Lynn. *The Romance of Risk: Why Teenagers Do the Things they Do*. New York: Basic Books, 1998.

Steinberg, Laurence and Wendy Steinberg. *Crossing Paths: How Your Child's Adolescence Triggers Your Own Crisis*. New York: Simon and Schuster, 1994.

ADOLESCENT SEXUALITY

Bouris, K. *The First Time*. Berkeley, CA: Conari Press, 1994.

Ponton, Lynn. *The Sex Lives of Teenagers: Revealing the Secret World of Adolescent Boys and Girls*. New York: E.P. Dutton, 2000.

Wolf, N. *Promiscuities*. New York: Random House, 1996.

ADULT DEVELOPMENT

Pogrebin, L. *Getting Over Getting Older: An Intimate Journey*. Boston: Little Brown, 1996.

Shapiro, Patricia. *My Turn: Women's Search for Self After the Children Leave*. Lawrenceville, NJ: Peterson's Guides, 1997.

BODY IMAGE/EATING DISORDERS

Siegal, M, J. Brisman, and M. Weinshel. *Surviving an Eating Disorder: New Perspectives and Strategies for Families and Friends*. New York: Harper & Row, 1988.

Wolf, N. *The Beauty Myth: How Images of Beauty are Used Against Women*. New York: William Morrow Co., 1991.

COLLEGE ADMISSION

Adler, Joe Anne. *100 Colleges Where Average Students Can Excel*. Arco Publishing, 1996.

Mayer, Bill. *The College Admissions Mystique*. New York: Farrar, Straus, and Giroux, 1998.

Pope, Lauren. *Looking Beyond the Ivy League: Finding the College That's Right for You*. New York: Penguin Books, 1995.

Pope, Lauren. *Colleges That Change Lives*. New York: Penguin Books, 1996.

COLLEGE ATHLETICS

Duderstadt, James J. *Intercollegiate Athletics and the American University: A University President's Perspective*. Ann Arbor: University of Michigan Press, 2000.

Schulman, James L. and William G. Bowen. *The Game of Life: College Sports and Educational Values*. Princeton, NJ: Princeton University Press, 2001.

Sperber, Murray. *Beer and Circus: How Big-Time College Sports Is Crippling Education*. New York: Henry Holt, 2000.

COLLEGE LIFE AND AFTER

Figler, Howard. *The Internship Bible*. New York: Random House, 1995.

Harris, Marcia and Sharon Jones. *The Parent's Crash Course in Career Planning*. Lincolnwood, IL: NTC Publishing Group, 1996.

Levine, Arthur and Jeanette S. Cureton. *When Hope and Fear Collide: A Portrait of Today's College Student*. San Francisco: Jossey-Bass Publishers, 1998.

Martz, Geoff. *How to Survive Without Your Parent's Money: Making It From College to the "Real World."* Princeton, NJ: The Princeton Review, 1996.

Schneider, Barbara and David Stevenson. *The Ambitious Generation: America's Teenagers, Motivated but Directionless*. New Haven: Yale University Press, 1999.

COLLEGE LIFE/SURVIVAL GUIDES

Combs, Patrick and Jack Canfield. *Major in Success: Make College*

*Easier, Fire Up Your Dreams &
Get a Very Cool Job*. Berkeley,
CA: Ten Speed Press, 2000.

Gottesman, Greg (editor), Daniel
Baer and Greg Gottesman. *College
Survival: A Crash Course for
Students by Students*, fifth edition.
Arco Publishers, 1999.

Grayson, Paul A. and Philip W.
Mechman. *Beating the College
Blues*, second edition. New York:
Checkmark Books, 1999.

Light, Richard J. *Making the Most
of College: Students Speak Their
Minds*. Cambridge, MA: Harvard
University Press, 2001.

Worthington, Janet Farrar and
Ronald T. Farrar. *The Ultimate
College Survival Guide*, fourth
edition. Lawrenceville, NJ:
Peterson's Guides, 1998.

EMOTIONAL PROBLEMS IN YOUNG PEOPLE

Clark, Hewitt B. and Maryann
Davis. *Transition to Adulthood: A
Resource for Assisting Young
People with Emotional or
Behavioral Difficulties*. Baltimore:
Paul H. Brooks, 2000.

Oster, Gerald and Sarah
Montgomery. *Helping Your
Depressed Teenager: A Guide for
Parents and Caregivers*. New York:
Wiley, 1995.

Maxym, Carol and Leslie York.
*Teens in Turmoil: A Path to
Change for Parents, Adolescents*

and Their Families. New York:
Viking, 2000.

GAY/LESBIAN ISSUE

Borhek, Mary V. *Coming Out to
Parents: A Two-Way Survival
Guide for Lesbians and Gay Men
and Their Parents*. New York:
Pilgrim Press, 1983.

Savin-Williams, Ritch C. *Mom,
Dad. I'm Gay: How Families
Negotiate Coming Out*.
Washington, D.C.: American
Psychological Association, 2001.

GENDER DEVELOPMENT

Apter, Terri. *Altered Loves:
Mothers and Daughters During
Adolescence*. New York: St.
Martin's Press, 1990.

Brown, Lyn Mikel and Carol
Gilligan. *Meeting at the
Crossroads: Women's Psychology
and Girls' Development*.
Cambridge, MA: Harvard
University Press, 1992.

Caron, Ann F. *Don't Stop Loving
Me: A Reassuring Guide for
Mothers of Adolescent Daughters*.
New York: HarperPerennial,
1992.

Caron, Ann F. *Strong Mothers,
Strong Sons: Raising the Next
Generation of Men*. New York:
HarperPerennial, 1994.

Pollock, William. *Real Boys:
Rescuing Our Sons from the Myths
of Boyhood*. New York: Random
House, 1998.

Kindlon, Daniel, Michael
Thompson, Dan Kindlon, and
Teresa Barker. *Raising Cain:
Protecting the Emotional Life of
Boys*. New York: Ballantine
Books, 2000.

LAUNCHING

Coburn, Karen L and Madge L.
Treeger. *Letting Go: A Parents'
Guide to Understanding the College
Years*. New York: HarperCollins,
1997.

Pasick, Patricia. *Almost Grown:
Launching Your Child from High
School to College,* New York:
W.W. Norton & Co., 1998.

MULTICULTURAL ISSUES

Allen, WR, E.G. Epp, and H.Z.
Haniff, eds. *College in Black and
White: African American students
in predominantly White and
historically Black public
universities*. Albany, NY: State
University of NY Press, 1991.

Tatum, Beverly. *Why Are All the
Black Kids Sitting Together in the
Cafeteria?* New York: Basic
Books, 1997.

INDEX

Photo by Scott Wyatt.

LAURA S. KASTNER, PH.D, AND
JENNIFER WYATT, PH.D.

Laura S. Kastner, Ph.D., is a clinical associate professor of psychiatry and behavioral sciences at the University of Washington. A psychologist and mother of two, she lectures widely on adolescence and family behavior.

Jennifer Wyatt, Ph.D., a Seattle-based writer and mother of four, contributes widely to a number of parenting publications.

They are the authors of *The Seven Year Stretch: How Families Work Together to Grow Through Adolescence*.

PRAISE FOR *THE SEVEN YEAR STRETCH*

"Required reading for parents, teachers, and therapists. Dr. Kastner's vignettes of family life will be recognized by all parents and they will treasure her clear, forthright advice."

—ANN F. CARON, ED.D.,
author of *Don't Stop Loving Me* and *Strong Mothers, Strong Sons*

"Has something to offer nearly all parents of teens."

—*Publishers Weekly*

"A valuable resource for both parents and others, including educators, who work with adolescents."

—*Library Journal*